MEXICO

From Montezuma to NAFTA and Beyond

Jamie Suchlicki

with a new preface by the author

Transaction Publishers

New Brunswick (U.S.A.) and London (U.K.)

First paperback edition 2000
New material in this edition copyright © 2000 by Transaction Publishers, New Brunswick, New Jersey. Originally published as Mexico: From Montezuma to NAFTA, Chiapas, and Beyond in 1996 by Brassey's, Inc., Washington.

This book is printed on acid-free paper that meets the American National Standard for Permanence of Paper for Printed Library Materials.

Library of Congress Catalog Number: 00-028702
ISBN: 0-7658-0652-5 (paper)
Printed in the United States of America

Library of Congress Cataloging-in-Publication Data

Suchlicki, Jaime.
    Mexico : from Montezuma to NAFTA and beyond / Jaime Suchlicki.
        p. cm.
    Originally published: Mexico: from Montezuma to NAFTA, Chiapas, and beyond. Washington: Brassey's, Inc., 1996. With new introd.
    Includes bibliographical references (p. -) and index.
    ISBN 0-7658-0652-5 (pbk. : alk. paper)
    1. Mexico—History.   I. Title.

F1226 .S83 2000
972—dc21   00-028702

MEXICO

From Montezuma to NAFTA and Beyond

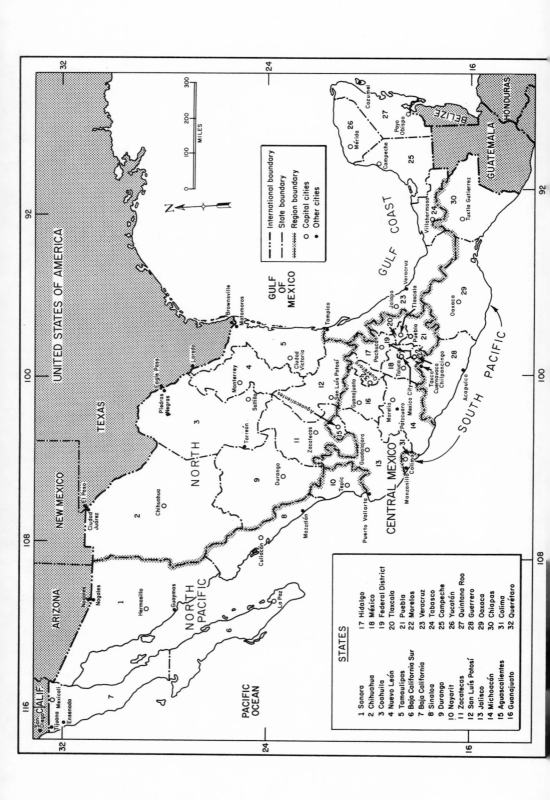

CONTENTS

Preface to the Transaction Edition

Since the publication of the first edition of *Mexico: From Montezuma to NAFTA, Chiapas, and Beyond* numerous changes have taken place in Mexico. For the first time in its seventy-year history, the *Partido Revolucionario Institucional* (PRI) lost its majority control over the lower house of the Mexican Congress, the Chamber of Deputies, in a bitterly contested election in 1997. The leader of the *Partido de la Revolución Democrática* (PRD), Cuauhtémoc Cárdenas, was elected mayor of Mexico City. The brother of former president Carlos Salinas de Gortari was indicted and jailed on charges of corruption, money laundering, and complicity in the murder of a rival political leader. New insurgencies, in addition to the one in Chiapas, developed in two other Mexican states, Oaxaca and Guerrero.

There were many reasons for the PRI's electoral defeat in 1997. First, Mexico still reeled over the economic mess inherited by President Ernesto Zedillo—businesses closed, unemployment and inflation soared, crime increased. Mexicans suffered and wondered about the ability of the government to deliver on its promises. Unhappiness and frustration increased. Then the assassination of political leaders and the corruption scandals within the PRI weakened its already tarnished image. Even the army general in charge of the anti-narcotics office was arrested, accused of complicity with major Mexican drug lords. Also, Mexico's propensity toward violence increased with rebellions in three states, Chiapas, Oaxaca, and Guerrero.

Mexico seemed to be coming unglued, and the PRI seemed to have run out of answers. Finally, the PRD mobilized discontented groups; it criticized Zedillo's neo-liberal policies and his closeness to the United States. Cárdenas was able to contrast his own austere and honest background with that of the corrupt PRI leadership.

Many saw the electoral defeat of the PRI as the beginning of a true multi-party system, a new democratic era and the end of PRI domination of Mexican politics. Pundits and scholars predicted a PRI defeat in the year 2000 presidential elections.

Yet the PRI seems to have one more life. Since 1997 the party has renovated its national and local leadership; supported reforms making the electoral system more transparent; called for an unprecedented electoral primary to select the next PRI presidential candidate; and attempted to respond to the social and economic ills afflicting Mexico. While lacking charisma, President Zedillo has projected an image of fairness, honesty, and efficiency, and has led his party in a remarkable comeback. In early 1999 the PRI won two important gubernatorial races, attesting to its renewed strength.

Given the unpredictability of Latin American, and Mexican politics in particular, it is difficult to forecast the outcome of the year 2000 elections. Personalities do play a role in Mexican politics. The selection of a populist, charismatic leader will help the PRI. If the PRD and the *Partido de Acción Nacional* (PAN)—the more conservative but still regional political party—continue to run independent of and against each other, it will help the PRI. If the economy remains steady or improves and if the ruling party spends—as it traditionally does before elections—in popular projects, particularly in rural areas, it will also help the PRI.

Betting on a PRI victory may not be a bad deal. After all, in addition to the above factors, the party has a well-greased political machinery throughout the country; a powerful media; and support from labor and other key groups. The party's front-running candidate, Interior Minister Francisco Labastida, is a well-known political figure, having served as governor of Sinaloa and minister of agriculture. What he lacks in charisma, he makes up in toughness and shrewdness. He is a hard-line politician, close to the old PRI stalwarts, able to bring the various party factions into line. On March 4, 1999, Zedillo seemed to endorse Labastida when he emphasized that what the PRI needs is "a strong candidate and a united party."

The PRD opposition candidate, Cárdenas, may flounder as it becomes obvious that his tenure as mayor of troubled Mexico City has not been successful. Solving the problems of Mexico City—crime, corruption, pollution, and overcrowding, to name a few—is a mission impossible. Perhaps Cárdenas would have been better off not winning in 1997.

The front-running PAN candidate, Vicente Fox, has gained in popularity recently. A charismatic and able businessman, he was a fairly successful governor of Guanajuato. Yet his pro-business views and his mostly northern base of support may not go down well with the masses of impoverished Mexicans, with labor, or with the indigenous population of the south.

No matter what the outcome, Mexico has made major progress. A more open society, a multi-party system, and a freer electoral process are all good signs. Yet democracy, even in a Mexican context, is difficult. A powerful presidential tradition; a weak congressional and judicial system; a highly illiterate population unaccustomed to individual responsibility; an unassimilated and poverty-stricken indigenous population; and a society riddled with corruption and narco-trafficking are all problems difficult to overcome. Mario Villanueva, governor of Quintana Roo, fearful of being arrested for drug trafficking, left his post and went into hiding only days before he was to turn power over to a newly elected governor. Building a democratic consensus under these circumstances is an awesome task.

Mexico is still far from having eradicated its authoritarian roots or having made major headway in solving its social and political problems. The next few years are going to be difficult and challenging, especially if the economy fails to improve significantly. Mexico's continuous reliance on petroleum and tourism are dangerous. Petroleum prices are not likely to remain high given the glut in world markets and the prospect of Iraq becoming again a major seller. Tourism is flaky. Crime and violence in Mexico City and around Acapulco may continue to frighten U.S. tourists and others. Any major decline in these two foreign exchange earners will impact Mexico negatively.

U.S. policy also may impact Mexico. The public campaigns in this country for our southern neighbor to clean-up its act with respect to drug trafficking and corruption, to move to a more democratic society, and to control its outward migration are irritants in a delicate relationship. Many in Mexico consider this to be interference in their country's internal affairs.

It is in the interest of the United States for Mexico to remain stable, prosperous, and friendly. Mexico is the third largest U.S. trading partner, a major source of energy, and a key destination for U.S. investments. A policy based on prudence and patience may be best. It would accept the evolution of Mexico's social, political and economic system; encourage continuous change to a more democratic society, and continue to build on the good will generated by NAFTA and recent cordial U.S.-Mexican relations.

I appreciate Irving L. Horowitz, chairman of the board, and Mary Curtis, publisher of Transaction Publishers, for their interest in, and support of, my work and their willingness to publish this paperback edition.

Jaime Suchlicki
Coral Gables, FL
May 1999

PREFACE

I began writing this book in 1992 partly because of the increasing importance of Mexico and partly because of my fascination with Mexican history and culture. I was also encouraged to undertake this effort by my publisher, Brassey's, Inc., who, along with Scribner's, had been very pleased with the strong acceptance in both bookstores and classrooms of the three editions of my earlier history, *Cuba: From Columbus to Castro.* Our common conclusion was that there would be an even greater demand for a brief, though comprehensive, history of Mexico.

My sense of the increasing importance of Mexico was stimulated by many sources. As a historian who is fluent in Spanish, I have studied and taught about Mexico at the University of Miami for almost three decades. I have traveled to Mexico frequently, both with my family and alone. While these trips provoked treasured memories of Mexican sights, scenes, and tastes, they also provided numerous meetings with Mexican officials, prominent scholars, and journalists. Additional insights were derived from my administration of the North-South Center at the University of Miami and from the editorship of the *Journal of Inter-American Studies and World Affairs.* On the U.S. side of the border, I was pleased to be consulted occasionally by members of the U.S. government foreign policy team in several administrations, which provided unique insights into official U.S. thinking about Mexico, its future, its problems, and U.S.-Mexican relations.

Mexico's change and modernization have been fascinating. I have watched in admiration as Mexico shrewdly offered its blazing sun, magnificent beaches, and long, beautiful coastlines in developing its

A contemporary view of the beautiful resort of Acapulco, with its clear ocean, modern high-rises, and impressive mountains. *Alyx Kellington*

potential as a travel and resort destination, which was particularly attractive to U.S. and Canadian visitors. Cozumel, Cancún, Puerto Vallarta, and some inland cities as well followed Acapulco in offering Mexico's architecture, ruins, interesting food, and friendly people to entertain and draw tourists. Northern Mexico was industrializing, with either direct or indirect help from foreign investment and technology, thus creating better paying and less menial jobs, which were desperately needed to offset Mexico's high unemployment and spiraling birthrate. Even the small economic and political elite that was so thoroughly enmeshed with the ruling political party appeared to acknowledge that a better educated and growing middle class deserved a more democratic system.

Despite all of these promising developments, I was fully aware of the less appealing aspect of the complete picture of Mexico. The leaders of the dominant political party—the Institutional Revolutionary Party (PRI)—appeared to be more tolerant of opposition, but still maintained autocratic control of the political process and its economic rewards. Those who were poor remained poor to the point of desperation. Wealth flowed to an expanding, but still narrow, slice of the population. The growing importance of drugs, drug transshipments, and enormous sums of money generated by this traffic could further corrupt Mexican officialdom, the police, the courts, and the military. At the southern borders, problems arose with both poor and neglected indigenous peoples and sometimes radical immigrants fleeing the wars in Central America and establishing camps in Mexico. In the northern areas, a large and increasing stream (perhaps over one million a year) of undocumented Mexicans entered the United States. Hostility simmered, particularly in the U.S. border states, over the grim cost of providing food, housing, education, and health care for these immigrants.

Mexico and my Mexican friends are complex and very enjoyable. As a dispassionate analyst and student of Mexican affairs, however, I was uncertain about the way in which a continuation of historical Mexican contradictions would express themselves in the coming decade. Suddenly, during 1994 and 1995, Mexico exploded into the center of the world's attention. Occasionally, news from Mexico dominated the world's concerns for days at a time. Neither I, nor obviously anyone else, publicly claimed to understand or predict each day's developments. Then, as a historian, I chastised myself, and reread the early chapters of this compilation of Mexico's colorful history. Although specific recent events were unpredictable, and important individual characters sometimes unidentifiable, little was totally new about Mexico's predicaments. Methodical attention to Mexico's historical patterns and trends has led me to believe that these unique events, dramatic and far-reaching though they have been, are merely the latest, if perhaps most intriguing and important, chapter in Mexico's long and exciting history. Suddenly, there was an urgency about completing and publishing this work, which hopefully will offer an explanation of Mexico's experience and its effect upon the world.

This is not a volume of political science, economics, international finance, or foreign policy. These aspects of the country are recorded in this historical chronicle of Mexico's major events and rhythms. This book is written for those who are merely curious, or deeply interested, or concerned about Mexico—its past and its future. It is written to explain Mexico to its neighbors, businesspeople, jet-set tourists, journalists, political leaders, workers and peasants, students, Hispanic Americans, and all those interested in learning about the fascinating, interesting, and sometimes boisterous history of this wonderful country and its people. Hopefully, readers of this volume will learn as much about Mexico as I did in the long years of research preceding its publication.

Many people helped in the preparation of this volume. I am particularly indebted to my friend, the president of Brassey's, Dr. Frank Margiotta, whose suggestions significantly improved the book. Professor Manuel Suarez-Mier made valuable comments. I am grateful for his insight as well as his endorsement of the book. Similarly, I am thankful to Mario Ojeda Gómez, president of El Colegio de Mexico, for his kind words. Several students at the University of Miami's Graduate School of International Studies, Franco Uccelli, and Carmen Hume contributed to the research, and I am most grateful to them. My able assistant, Maria Urizar, typed the original manuscript and dealt with my numerous revisions and changes, for which I am most appreciative. Diane Hamilton worked tirelessly in obtaining the photos for this book, primarily from the Library of Congress. To her and the library I am most grateful. My wife, Carol, and my children, Michael and his wife, Laura, Kevin, and Joy tolerated my moods, ignored me when I was immersed in writing, and demanded very little. To them, all my love and appreciation.

J.S.
Coral Gables, Florida
1995

MEXICO

CHAPTER 1

UNDERSTANDING MEXICO

Millions of tourists around the world fondly remember the beaches and burning sun of the Mexican coastline, the excellent creative food, the mariachi bands blaring in the streets, the soft music of romantic violins under a moonlit sky, and the ruins of ancient civilizations whose monuments remind one of the Egyptians. Foreigners have a benign and warm feeling about the Mexican people and vacationing in Mexico. Other millions have eaten vegetables and fruit grown in Mexico and have used products made in Mexico. International business people have evaluated Mexico eagerly as a place to invest money, to start new businesses, and to establish franchises of stores and restaurants popular worldwide. Manufacturing companies looked toward Mexico for its less expensive and reliable labor and to its growing markets for their products. Businesses and individuals in the American cities bordering Mexico have counted on Mexican labor and purchases by Mexican citizens, as Mexicans on their side of the border have counted on the business generated for them by Americans in Mexico. Worldwide, investors have sought quick profits by purchasing shares in Mexican companies available for sale in foreign stock markets or through international mutual funds. Teléfonos de Mexico, hotly traded on the New York Stock Exchange, soared upward in price. Banks invested in, and loaned money to, the Mexican government, businesses, financial institutions, and individuals.

Mexico's image had become one of a developing country nearing economic takeoff—willing to open and integrate its economy into the major trading blocs, and moving toward a more democratic political system, that would recognize pluralism and tolerate opposition. Suddenly, dramatic shocks began to crack the façade of Mexico's growth, modernity, and stability. Step by step, a series of explosive, almost frightening, events scarred Mexican progress. These built to a crescendo of doubt and fear about Mexico's future, both within and outside the country.

On January 1, 1994, celebrations for the implementation of the North American Free Trade Agreement (NAFTA) were diluted by an unexpected, but carefully organized, guerrilla uprising in the southernmost state of Chiapas. This quickly developed into a challenge to national stability with smaller echoes of bombings in the capital city. The stunned world watched as towns were occupied, the army was rushed in, battles took place, and hundreds were killed and wounded. Scenes of extreme poverty and determined Mexican revolutionaries appeared around the world on local television. A resolution of this revolt seemed elusive.

In March 1994, the country was rocked again as the PRI nominee and, thus, the next president of Mexico, Luis Donaldo Colosio, was assassinated. Although the substitute PRI candidate won a surprisingly strong and relatively honest victory in August, this triumph was soon marred by the assassination of the head of the dominant PRI party. Three weeks into December 1994 and into his term, the new president, Ernesto Zedillo, surprised everyone and drastically devalued the peso because Mexican foreign exchange holdings had been depleted by his predecessor. The Mexican economy and people were thrown into chaos, and world financial and business leaders were stunned. Investors lost fortunes as stock prices tumbled. Mexico's new importance was evident through worldwide efforts to support the Mexican currency and economic system and through the deep personal involvement of the American president in this effort.

Additional surprises were not far behind. Early in 1995, the violent uprising in Chiapas flared again. The army was initially dispatched to snuff out this rebellion, and then suddenly it was withdrawn. Rumors of a coup by angry military officers raced through the capital. In March 1995, the Mexican president again shocked the country and the world. He publicly assailed former President Salinas by arresting Salinas's brother in the murder of the PRI head, accusing Salinas of a cover-up in the investigation of the assassination of presidential candidate Colosio, and blaming the former president for the peso devaluation and economic wreckage. Also in March, the former assistant attorney general and brother of the assassinated head of the PRI was arrested in the United States when it was discovered he had laundered millions of dollars from Mexico into the United States and may have helped cover up the murder of his own brother. A drug dealers' conspiracy was whispered to be behind the two assassinations. Mexico began to resemble a tragic soap opera, with almost daily plot twists and turns, as the world figuratively shook its head in bewilderment. By the time this book is published, undoubtedly there will have been further occurrences and discoveries that will be equally unexpected and surprising.

What is an astonished and fascinated world to make of all of this? Is there any coherent explanation? What should one think of Mexico now? Is Mexico to be avoided? This is not a book of current events or of predictions. Rather, it is a history that contends that to understand Mexico today and tomorrow one has to look at Mexico yesterday. Revolutionary peasants, violence, and assassinations are an integral part of the rich and colorful tapestry of Mexico's history. They, along with the continuing concerns over NAFTA, financial chaos, and the victory of the PRI presidential candidate, flow from the basic currents that have shaped Mexican life for more than one thousand years.

Although this volume is naturally organized as a chronological history, there are several major themes that are key to understanding the forces and contradictions that have shaped Mexico, its culture, its people, and its history. These patterns will continue to affect Mexico's future. As one reads about Mexico's turbulent past, one should note several themes and elements recurring and affecting the history of Mexico:

Struggles between north and south, urban and rural, rich and poor, Mexico City and the rest of the country. In many respects, these tensions reinforce one another and help to explain some of the violence as different regions and groupings have tried to capture national power at the center in Mexico City. In general, the south of Mexico is poor, agricultural, rural, provincial, peasant, and alienated from Mexico City. The north is more industrialized, urban, unionized, and richer; it receives attention and benefits from Mexico City. The capital dominates the country and has accrued financial, economic, and political power at the expense of the rest of the country, particularly the rural areas.

Attraction to, and rejection of, the United States and its influence. A famous Mexican writer once aptly summed up the historic Mexican view of the United States: "So far from God, so near to the United States." Mexicans admire the United States. Mexicans are quite hospitable to millions of U.S. citizens who work within or visit Mexico each year. Mexicans share a vast U.S. border, desire to own U.S. products, sell more goods to the United States than to any other country, solicit U.S. investment for growth, have millions of relatives living in the Colossus of the North, have joined the North American Free Trade Agreement, and wish for a democracy as it exists in the United States. Mexicans also remember, however, that Americans took more than one third of Mexico's territory, have invaded Mexico several times, have meddled frequently in Mexican affairs, and have often exercised undue influence over the Mexican economy and government. Then, there are the issues surrounding undocumented Mexicans who violate U.S. law by entering and remaining in the United States. Mexican history is rife with ambivalence on the part of Mexico and Mexicans about the United States. It is an unequal relationship, which has sometimes erupted in outbursts of violence on both sides. This history of cross-border relations has often been mixed into the struggles among the groups mentioned above.

Liberal and conservative swings in an autocratic political system. Mexico has rarely had a widely accepted method of transferring legitimacy to new governments and leaders. During the nineteenth century, small elite cliques made the choices of who governs, and, because the governments or parties in power tried to smother serious opposition, violence often resulted. Government figures or opponents were removed by bullets, and broader rebellions and revolutions seemed necessary to overthrow unacceptable governments. Because government is a path to riches and to rewarding particular groups, those out of power have had strong incentives to seize the reins. Even within the six decades of relative stability provided by the dominant party—PRI—in this century, there have been pendulum swings between left and right. A conservative president may tend to favor decreasing government's role, reducing spending on the poor, and encouraging the business and professional classes. A more liberal leader would swing the pendulum toward the rural classes, labor, social spending, and a larger direct government role in the economy, including ownership of important sectors. This cyle has been repeated continually throughout Mexican history during struggles between the rich and the poor, the capital and the rest of Mexico, the north and the south, and the rural and urban areas.

A major political role for the military. Because Mexican national unity was historically hampered by geographic and ethnic divisions, and because violence was often used as a solution to political succession issues, military leaders have played a historic and important role in governing Mexico. From the landing of Cortés until the 1930s, power most often came from the barrel of a gun. Mexican history is thus replete with storied and colorful military presidents, pretenders, and insurgent peasant guerrilla leaders. Again, the strains between the groups mentioned above have often been acted out through military or revolutionary leaders representing different classes, interests, and regions. The direct role of the military has been significantly reduced since 1940 by co-optation and consultation within the councils of the ruling party and government. Unless there are satisfactory resolutions of the recent Chiapas uprising and assassinations of major political figures, however, one can predict that the role of the military will increase.

The Catholic Church versus the political system. There has been a natural tension between an international and powerful Catholic Church and the leaders of Mexico. This has ranged from the later years of colonial rule when clergymen led rebellions against the Spanish state, to prohibition and persecution of the Church after the 1910 Revolution, to a peaceful accommodation during the late twentieth century. One can sometimes see a pattern of local clergy aligning with the abused and neglected rural peasants, while at higher levels, the Church sometimes has supported the ruling classes of the larger cities. In 1995, church versus state does not appear to be a source of major friction, but one should not be surprised if this tension develops in a severely distressed Mexico.

Competition between the needs of different races and ethnicities. The Mexican population is composed of three major groups—Indians, the indigenous Mexicans; mestizos, those of mixed Indian and Spanish ancestors; and direct descendants of the conquering Spaniards. The Indian population has often been out of mainstream Mexico and has been predominantly poor, rural, and located in the south and other regions of the country distant from the center. Abused, exploited, and lacking enough land to do more than subsist, Indian peasant rebellions and guerrilla armies are such a persistent feature of Mexican history as to have become mythological. Spanish descendants are more likely to live in the city and be more prosperous and better educated professionals or owners of land. Mestizos are the largest part of the population and are caught between two cultures. They are the most likely to migrate to the United States. These three groupings at times find themselves on opposite sides of issues that surface because of other splits in the society. Many major struggles of Mexican history have resulted from the competition between the differing needs and values of these three groups.

A divided land: Mexico's natural environment. Mexico has been both blessed and cursed by its natural environment. Its geography and climate often divide and isolate groups and foster growth and development in some regions while making it difficult in others. It is appropriate to precede our story of Mexican history with a brief introduction to the landscape and the early peoples that so shape the Mexican experience.

CHAPTER 2

A Divided Land: Mexico's Natural Environment and Native Peoples

Mexico is a contrasting and beautiful blend of past and present. It is a land where the influences of highly developed Indian civilizations and old Spain flourish visibly in a modernized society. Rich in culture, history, and tradition, the people of Mexico are a unique mixture of Indian and Spanish descent. They are as varied as the land they inhabit. The history of Mexico, deeply engraved by its Indian past and its Spanish colonial experience, has created a dynamic people, a unique country, and an exciting culture.

Those who visit Mexico are instantly captivated by its charm and diversity. There is not one but many Mexicos—a kaleidoscope of different peoples living in various phases of cultural and economic development, some still in virtual isolation, populating pockets of land in faraway mountains, villages, and jungles.

At first glance, one immediately sees the differences in Mexico's landscape. Its natural scenery is a composition of majestic mountains, jungles, deserts, valleys, lakes, and, of course, beaches. With the exception of the northern mesa and the Yucatán Peninsula, much of Mexico is divided by mountain ranges. The eastern Sierra Madre and the western Sierra Madre run north to south across the country, forming numerous valleys and plateaus. In between these two great mountain chains lies the central plateau, which contains the northern and central portions of Mexico. It is here that the majority of Mexico's eighty-seven million people are located and where agriculture thrives. These mountain chains and the Sierra Madre del Sur, another cluster of mountains that further divides the south of Mexico, determine Mexico's geographic fractionalism. They highlight the difficulty that has existed in communication and transportation. In part, geography has contributed to Mexico's economic problems, past and present, and has had a significant impact on the culture of people physically separated from one another.

Geographically distinct from the three main Sierra Madres is one of the world's most notable volcanic belts, which crosses the country in an east-west direction from about Colima on the Pacific to near Mexico City in the middle of the country to Veracruz on the Atlantic. For Mexicans, volcanoes are both a curse and a blessing. Constant minor tremors, with an occasional major earthquake, make life on the plateau exciting and often dangerous. Yet, volcanic soil is extremely fertile and has made the regions flanking this volcanic belt the richest agricultural areas of Mexico.

Mexico is relatively large, encompassing 760,600 square miles, about one fourth the size of the United States. In Latin America, only Brazil and Argentina are larger. Much of the country is either mountainous or wilderness, lacks water, and has limited arable land, which are critical elements in its human geography. Half of the land—all through the north, along the coasts, and in the Yucatán—is arid and must be irrigated before it can produce any crops. Another third is semiarid. Only a small percentage of the land is capable of yielding a harvest without irrigation. Wherever water is abundant from rainfall or rivers, great care and resources must be expended to prevent recurrent floods.

Two principal bodies of water bound Mexico—the Pacific Ocean on the west coast and the Gulf of Mexico on the east. In addition to these two, the Gulf of California is a smaller body of water that lies between the Baja peninsula and the mainland. Although many rivers run throughout Mexico, very few can be used for navigation, and most flow through the least populated areas. The Rio Grande is a well-known river that runs for one thousand miles between the United States and Mexico. Throughout most of the year, it, too, is unnavigable.

Most of the rivers can be used for irrigation or as a source of generating electricity.

Many people are undoubtedly drawn to Mexico for its warm, temperate climate, but here, too, the temperature varies almost as much as the land and its people. Mexico gets hotter as one proceeds southeast toward the equator. At the same time, the higher one goes, the cooler it becomes. Half of Mexico falls within the northern temperature zone, while the other half lies south of the Tropic of Cancer. These two temperature zones produce very different climates, ranging from very hot through temperate to relatively cool, depending upon factors such as altitude, latitude, and rainfall. Most of the population lives in the temperate lands in the central plateau in and around Mexico City, where temperatures range from seventy to seventy-five degrees Fahrenheit. The highlands are usually too cold and the coastal areas around the Gulf of Mexico are too hot, with rapidly leaching soils. This, together with the location of Mexico's major Indian civilization during the 1500s, explains why the Spaniards settled and established their capital in present-day Mexico City rather than on the coast.

Rainfall is also important for living conditions, and in most of Mexico it is insufficient. Large areas receive little rain, while others are frequently drenched. From one year to another, farmers wonder whether drought will destroy their crops. The subtropic zone, where Mexico City is located, combines good soil with sufficient rainfall.

In addition to the diversity of its land and the nature of its climate, Mexico has much to offer in natural resources. Lush forests occupy vast regions of the country. Trees of great stature, age, and variety, such as pine and oak, populate the national parks set aside by the government to preserve these valuable reserves.

Minerals are yet another extremely important Mexican resource. As far back as the conquistadores, Mexico's mineral deposits have been of great interest to other countries. Today, Mexico is still a leading producer of silver. Anyone who travels to the country is immediately aware of the abundance of silver and is surprisingly pleased to discover its reasonable price. Other minerals that contribute to Mexico's well-developed mining industry are lead, zinc, copper, and gold. Besides these resources, Mexico has a plentiful supply of iron ore and is one of the world's largest producers of oil.

Mexico truly has been given a landscape of contrasts and contradictions to shape its history, and the same can be said of its diverse populations. To fully appreciate the complexity and richness of Mexican culture and history, one must understand their roots in the Mexican people. The Indians who inhabited early Mexico had created (along with the Incas of Peru) the most advanced and sophisticated civilizations in all of North and South America.

When the Spaniards arrived at the great Aztec city of Tenochtitlán, they encountered only the last of a long series of indigenous civilizations. While the Aztecs dominated immediately before the Spanish conquest, they did not represent the zenith of cultural development achieved in Mexico. The Aztecs themselves had myths and legends that told of the great civilizations that preceded their own. The ancient history of Mexico is replete with the ruins of civilizations that rose, became dominant, and later fell. The development of pre-Hispanic Mexico is not the history of a single and continuous culture that developed and expanded or contracted depending on the whims of nature or warfare. It is a complex patchwork of cultures that rose and fell independently of one another but that often merged through trade or war.

The rugged terrain of Mesoamerica, which embraces much of Mexico, has been host to several cultures, all of which had their start with the first migration of *Homo sapiens* into the Western Hemisphere between twenty thousand and fifty thousand years ago. These first Americans are believed to have been Asian hunters who unknowingly crossed the Bering Strait in pursuit of big game during the Wisconsin Ice Age. At this time, the polar ice caps swelled in size and the Bering Strait, a narrow, relatively shallow channel of water, was exposed as the ocean's water level dropped, frozen in polar ice. Successive waves of Asian nomads advanced across this ice land bridge into North America. Eventually, the ice caps began to melt, and by 8000 B.C. the land bridge had disappeared. Although it was still possible to cross over from Asia by water, and a few Asians probably did, their numbers were relatively insignificant.

These first migrants are believed to have traveled in small bands. Following their prey, these nomads slowly inhabited the Americas, working their way south. By 16,000 B.C., the Western Hemisphere was unevenly and sparsely populated from Alaska to Tierra del Fuego. These early Americans' livelihoods depended on their geographic location. All of them relied on the gathering of wild plants and small animals; some were proficient hunters of large game; other, near lakes or the sea, were fishermen. They were acquainted with fire and produced stone tools, carvings of bone and wood, and probably baskets and nets. These primitive people lived in small, family-based groups, moving as the need arose, in search of more bountiful territory.

Although they were relatively nomadic, they tended to remain within a specific range. These familial groups expanded and became more settled. With a more sedentary lifestyle came simple plant cultivation based on maize, beans, squash, chili peppers, and, perhaps, fruit trees. Dogs were also domesticated around this time. The transformation from nomadic hunter-gatherers to settled agriculturalists was slow and uneven, but an agricultural economy based on year-round farming was consolidated in Mesoamerica about 2000 B.C.

The agricultural techniques used by the first Mesoamericans were established early. The most common method was milpa, or slash-and-burn agriculture. This method is believed to have been very productive and able to support large populations. Slash-and-burn farming tended to exhaust the soil quickly—within two or three years—so farmers often moved into new territory or left fallow a portion of a cleared land. Although productive, milpa agriculture required large tracts of land; the highland regions required a more intensive system using terraces and irrigation systems. In marshy areas and around the edges of lakes, *chinampas* (small artificial islands), sometimes called "floating gardens," were used. Despite the advances and various agricultural methods used throughout the region, the Mesoamericans were seriously limited by the lack of draft animals.

These early farmers lived in small villages of modest scattered dwellings. In the highlands, their houses were made of wattle and daub with thatched palm roofs, and in the lowlands, they were constructed of wood. These villagers produced various crafts, such as weaving, ceramics, and woodworking. Pottery and clay figurines were common throughout Mesoamerica.

Village communities were organized around centers with distinctive ceremonial structures, which were apparently occupied by specialized elites with the power to appropriate agricultural surpluses and labor. Only societies governed by powerful elites and a dominant ideology could have compelled the peasantry to provide the labor necessary to build and maintain such centers with their massive temples and palaces and to support the nonfarming elites.

These early societies were pantheistic, although a single sect tended to dominate, and within society, the elite leaders served as intermediaries between gods and men. This hierarchy of warrior kings and their subordinate priests designed and built the cities, developed art and science, engaged in trade and war, and controlled the government and religion, which could explain the rise and rapid fall of several Mesoamerican societies. When the elites were either defeated in battle or overthrown in revolt, their cultures faded with them, while the rural masses' lives continued basically unchanged.

The oldest of the early civilizations in the New World was Olmec. Actually, Olmec refers to an art form and culture rather than to a particular people. The Olmecs are considered the "mother culture" of Mesoamerica, as nearly all succeeding civilizations share some aspect of the political, social, economic, or religious patterns first developed by them.

Little is known about their origins, as ruins of their civilization provide nearly all that is known. Olmec culture flourished between 1200 and 400 B.C. near the Gulf coast in the lowlands of southern Veracruz and western Tabasco.

They were excellent architects, and their prominent use of platforms and north-south orientation became the model for later Mesoamerican cities. The carefully planned Olmec ceremonial complexes demonstrate notable engineering and construction skills. Through the construction of stone-lined pools, their cities had a year-round water supply. In addition, the oldest ball court is found here, which suggests that the ceremonial game played throughout Mesoamerica originated with the Olmecs.

Olmec art was both abstract and realistic; it portrayed religious myths and real persons. Olmec artists used various materials and produced numerous objects from tiny jade figurines to massive stone sculptures. The colossal stone heads are the most striking. They depict subjects with infantile features—wearing what appear to be North American football helmets. The heads are believed to depict chieftains, warriors, or perhaps gods. The Olmec also produced many stone altars and stelae. Stelae are huge stone slabs carved in relief, which often depict historical scenes and hieroglyphic information.

Trade and conquest featured significantly in the Olmec society, but religion was the force behind the spread of its culture throughout the region. Olmec religion exhibits two cults—the jaguar cult and the serpent cult—which influenced all subsequent Mesoamerican religious thought. The jaguar cult dominated Olmec society and art. Representations of jaguars and ma-jaguars are found throughout. Quetzalcóatl, the feathered serpent, later god of the Aztecs, came from the Olmec serpent cult. The cult of Quetzalcóatl ultimately spread throughout Mesoamerica, and the feathered serpent became one of the most powerful gods. In fact, more than a thousand years later, Quetzalcóatl still had a profound effect upon Mexico's history; upon Cortés's arrival,

Olmec culture, the oldest of the early civilizations in the New World, flourished around 1200 B.C. on the Gulf coast around Veracruz. *Library of Congress*

Montezuma II believed that Cortés was Quetzalcóatl returning to claim the Aztec throne.

The greatest achievements of the Olmecs were cultural. They developed mathematics, astronomy, and a calendar. The calendar system invented by the Olmecs was highly accurate and tracked time back nearly three thousand years. The Mesoamerican calendar system that the Olmecs originally developed was based on both a 365-day solar year and a 260-day lunar year. These two cycles together generated a fifty-two-year cycle marking the end of an era. The end of a fifty-two-year cycle was believed to be a significant and dangerous time.

The Olmec calendar system required an advanced understanding of mathematics. The Olmec number system was vigesimal (based on twenty) instead of decimal and used three symbols—a dot for one, a bar for five, and a shell-like symbol for zero. The concept of zero is one of the Olmecs' greatest achievements. It permitted numbers to be written by position and allowed for complex calculations. Although the invention of zero is often attributed to the Mayans, it was originally conceived by the Olmecs. Even the Europeans lacked the concept of zero, until it was imported from the Middle East during the Middle Ages.

The decline of the Olmec civilization began around 900 B.C. Owing to the apparent violence involved in the destruction, some scholars speculate that the fall of the Olmecs was caused by social upheaval. Perhaps the ruling Olmec elite became oppressive and progressively demanded more labor and tribute from the commoners, which ultimately precipitated a revolt. The end arrived around 400 B.C.

From the Olmecs' ruins developed a series of distinct, but related cultures. Over the centuries, trade and religion promoted Olmec culture throughout Mesoamerica, and other societies adopted aspects of Olmec culture. Archaeologists believe that Izapa, in the state of Chiapas in southern Mexico, served as a cultural link between the Olmecs and the classical Mayan civilizations, which would later flourish and control parts of southern Mexico and Central America. The Zapotecs, whose supreme capital was at Monte Albán in the present state of Oaxaca, also were influenced by the Olmecs. After the fall of the Olmecs, the Mayan civilization and those centered at Monte Albán and Teotihuacán would dominate the region from the start of the Christian era to the year A.D. 900.

This represents the classic period of development when pre-Hispanic Indian civilization flourished, and architecture, artistic expression, and science were at their zenith. Advanced crafts and skills were required to provide for complex communities. The burgeoning population required strict measures to provide for it. Human sacrifice, which would be so common under the Aztecs, was far less frequent. The classic period is marked by relative peace, and a sense of order, progress, and regimentation guided the leadership. Farming became more scientific, and abstract thinking increased as emphasis was placed on planting cycles and seasonal calculations to determine those cycles.

In the central valley of Mexico at Teotihuacán, the Olmecs' advances were incorporated into a culture and civilization believed to have been the greatest in pre-Hispanic America. Teotihuacán has been compared with ancient Rome because of its monumental size, widespread influence, and imposing structures. At its peak, Teotihuacán's population was between 125,000 and 250,000; the city covered more than twelve square miles. It was the bustling metropolis of an empire that controlled much of Mesoamerica. Evidence of its influence has been found as far south as the Mayan outpost on the outskirts of Guatemala City and into northern Mexico. Despite Teotihuacán's size and influence, Monte Albán and the Mayans remained relatively independent of it.

The Aztecs referred to Teotihuacán as "the place of the gods," and it inspired reverential awe. Aztec legend said that the gods lived there

Not unlike the Egyptians, the early peoples of Latin America also built pyramids. This one at Teotihuacán and others found outside Mexico City and in the Yucatán are prime examples of indigenous architecture. *Diane Hamilton*

and that the sun and moon were created there as well. Owing to the city's immense size, the Aztecs believed that it must have been built by a race of giants, although it was in ruins long before the Aztecs arrived. Like most pre-Hispanic Mesoamerican ancient cities, it was divided into four quadrants representing the four corners of the universe. Teotihuacán was an important religious and commercial center, that contained many ceremonial buildings, pyramids, and an immense marketplace.

The size of Teotihuacán and the density of its population required a sophisticated social system to organize and ensure the well-being of its inhabitants and those of the outlying territories. The society was composed of various social strata. The lower classes lived in barrios grouped according to familial ties and trades or function. Numerous barrios would be present in each of the city's four quadrants. The imperial society, which possessed authority, knowledge, and religious privilege, crowned this organizational structure. Between the lowest and the highest classes, however, existed merchants, soldiers, and priests. The merchants traveled throughout the empire, trading in cacao, cotton, quetzal feathers, and luxury objects of fine stone. These powerful merchants may have collected tribute from subject populations or acted as diplomats for the ruling elite on their travels, which increased their power and prestige in the social system. War was not as chronic as it was later, but a powerful state such as Teotihuacán still relied on soldiers to maintain order. The priests held the greatest power and influence of these middle groups. They possessed the highest culture and learning, planned the buildings, and were responsible for maintaining the calendar, all of which were related to religion. Religion was the center of life in Teotihuacán as in all Mesoamerican civilizations. Residents of the surrounding areas were drawn to Teotihuacán, much as tourists or pilgrims are drawn to particular cities today, which contributed to its status and prosperity.

Probably owing to agricultural failure, Teotihuacán began to decline. Around A.D. 640, Teotihuacán was invaded, looted, burned, and, in part, deliberately destroyed. The fall of Teotihuacán initiated a period of confusion and migrating populations throughout central Mexico. While disorder dominated in the north, Mayan culture entered a period of great expansion and progress.

The Mayans had many important centers, none of which completely dominated the others. The Petén region of Guatemala, however, is generally considered the heart of Mayan culture. The great city of Tikal, with a population of one hundred thousand people, contains six pyramids, among which was the tallest of the Mayans. Beautified by lakes, palaces, temples, and ball courts, Tikal represents an example of Mayan grandeur. There were, however, other significant Mayan centers located in southern Mexico and Yucatán.

The Mayans were the premier scientists of pre-Hispanic America. Under their direction, writing and calendars were taken to new heights. Although only about two thirds of Mayan hieroglyphs have been deciphered, they have revealed some fascinating insights into the refinement of Mayan learning. Under the Mayan calendar system, symbols used to record dates were extremely distinctive. The Mayans also had a mathematical unit that was the equivalent of sixty-four million.

There is no consensus regarding the decline of the Mayans, which occurred around A.D. 900. Perhaps it was a lack of food resulting from pestilence, insects, or some other natural disaster. Some scholars suggest internal rebellion or that invaders from the north imparted the Mayans with warlike characteristics, which ultimately resulted in their self-destruction.

The rise and fall of the Mayans in the southern regions of Mexico had little impact on the central highlands. Violent invaders from the north, however, would radically change the features of pre-Hispanic

Located at Chichén Itzá in the Yucatán Peninsula, this is one of the most remarkable pyramids in the New World. The Mayans were the premier scientists of pre-Hispanic America and developed an accurate calendar and a superior writing system. *Library of Congress*

Mexico. Although metallurgy was introduced, perhaps from South America, there was little scientific advancement. They produced gold and silver jewelry and used copper to fashion weapons, but otherwise the use of metal was very limited. Written records were introduced, which provided a more substantial base of inquiry, but the historical accounts of the period are permeated with myth and legend and often are fragmentary at best.

The most striking change involved the political systems that dominated. Societies became more militant and violent. Wars were waged for tribute instead of territory. Wars also were fought simply to collect subjects for methodical sacrifices that, along with the importance of fearful gods, had begun to dominate religion.

While the civilization centered at Teotihuacán dominated the region, the barbaric northern tribes were kept from the central valley. With the fall of Teotihuacán, however, the valley was subjected to periodic invasions from the north. The northern tribes, consisting of various groups, were known by the generic term *Chichimec*. Perhaps the most important group of these nomadic tribes was the Tolteca-Chichimeca, or Toltecs.

The available written history concerning the Toltecs permits a more distinct depiction. It is generally believed that the Toltecs arrived in the central valley during the tenth century with their leader Mixcóatl. The Toltecs' history is filled with accounts of court intrigue and politics surrounding Mixcóatl's son Topiltzin and his battle to control the empire. Topiltzin became a devoted follower of the ancient god Quetzalcóatl, and eventually assumed the god's name in addition to his own. He gained control of the empire and founded Tula in A.D. 968. The Toltecs, originally a semibarbarous people, assimilated the more advanced ways of the central valley and flourished under his benevolent reign.

Tula's influence and the prestige of the Toltecs would endure well beyond their fall. Although not as large as Teotihuacán, Tula is believed to have been more majestic and extravagant. Palaces were decorated with colorful plumage, gold sheeting, jewels, and seashells. Much of the Toltecs' history was embellished by the Aztecs, who attributed Topiltzin with great powers and merged his mythical achievements with the serpent god himself. According to tradition, Topiltzin was believed to possess boundless knowledge and was considered to be the originator of all benefits to mankind. He showed his people how to plant corn, which grew to incredible size, and he is credited with having invented writing, the ritual calendar, and the architectural marvels of Tula.

Toltec society was not homogeneous. Diverse tribes lived within the city, and dissident factions developed. These factions ultimately evolved into competition between those who championed war and those who advocated peace. This conflict was personified through tales of Tezcatlipoca and Quetzalcóatl. The ancestral supreme deity of the Toltecs was Tezcatlipoca (Smoking Mirror)—an unpredictable, fierce god who was never to be crossed. Followers of Tezcatlipoca advocated human sacrifice and war, while the more peaceful followers of Quetzalcóatl preferred more symbolic sacrifice such as butterflies. The ascendancy of the followers of Tezcatlipoca and the flight of Topiltzin had profound consequences on the future of the Toltecs and Mexico.

The militant Tezcatlipoca faction in Tula established a new order, which would persist in Mexico until the Spanish arrived—excessive human sacrifice and forceful conquest of other societies. A new fearsome image also appears in their remaining works. Huge statues of warriors symbolize the knightly orders of jaguar and eagle.

Toltec influence on the Mayan cities of the Yucatán is manifest in the architecture and what is known about the hybrid Toltec-Mayan society that prospered at Chichén Itzá. Even the city itself bears record of the intense Toltec influence. "Itzá" is a Mayan name for the Toltecs. Despite the advances made in the Yucatán, by the time the Spanish arrived, the region had deteriorated into an anarchic array of impoverished city states.

By the twelfth century, the Toltecs' power waned as droughts and attacks by the northern barbarians increasingly took their toll. Tula was finally destroyed, and the Toltecs were dispersed throughout the region. Although they were no longer powerful as a society, their influence endured throughout Mexico's central valley.

After the Toltecs' fall, another period of confusion and instability pervaded central Mexico. Waves of barbaric Chichimecs pressed down and were incorporated into the competing communities, which were the legacy of the Toltec empire. City states rose and fell throughout the region as each vied for hegemony. From this chaos emerged the Aztecs, who would eventually dominate the central valley of Mexico and represent all Mexican Indians to the peoples of Europe.

Ironically, Mexico received its name from the Mexica, commonly known as the Aztecs. The Aztecs were relative latecomers to the valley of central Mexico—and unwelcome latecomers, too. When they arrived, the valley was divided into city-states. These relatively small cities were populated by peoples whose culture derived more from the descendants of Teotihuacán and the Toltecs than did that of the new arrivals from the north. These refined farmers regarded the Aztecs with profound distaste. The Aztecs were perceived as crude, boorish interlopers. Part of this perception derived from their custom of gruesome human sacrifice, but stealing their neighbors' wives surely contributed, also.

Despite the repulsiveness of the Aztecs, the farming peoples of the valley learned to tolerate them or to respect their ruthlessness. The Aztecs were ambitious, excellent warriors, whose ability was appreciated by the valley's ruling warlords.

The Aztecs found the shores of Lake Texcoco a useful place to hide. Along the marshy edges of the lake, considered unsuitable by others in the area, no one bothered them, and the region was abundant in fish. The Aztecs finally settled on a small island in the lake from which, through great ingenuity and great labor, they founded the great city of Tenochtitlán. Through a sequence of alliances and marriages, the Mexica-Aztecs had a real monarchy descended from the royal house of the Toltecs. Following a power struggle, Tenochtitlán joined the cities of Texcoco and Tlacopan in a triple alliance, which would eventually control central Mexico.

During the middle of the fifteenth century, the densely populated kingdom was wracked by a series of natural disasters. The resulting famine caused thousands to flee or die. These natural disasters had
a lasting effect on Aztec society. The Aztec leadership realized that, to
ensure the viability of the metropolis, they must gain access to food
sources by expanding and broadening their control beyond Mexico's
central valley. This military expansion had the combined effect of
solidifying Aztec domination and making bloody, large-scale sacrifice
an important element in the Aztec state. By the end of the fifteenth
century, through intimidation and warfare, the Aztecs dominated the
triple alliance and most of Mesoamerica—a position they would maintain until the arrival of Cortés.

Aztec civilization embodied bits and pieces of the many Indian
cultures preceding it, although it did not represent the peak of pre-
Hispanic culture in Mexico. The island-city of Tenochtitlán appeared
enormous and impressive. Estimates of the city's population ran from
80,000 to 250,000—more than six times larger than Seville, which was
the largest city in Spain at the time. Throughout the city were tall pyramids crowned with temples. The city itself was pyramid shaped; the
height of the buildings gradually increased as one approached the center of the city, passing first houses, then palaces, and finally the Great
Temple, which was the city's center and highest point. Lush trees and
gardens were everywhere, and there were large ponds for ducks and
swans. Great dikes spanned the lake to regulate its level and keep fresh
water separate from brackish. Fresh water also was brought into the city
by aqueducts from mountain springs.

In addition to their architectural and engineering accomplishments,
the Aztecs were quite advanced culturally. Although the Aztec's written
language was still a mixture of pictographs, ideograms, and phonetic
writing, their spoken language, Náhuatl, was quite refined. A pleasant-
sounding language, with a rich vocabulary and flexible construction,
Náhuatl allowed its speakers to express intricate concepts and feelings.
Perhaps as a result of this, the Aztecs preferred repetitious, rhyming
poetry over prose. Poetic orations were used to preserve customs and
social ideals, and dancing and music also were intimately connected
with social and religious rituals.

Aztec society was highly stratified. On the top was the emperor. The
last emperor, Montezuma II, was a semidivine despot with thousands of
servants and an unlimited number of concubines. The other extreme
of society encompassed the largest groups—the commoners, or *macehualtes,* and the slaves. The *macehualtes* were divided into administra-

tive clans, called *calpulli,* whose membership was based on extended familial ties. A *calpulli,* similar to a district or ward with a chosen spokesman, provided for the basic unit of control for Aztec society. Members worked a common piece of land and, in times of war, would fight together.

Merchants and craftsmen had certain privileges and prestige, but they were legally commoners and were not strictly part of the noble class. The *pochteca* organized caravans and traded throughout the empire and beyond. They often passed through hostile territory, so the empire used them as spies and diplomats. Next came the skilled craftsmen. Within this class, there were degrees of status. Those who were jewelers and those who created intricate featherwork were held in higher regard than stonecutters, for example.

The nobles, or *tecuhtli,* provided the administrative expertise to run Aztec society. Membership in this class was not technically hereditary but it did have certain hereditary aspects. Being born into the nobility afforded certain advantages that helped to ensure a suitable societal position, and consequently many positions were passed from father to son. The *tecuhtli* was dominated by two groups—the military and the priesthood. These two career paths were not mutually exclusive and gave Aztec society its character of theocratic militarism. The priesthood and military shared a common bond in that they both dominated the Aztec realm. The warriors conquered new lands and used the vanquished people to work the land and obtain tribute. They also collected victims who were given to the priests for religious sacrifice.

Religion permeated Aztec society. Nearly every aspect of everyday life, from planting corn to warfare, held some religious significance. Although the Aztecs worshiped a pantheon of gods, Huitzilopochtli, the god of sun and war, was their chief deity. According to Aztec legend, the sun and earth had previously been destroyed four separate times. They were living in the fifth sun and felt that final destruction was imminent.

There were strange, mysterious forces at work everywhere in Aztec daily life. The Aztecs considered themselves to be at the mercy of the elements and constantly on the brink of doom. Natural disasters were signs of the gods' displeasure. To prevent this destruction, they had to feed Huitzilopochtli human blood. Human sacrifice did not ensure survival, however; it only bought time. This dread of the inevitable destruction of the Mexica-Aztec, and perhaps the world, only resulted in the zealous and ever-increasing amount of human sacrifice. In this atmosphere of superstition and mystery, the people took no chances.

Every aspect of Aztec life—from planting corn to warfare—had religious significance. In an atmosphere of superstition and fear, human sacrifices served to placate the gods. *Library of Congress*

Massive human sacrifice served to impede the inevitable destruction of their world and to placate the gods, but other more personal measures were also required to ensure a relatively smooth passage through an often difficult life.

Attention to religious ritual, self-control, and conformity were key to Aztec life. Ideal civilized behavior required the restraint of emotions and conformity of behavior and dress. Emotion was seen as destructive because it loosened an already tenuous control on a precarious life and was a sign of moral weakness. Aztec life was designed to minimize this potential weakness. Male and female roles conformed to patterns that were defined through ceremony and ritual and that met the needs of the empire. Simple breaches of etiquette, such as looking at the face of the king, were often seen as spiritual failings, punishable by death. From birth, females were raised behind rigid domestic barriers and were to remain in the home as weavers and cooks. Males were to be farmers, warriors, and heads of households. By the time of Montezuma II, the empire's religious demands were becoming insupportable by the *macehualtes.*

The structure of Aztec society, which was based on intimidation rather than loyalty, served to keep the *macehualtes* under control, but, by the early sixteenth century, they were under increasing pressure. Crop failures and political restructuring that placed more power and resources in the hands of the emperor and nobles increased the burden of the lower classes. As the burden increased, the commoners in outlying areas revolted more frequently, and the power of the army was spread over ever-larger territories far from Tenochtitlán. Although these factors alone would probably not have been sufficient to force the collapse of the Aztec empire, they facilitated its conquest.

CHAPTER 3

ENTER THE SPANIARDS

The native population of Mexico seemed preconditioned to succumb to Spanish domination. Despite his power, the Aztec emperor Montezuma II was a product of Indian culture. He was superstitious and affected by the same foreboding about the future as his subjects. Although he ruled with great authority, events appeared ominous. In addition to social unrest throughout the empire, lightning had struck and damaged his major temple, and a comet appeared, which frightened the Indian population. Indian mythology also spoke of the imminent return from the east of the Aztec god Quetzalcóatl, who would come to reclaim his kingdom. When in 1519 emissaries arrived to tell of bearded white men landing in Yucatán on the eastern coast of Mexico, panic struck the emperor and his subjects.

The bearded white men who landed at Veracruz were not led by Quetzalcóatl, however. Instead, the audacious and daring Spaniard, Hernán Cortés, burned his ships to prevent any defectors among his men from returning to Cuba, planted the cross of Christ, and began the almost incredible task of conquering the Aztec empire. After an initial successful skirmish with Indian warriors he acquired Doña Marina, the beautiful daughter of an Indian cacique. This young woman was adored by the Indians of the area and served Cortés well in the difficult task ahead of dealing with the Indian population.

Upon hearing of the impending arrival of the conquistadores,

Montezuma attempted to appease them by sending gifts and offering homage, which only whetted their appetite. In a bold move, Cortés allied himself with the Tlaxcalans Indians, who had remained independent from the Aztecs, and marched toward Tenochtitlán, capital of the Aztec empire. En route, many Indians welcomed Cortés as a deliverer from brutal Aztec control. Gripped by fear and indecision, Montezuma refused to fight Quetzalcóatl emissaries and invited Cortés into the capital.

When Cortés entered the city, he realized that the monarch was incapable of resisting. Because he feared that the far more numerous Aztecs might eventually rebel against the Spanish presence, Cortés seized Montezuma and made him his prisoner. Montezuma summoned all his caciques and ordered them to obey the Spaniards and to collect tribute and gold for the Spanish monarch. Using Montezuma as his mouthpiece, Cortés controlled the Indian masses and governed from behind the throne.

Cortés remained in Tenochtitlán for several months. By then, a new Spanish expedition from Cuba reached the Mexican shore with orders to limit Cortés's power. Leaving one of his lieutenants in command, Cortés marched to the coast and persuaded his compatriots to join him. Meanwhile, an Indian uprising occurred in Tenochtitlán, which was partly the result of the ruthless policies followed by Cortés's lieutenants.

Cortés hastened back, only to find that the Indians were in open revolt and that his men were barricaded in the palace and threatened with starvation. He ordered Montezuma to arrange for supplies, but the emperor refused. Cortés then released one of the Aztec chiefs, Cuitlahuac, with orders to open the markets and bring food to the palace. Instead, Cuitlahuac assumed leadership of the revolt. There was furious fighting in the capital. Cortés finally convinced Montezuma to address his people and to order them to obey the Spaniards. The angry Indians, however, refused to listen to their captive emperor and showered him with stones. Montezuma died several days later. Hungry and pursued by the angry mob, Cortés and his men were forced to leave the capital and retreat to the coast in the gloom of *la noche triste,* the night of sorrow.

The Aztecs had succeeded in driving out the Spaniards from their capital. A new courageous and determined leader, Cuauhtémoc, inherited the throne. Spanish prisoners were executed, and Indians who were friendly toward the invaders were killed. The capital was put in a state

The able and daring Spanish conquistador Hernán Cortés captured Montezuma and made him his prisoner. Using the Aztec ruler as his spokesman, Cortés controlled the Indian masses from behind the throne. *Library of Congress*

of war, and garrisons throughout the empire were fortified. Cuauhté-moc knew that the Spaniards would return and that the struggle now was for his own survival as well as that of Aztec civilization.

In May 1521, Cortés and his men began the siege of the city. The Aztecs fought valiantly. Corpses piled high in the streets. Food supplies were scarce, and water supplies dwindled when the Spaniards shut down the aqueduct. Yet, Cuauhtémoc would not surrender. The Spaniards then began a systematic destruction of the city. By midyear, with most of the city in ruins, the Aztec defense finally collapsed. Cuauhtémoc attempted to escape but was captured. Brought before Cortés, he asked to be killed, but Cortés refused and placed him under house arrest.

There he remained in captivity for a long time and was frequently subjected to brutal torture. Believing that the emperor knew where Aztec treasures were hidden, the Spanish conquistadores tried to force Cuauhtémoc to reveal the hiding place for the gold. Yet, the brave Cuauhtémoc endured tortures but refused to reveal any secrets. While in captivity, he also accompanied Cortés on several expeditions. During one of these expeditions to Central America, Cortés became convinced that Cuauhtémoc was urging Indians to rebel. Although Cuauhtémoc insisted that he was innocent, he was hung in 1525.

The elimination of the last Aztec emperor and the virtual destruction of Aztec power brought the entire empire under Spanish control. Because the Aztecs had consolidated their power throughout the region, and most of the tribes considered Cortés to be their deliverer from Aztec tyranny, they now submitted to the new rulers.

Yet, the relative ease with which the Spaniards conquered a much larger and better organized civilization has captivated the imagination of those interested in Mexican history. The reason derives partly from the genius and tenacity of Cortés. His bold move in capturing Montezuma and in ruling from behind the throne allowed for the gradual transition from Aztec to Spanish power. The oppressive nature of Aztec rule also created a favorable climate in which other tribes would accept and then ally themselves with the conquistadores.

Other factors contributed to facilitating the conquest. Indian religion and superstition played a key role. Fatalism—the belief that periodically a major catastrophe would afflict their civilization—increased conformity to, and acceptance of, their new situation. Spanish firearms and horses also terrorized the Indians. One can only wonder how the Indians must have reacted to seeing those white men with beards and metal uniforms riding on strange animals and spitting death from unfamiliar weapons.

The end of the conquest soon paved the way for the beginning of exploration and colonization. Cortés the conqueror became Cortés the builder. He built a fleet to explore the west coast of Central America and to try to discover a route to the Spice Islands. He erected graceful

Conquest and colonization took their toll on the native civilizations in the New
World. While Spanish cruelty was most pronounced in the conquest of the
Caribbean, the subjugation and control of large numbers of Indians in Mexico
and Central America were accomplished by harsh discipline and, at times, cruel
methods. The Catholic Church often opposed abuses, seeking conversion rather
than oppression. *Library of Congress*

structures—palaces and churches. He brought cattle and sheep from
Spain and encouraged silk production. He planted wheat and sugar-
cane. His two sugar mills were the first on the continent. He christened
his domain New Spain and so communicated it to King Charles of
Spain.

Cortés's significant power and deeds soon increased the jealousy of
influential Spaniards. While many lusted for his glory and power, others feared his independence and stubbornness. The newly appointed
viceroy of New Spain, Antonio de Mendoza, who was the most influential representative of the king in the New World, blocked his projects
and made his life increasingly difficult. Cortés returned to Spain and
appealed to the emperor, but he was continuously ignored. His work
was completed, and his moment of glory had passed. He had served his
country with distinction by adding lands of unparalleled wealth to the

Spanish empire. Neglected by the people he had served so well, he died a bitter and disillusioned man in 1547.

The rulers of New Spain faced numerous problems in consolidating power over the vast territories that they had inherited from the conquest. Perhaps the thorniest one was the organization and control of the large Indian masses. In the Caribbean, the Spaniards had found smaller groups of Indians, many of whom were nomadic. A process of elimination occurred that was partly a result of diseases, overwork, abuses, and the actual shock of conquest. The dwindling population in the Caribbean prevented the creation of a large agricultural base in the region and the effective settlement of these islands. With the exception of Cuba and Hispaniola, most of the Caribbean remained uncolonized by the Spaniards and underpopulated. The fact that little mineral wealth was found shifted attention away from this region and toward the mainland, where there was greater mineral wealth and a larger population.

For the next three centuries, the Caribbean remained a bridge—a stopping point—for the Spanish fleets visiting the mainland. The center of the Spanish empire moved very easily on to New Spain and Peru. The vacuum left by Spain in the Caribbean was filled later by the Dutch, the English, and the French—latecomers to the game of colonization. Unable to challenge Spanish power, they were forced to settle the smaller islands on the eastern Caribbean.

Toward the eighteenth century, black slaves from Africa were brought to the Caribbean, particularly to Haiti and later to Cuba, to work the fields and mines and to help develop the sugar industry. As sugar became more important, more and more slaves were brought in, and the Caribbean took the form of a typical plantation society, dominated by a minority of white foreigners, where black slaves worked and produced a needed commodity for the outside world.

New Spain developed very differently. Although the Indian population decreased significantly during the first century of Spanish occupation, the Spanish found here very large sedentary and organized masses with a richly developed culture. The very abundance of a native labor population precluded the need to import labor from Africa or elsewhere. In fact, aside from the silver and gold mines found by the Spaniards, the greatest wealth found in New Spain was labor. There was a fairly well-organized and disciplined population accustomed to paying tribute and working for their native overlords. The transfer of this labor to the Spanish overlords was relatively smooth.

Yet, the Spaniards faced the massive task of Christianizing this large

The Indians provided not only tribute but, most important, the labor force
necessary to work the mines and fields of Mexico. Famed muralist Diego Rivera
depicted some of the themes of the twentieth-century Mexican revolution: nationalism, the glory of Indian civilization, the struggle between capital and labor, and
Spanish abuses of the indigenous people. *Library of Congress*

population. In the sixteenth century, religion played a key role in the
lives of most Spaniards. With the Reformation brewing in Europe,
conquering souls became as important as conquering lands. The experience of the Caribbean, where the Indian population virtually disappeared after the conquest, influenced Crown policies. In the Caribbean,
Father Bartolomé de las Casas had written extensively condemning
Spanish cruelty and claiming that the Indians were rational and free
and, therefore, entitled to retain their lands and become Christians.
He clashed with those who defended the doctrine of just conquest,
which advanced the idea that the Spaniards were naturally superior and
had divine authorization to use force to convert the natives or even to
enslave them. The writings of Las Casas received widespread attention
throughout Europe. They influenced Spanish-Indian policy in the New
World and underlay the "black legend" about exaggerated Spanish
cruelty.

The initial Crown policy in dealing with the Indian population took shape in the *encomienda,* which entailed assigning Indian groups or inhabitants of a town or village to a Spaniard who would extract labor and tribute from them while providing for their Christianization. The granting of an *encomienda* involved neither title to the land on which the Indians lived and labored nor ownership of the Indians. The Crown took the position that the natives were "free" subjects, although they could be compelled to pay tribute and to work like other such subjects.

Many *encomenderos,* however, interested only in exploiting the resources of the land, disregarded their moral, religious, and legal obligations to the Indians, as did others elsewhere in the New World. Acting as absentee owners, in many instances, they delegated actual control of their *encomiendas* to overseers who overlooked the provision about Christianization, abused the Indians, and extracted from them an unreasonable amount of labor.

A conflict soon developed between the Crown and the Spanish settlers over the control and utilization of the labor as well as between the Crown's stated objective to Christianize the natives and its own economic motivations. It was not that Christianizing and extracting labor were incompatible, but, in the reality of the New World, the sixteenth-century Christian ideal of converting souls was frequently sacrificed for a profit. Christianization was reduced to mass baptism, and, despite the Crown's insistence that Indians were not slaves, many were bought and sold as chattel. The Spanish monarchy itself profited from the *encomienda* system, using Indians as miners and taxing the *encomenderos* for the number of Indians they received. Despite attempts to regulate the functioning of the *encomienda* and prevent further abuses, the Crown lacked a means of enforcement. Such legislation as the Law of Burgos (1512–1513) or, later, the New Laws (1542), which sought to end the *encomienda,* were intended more as statements of purpose than as practical legislation that could be implemented in the New World wilderness.

The *encomienda* was used by the Crown as a political instrument to consolidate its control over the Indian population. Undoubtedly, Ferdinand of Aragon and later Spanish rulers were initially greatly motivated by the religious influence of the sixteenth century, but they also may have recalled the profitable financial and political results brought about in Spain by the conversion of the Moors and the Jews and, in so doing, hoped perhaps that the conversion of the Indians would lead to similar political control and financial gain.

CHAPTER 4

THE EMERGING
COLONY

By the end of the sixteenth century, the conquest and pacification of the Indians was almost complete, exploration and colonization had advanced in all directions, and the boundaries of New Spain were set. Indeed it was a vast territory—from present-day Honduras in the south to the vast hinterlands of Texas and northern Florida in the north; on the west, it included not only all of the coastal areas of present-day Mexico and Central America, but also islands beyond the western coast of New Spain. An expedition organized in Mexico had taken possession of the Philippine Islands and incorporated them into the Spanish empire.

Despite this vast occupation, many areas remained sparsely populated. Spanish power particularly in the north and outlying regions was sometimes weak and ineffective. Numerous explorations and settlements were undertaken in present-day California, Arizona, and New Mexico, but no large centers of population developed, and these regions were not effectively occupied through most of the colonial period.

To govern this vast territory, the Crown introduced a complicated, and occasionally cumbersome, institutional apparatus. In Spain, the Council of the Indies was established, which had the responsibility of governing all of the Spanish possessions. In New Spain, the highest representative of the king was the viceroy or viceregent who ruled with almost complete authority over administrative, political, and judicial affairs. Until the eighteenth century, there were only two viceroyalties in the New World—New Spain (Mexico) and Lima (Peru). Later additions were the viceroyalty of New Granada in 1739 and the viceroyalty of La Plata in 1776. Under the viceroy, a series of governorships were created to administer the various territories. The governors were subject to the *audiencia.*

The *audiencia* was a peculiarly Spanish institution that combined judicial, advisory, and executive powers. In 1527, the Crown appointed the first *audiencia,* which originally was composed of four justices *(oidores)* and a president. The *audiencia* also exercised the right to supervise and investigate the administrative actions of various officials. This was sometimes accomplished by a royal order to conduct a *residencia,* or formal hearing, held at the end of an official's term of office. At such time, witnesses testified before an appointed judge concerning the performance of the official. If found guilty of any misbehavior while in office, he was required to make restitution to those whom he had mistreated; in some instances, harsher punishments were administered. Another important check on the power of higher officials was the *visita,* or inspection, performed by a special Crown-appointed official who reported back to the monarch and the council concerning the operation of the colony and the performance of its official.

At the local level, the most important institution was the *cabildo.* Presided over by the governor or his lieutenant and composed of *alcaldes* (judges), *regidores* (councilmen), and other minor officials, the *cabildo* was the political, judicial, and administrative unit of each new settlement. It imposed local taxes, provided for local police, and maintained public buildings, jails, and roads. The *alcaldes* acted as judges of first instance, and, in the absence of the governor or his lieutenant, they presided at meetings of the *cabildo.* They also visited the territories under their jurisdiction and dispensed justice in the rural areas.

During the early days, the *cabildo* emerged as a fairly representative institution of local government. Although the governor appointed its president, the *teniente de guerra,* members were either elected by the settlers or appointed by the *conquistadores.* Away from the direct control of the governor and following the Spanish tradition of independence, these Spaniards exercised a significant amount of autonomy.

The *cabildos* selected a *procurador* (solicitor) who represented the interests and desires of the community and served as liaison between the settlers and the Spanish crown. *Procuradores* from various towns met to discuss their needs and to select a general *procurador* to present their grievances and requests to the king. Yet, this budding development of representative government was soon crushed by various governors' attempts to centralize authority.

By midcentury, representative and autonomous government gave way to centralization and political interference from Spain. The Crown began to appoint *regidores* for life and initiated the practice of selling offices. *Regidores* in turn appointed the *alcaldes.* These changes were accompanied by frequent quarrels between the *cabildo* members and the *teniente de guerra* over the distribution of power. Differences also occurred between the *cabildo* and the governors. The latter were not at all content to allow local government to be conducted independently of them. They also complained that councilmen, under the protection of their office, were speculating, organizing monopolies of necessary commodities, and hoarding groups of Indians for their personal benefit. In an attempt to reassert their authority, some governors appointed deputies—*tenientes de gobernadores*—with extensive powers to represent them in faraway towns.

As royal government became better organized and more entrenched, the powers and prerogatives of the *cabildos* were progressively curtailed. By the end of the colonial period, few responsible citizens wanted to become involved in local government. Those who did were more interested in their personal well-being than in the affairs of the colony. Spaniards who bought their offices sought reward for their investments and enriched themselves at the expense of public funds. Creoles, who were Spaniards born in the New World, also joined the lower ranks of the Spanish bureaucracy. To secure wealth and other opportunities that were controlled by peninsular Spaniards, they looked to local government as one of the few potential areas of employment in which they could succeed.

The Catholic Church played an important role in this society. As in the rest of Spanish America, the Church was under the direct control of the Crown, except for doctrinal affairs. The *patronato real,* which was a body of rights and privileges granted by the pope, permitted the Spanish monarch to nominate all higher church dignitaries who came to the New World; it also gave him control of administering ecclesiastical taxation. In practice, the king and his officials became the secular heads of the Church, which was a political arm of the state that dominated Indians as well as colonists.

In the early colonial period, the work of conversion and pacification fell primarily on the Franciscans. These friars studied Indian languages and traveled throughout New Spain teaching Christianity and converting Indians. To accomplish this task, Indian temples, idols, and paintings that represented idolatry were destroyed. Indian historical records were eliminated and replaced with works on the history of Spain and Western society. The efforts of the Franciscans paid off. Not only did the Indians convert to the new religion, but they also learned Spanish and abandoned many of their bloody rituals and superstitions.

Throughout this period, the friars and missionaries were the shock troops that penetrated Indian villages, while the secular priests followed as the army of occupation. In addition to the task of conversion, they strengthened the political power of the Crown in expanding and holding together the empire. They also preached obedience and loyalty to the monarch and his officials, and finally acted as an intelligence service that reported on activities and problems in the region under their supervision.

Conquering souls instigated significant quarreling both among the various orders and between the orders and the hierarchy of the Church. The Franciscans wrangled with the Dominicans, who arrived later. The Church tried to displace the friars from the parishes and replace them with priests. By the end of the sixteenth century, the secular clergy had reasserted its authority in most of the areas close to major cities and enjoyed its privileged position and the obedience of the great majority of the native population.

Although the task of conversion and pacification was far from easy, the Spaniards did a monumental job. Millions of Indians were converted to Christianity, and, although the depth of their understanding about the new religion was debatable, the masses certainly adopted the symbolism of the religion, paid tribute to the Church, and remained loyal to the Spanish crown for three centuries.

The Church benefited from conversion and became a wealthy institution. Its primary means of support was a tax—the tithe. In addition, wealthy hacendados paid salaries to priests. Gifts and bequests from pious Christians enriched the coffers of the Church. Property owned by the Church was exempt from taxation, so the colonial period witnessed great accumulation of property. By the nineteenth century, the Church was a wealthy and powerful institution, and priests shared the psychology of the landed classes in Mexico, which induced obedience among the workers and exploitation of the native population. In the

The cathedral in Mexico City. The Catholic Church benefited from the protection of the Spanish Crown, converted the Indian masses to Christianity, built numerous churches throughout the country, and grew into a wealthy and not universally liked institution, particularly after Mexican independence. *Library of Congress*

later colonial period, the ideal of Christianization and the teachings of the Church were sacrificed to profit.

Throughout the colonial period, education was in the hands of the Church, and all schools were ecclesiastical. More than forty colleges and seminaries existed in New Spain, and the Jesuits reigned supreme in education. Granting a higher degree was left to the University of Mexico, which was founded in 1553. Learning was based on an authoritarian concept of the universe. Knowledge was either revealed in the Scriptures, established by the Church, or handed down from ancient writers such as Aristotle. Observation as a means of acquiring knowledge was discouraged, and experimentation was nonexistent. Instruction was conducted in Latin. The university trained primarily clergymen for the task of conversion. Higher education was restricted to those without any blood taint. Jews, blacks, and those of Moorish ancestry were excluded. Indian nobles received special education.

The spirit of conformity was also encouraged by the Inquisition. Introduced in New Spain during the middle of the sixteenth century, its function was to maintain the purity of the faith and to preserve religious orthodoxy. Yet, it also assumed broader power, which included rooting out *conversos*—those of Jewish origin who had converted to

Christianity—as well as Protestants who entered the colony. Indians were exempted, as they were considered irresponsible and childlike.

The Holy Office of the Inquisition also exercised control and supervision over literature entering the colony. Spain feared liberal and Protestant writings, which were spreading throughout Europe, for their potentially corrupting influence upon both the native populations and Spaniards themselves. During the earlier colonial period, the Inquisition had successfully prevented European ideas from infecting New Spain. By the end of the colonial period, however, the writings of the Enlightenment had penetrated into the homes of the elite in Spanish America, including those of members of the clergy.

Although few people were actually executed as a result of the Inquisition, many were jailed, flogged, or exiled for various crimes, which included—besides heresy—adultery, bigamy, and blasphemy. Those found guilty of even minor crimes were ridiculed and ostracized by the population. As time passed, the Crown also used the Inquisition as an instrument of royal control to investigate both political and religious dissidents and to ensure loyalty and obedience to Spain.

Despite this somewhat suffocating intellectual climate, New Spain produced two world-class literary and scientific figures. Sor Juana Inés de la Cruz, who lived in the seventeenth century, is considered the first and, perhaps, the best of Mexico's early poets. Although her poetry has no traces of Mexicanism and reflects much of the artificiality and religiosity of the times, she linked the two continents with her poetry and insatiable curiosity. From the convent of St. Jerome, she wrote beautiful and charming verses that captivated the hearts of her generation.

In the scientific field, Carlos de Sigüenza y Góngora is outstanding. Educated by the Jesuits in Mexico, Sigüenza displayed an astonishing proficiency in science and mathematics. During the late seventeenth century he won the chair of mathematics and astronomy at the University of Mexico. Sigüenza challenged the official doctrine that comets were divine portents of disaster and argued for their natural origin. He is considered the first scientist of colonial Mexico to question the scholasticism that permeated the university and most of society.

Colonial society in New Spain exhibited very special characteristics. The absorption and almost total disappearance of native languages is apparent to the modern traveler to Mexico. The length of the colonial period—more than three hundred years—the absolutist character of the Spaniards, the work of the missionaries and the Church, and the difficulty in transmitting Indian languages, which were composed of hieroglyphics, explain the dominance and survival of Spanish as the prevailing language. Although in some smaller towns of Mexico some Indian dialects have survived, Spanish was universally spoken.

Another interesting characteristic is the crossbreeding that occurred more rapidly in New Spain than in any other part of the Western Hemisphere. In the valley of Mexico, the Spaniards found a complex and sedentary society. As the colonial period progressed, a new class—the mestizo, the mixture of whites and Indians—began to grow. Their lot was not much better than that of the Indian. Some lived like Indians; others lived as rancheros or worked the mines; still others became bandits or beggars; a few entered the lower ranks of the clergy. Neither white nor Indian, the mestizos resented the Spaniards' attitude of superiority, while not identifying with the masses of Indians. They inherited the individualism of the Spaniards and the fatalism of the Indians, coming to believe, as did the Indians, that life and historical periods usually ended in tragedy. Also similar to the Indians, their hermetic, introverted personalities and attitudes prevented outsiders from penetrating their outer layers and learning their true feelings and attitudes.

Throughout the colonial period, Indian and mestizo protests and rebellions were common in New Spain. A tradition of violence existed before the conquest in both Indian and Spanish societies. Frustration with existing conditions and class and racial antagonism may have also increased the propensity toward violence. Mutinies against taxes and ill-treatment were common. In 1598, Tepic miners rebelled; in 1680, Indians of Tehuantepec rose in arms and controlled the Isthmus for several years; in 1692, roaming mobs of Indians set fire to large sections of Mexico City; in 1761, Mayan descendants rebelled in Yucatán. All of these ended in defeat for the native populations.

While the Indians and mestizos lived in miserable conditions struggling to eke out an existence, another class, the Creole—the Spaniard born in New Spain—prospered and enjoyed colonial life. The children of the Spanish owned mines, shops, and haciendas, and many grew wealthy. Yet, they were excluded from government. Fearing that these Spaniards born in the New World would develop an attachment to their birthplace and eventually would become disloyal to Spain, the Crown followed the practice of appointing only Spanish-born—called *peninsulares* or *gachupines*—to high governmental positions. This practice was partially responsible for preserving the empire's loyalty to the remote Crown in Spain for three centuries. Yet, it simultaneously increased resentment and frustration among the Creoles who felt discriminated against merely because of their birthplace. This tension came to the forefront during the early nineteenth century, when many Creoles joined the struggle for independence from Spain and helped to overthrow Spanish power not only in Mexico but throughout most of Latin America.

CHAPTER 5

COLONIAL ECONOMY AND LABOR

The mineral and human wealth found in New Spain shaped Spanish economic policy for the next three centuries. Spain believed, as did other European powers, that colonies existed for the benefit of the mother country. The objective of this policy of mercantilism was to strengthen Spain and to protect Spanish industry and manufacturing. The colonies were to supply minerals and raw materials that could be converted into manufactured products and sold back to the colonists. Local manufacture and industry were discouraged.

The basic nature of the economy of New Spain was extractive and dependent, with a distant authoritarian Crown controlling and dictating the economic development of its possessions. To achieve this end, Spain elaborated a protectionist and monopolistic policy centered on the Casa de Contratación, or House of Trade, located first in Seville and eventually in Cádiz. All trade with the colonies was conducted from these ports; once or twice yearly fleets traveled to and from the colonies bringing all items of trade. The Casa supervised commerce and navigation, issued ordinances to regulate trade, and tried cases that resulted from violations of Casa regulations.

To control the movement of goods, in addition to the Casa, Spain relied on powerful merchant guilds—*Consulados*—composed of prominent Spanish businessmen who monopolized most transactions. The Casa protected the merchants and excluded competition. The *Consulados* sold and bought goods and furnished capital for commercial enterprises. The *Consulado* became a monopoly of influential merchants with far-reaching privileges. The Crown also exercised direct control over certain products, such as mercury, gunpowder, and salt, taxing their sale for the benefit of the Spanish coffers.

Spain also benefited from various taxes and duties that were imposed on the colonies. Altogether, there were more than fifty different taxes, among which the most disliked was the *alcabala* or sales tax, payable on most items sold. The *almojarifazgo* was a tax on imports and exports. The *arrería* was a tax to pay for the cost of the fleets. Colonists also paid export and import duties on goods shipped to, and brought from, Spain. The Crown also collected tribute from the Indians and sold licenses, offices, and land. The *quinto,* or a fifth of all extracted metals, was collected from the miners as the cost for the concession to extract silver and gold.

A 1671 Dutch engraving of the port of Acapulco. Throughout most of the colonial period, Mexico traded exclusively with Spain. Spanish fleets visited Mexico bringing manufactured products from Europe and returning with silver and gold from Mexican mines. On the Pacific coast, Acapulco flourished as a small trading center. *Library of Congress*

The biggest challenge to Spanish monopolistic policies was smuggling. The high prices of Spanish products, the desire for a variety of European goods, and the decline of Spain as a major maritime power encouraged the Europeans, particularly the Dutch, English, and French, to challenge Spanish control. The Caribbean became the center of operations for these smugglers. Smuggling, particularly in the sixteenth and seventeenth centuries, became a profitable and important commercial activity, usually welcomed by colonial settlers, frequently tolerated by greedy Spanish officials, and always opposed by the Spanish Crown.

The next biggest challenge was piracy. Using the Caribbean as their base of operations, French, English, and Dutch pirates terrorized coastal Spanish towns, plundering and seizing Spanish gold and silver. Perhaps the most daring, and probably the most profitable, pirate attack occurred in 1627, when the Dutch pirate Piet Heyn captured the entire Spanish fleet, after it had sailed from Mexico on the way to Spain. Although bothersome to the colonists and costly to Spain, none of these attacks challenged the territorial possessions of Spain in the New World. Only wars, of which there were many, changed the map of the Caribbean, and then in a very limited manner. All of the lands occupied by Spain on the continent remained in the Spanish fold until their independence during the early nineteenth century.

Mining played a key role in the early development of New Spain. A major gold and silver rush occurred when the first mines were discovered in Zacatecas in the north and Taxco and Sultepec in the south. Great mining centers were established, and around them haciendas, or large farms, developed that provided cattle and other needs to the mining communities. According to Spanish law, the land belonged to the Crown, but subjects were allowed to work it as long as they paid taxes. The initial mining booms lasted until the early seventeenth century, when New Spain silver mining declined, and new production flourished in other parts of the empire such as Peru. Yet, Mexico continued to produce moderate amounts of silver during the balance of the colonial period and even today.

The initial wealth produced by the Mexican mines discouraged other productive activities in the colony and encouraged Spain to rely heavily on mineral wealth for its economic well-being to the detriment of industry. Spain, furthermore, squandered much of the wealth from the New World in futile dynastic, religious, and territorial wars in Europe. Instead of emerging from the colonial experience as a powerful and wealthy nation, Spain remained an impoverished and greedy nation that hoped for greater wealth to satisfy the ambitions of mediocre monarchs.

In addition to mining, cattle and sheep raising became important and prosperous businesses. Although the activity called for daring horsemanship, it required no sustained effort, for Mexico's abundant lands facilitated breeding. The cattle were let loose on northern savannahs where they rapidly multiplied. They were used as a means of transportation as well as a source of food.

Spaniards preferred such pastoral pursuits as cattle and sheep raising to farming. Tilling the soil required manual labor and had been the work primarily of the Moors in Spain. Now, this work would be left to the Indians or the blacks in the New World. Besides, as a result of the Reconquest, the Spanish struggle that culminated in the expulsion of the Moors from Spain during the late fifteenth century, Spaniards had become accustomed to cattle, which could be transported to the new lands as these were captured from the Moors. Enterprising Spaniards brought cattle and sheep to Mexico and received large grants of lands from the Crown, which was interested in encouraging the settlement of vast unpopulated areas, particularly in the northern regions.

Foodstuffs also were an important part of the economy. Indian agricultural practices were continued for the production of corn. Other crops and cereals such as citrus, sugar, and wheat were introduced from the Old World. Settlers were given small plots of land to be cultivated by themselves or with the help of Indians. The natives retained some of their own lands, which they held privately or in common to provide food for themselves.

Several export crops became important for royal income. Essential to the growing textile industry in Europe were good dyes, and New Spain produced one of the finest with a native product, cochineal. Extracted from small insects, this dye and another one that was extracted from indigo plants became important export items.

While the main productive centers in rural areas were the mines and the haciendas, in urban areas the *obraje,* or textile sweatshop, became important. All luxury items, including expensive fabrics, were imported by Spain from European countries and then shipped to the colonies at inflated prices. Because most of the population in Mexico could not afford these expensive fabrics, local mills developed throughout the major cities of New Spain. In addition to textiles, these *obrajes* produced smaller crafts and products and became a major source of employment for Indians, black slaves, and common criminals, who were assigned to *obrajes* to fulfill their sentences.

Naturally, conditions in such sweatshops were miserable at best. Workers were placed behind locked doors and forced to work long hours with little rest and poor food. Often, they were locked in the *obrajes* for weeks at a time with little opportunity for visiting their families or recreation. Although conditions in the mines and the haciendas were difficult, and the native population suffered untold abuses, conditions in the *obrajes* seem to have been worse, probably only a notch above being in prison. After visiting the *obrajes* in the early nineteenth century, Alexander von Humboldt criticized the unhealthiness of the situation and the bad treatment received by the workers. "All appear half naked and deformed. The doors remain constantly shut. All are unmercifully flogged if they commit the smallest trespass."

The decline in Indian population, the abolition of the *encomienda,* and the need to organize and tighten control over the dwindling native population to provide needed labor gave rise to a new invention—the *repartimiento* or apportionment. It was based on the principle that the Crown could force its citizens, namely Indians or black slaves, to do work for the benefit of the colony. The *repartimiento* consisted in an allotment of laborers by Spanish officials to a Spaniard or Creole, for a specified period of time, to work in the mines, produce foodstuffs, or build highways, churches, and other public facilities. The Indians were to be paid and not abused. Yet, as with other labor systems introduced by the Crown, there was a gap between theory and practice. In the reality of the New World, Indians were overworked, abused, and frequently not even paid.

After the Crown issued numerous laws to regulate the *repartimiento,* conditions seem to have improved somewhat. Because the Indians were accustomed to paying tribute and to rendering personal services to support their rulers, this system, as it evolved, seemed more compatible with their traditions. As mine production decreased, the need for labor became more acute, and a permanent labor supply seemed more desirable than a coercive and unreliable system that depended on Spanish officials. Miners hired Indians on a permanent basis and paid them slightly better wages to retain them in the mines. By the end of the colonial period, the *repartimiento* had declined as a form of organizing labor, giving way to a more insidious and longer lasting system—debt peonage.

Debt peonage became widespread in the late colonial period, particularly in the mines and the haciendas, and survived well into the national period. Employers induced Indians to work for wages and advanced them money and goods on their salaries. Because enough money was advanced, the workers could never hope to pay off the debt. In addition, because they legally could not abandon their place of employment until all debts were paid, they became debt peons and were tied to their bosses for life. Their debts were inherited by their children, which perpetuated the system indefinitely.

Despite problems and abuses, the economic system imposed by Spain on Spanish America was significant in various aspects. It helped preserve the colonies under Spanish control for more than three centuries, it prevented other European powers from challenging Spanish supremacy, it allowed for the extraction of significant wealth, and it subdued and organized a large population that worked for the Crown and its subjects, paid taxes and tribute, and enabled colonial exploitation for the benefit of the mother country.

Yet, the system created numerous problems, many that still beset Mexico today. It created an economy that is dependent upon the outside world, one that stifled innovation, commerce, and industry; it permitted, and even fostered, social and ethnic inequalities, which surfaced violently during the wars for independence; it promoted a landed elite whose power was based on the large haciendas and the bondage of the Indians. This landed oligarchy encouraged regionalism and localism, preferring to develop estates away from the supervising central authority. They worked with local officials, the forerunners of the local caciques or political bosses of the nineteenth century, who enriched themselves and greatly benefited from their alliance with the hacendados.

By the end of the eighteenth century, the Hapsburgs who ruled Spain were weak and inefficient; their rule over the New World was ineffective and outdated. The glory of the early days had faded, and the colonies languished as decaying remnants of a once powerful and prosperous empire.

CHAPTER 6

THE BOURBON CENTURY

As the eighteenth century began, changes in Europe greatly influenced Spain and its colonies in Spanish America. The last of the Spanish Hapsburgs—"the bewitched" Charles II or the "imbecile" monarch, as he was better known—died without an heir. The Bourbons of France had the best claim to the Spanish throne, and in 1701, Philip of Anjou, grandson of Louis XIV of France, was proclaimed king of Spain. The rise of French hegemony in the Spanish peninsula was followed by the Austrian Hapsburgs' declaration of war, as they, too, claimed the Spanish throne. The War of the Spanish Succession, between Spain and France against Austria and its allies, lasted until 1713 and ended with Philip V on the Spanish throne.

The Bourbons found an impoverished and demoralized Spain. The country was ravaged by wars, ruined by inefficiency and corruption, economically dependent on other European powers or merchants, and estranged from its declining colonial empire. Philip and later his successor, Charles III (1759–1788), were bent on rectifying the situation. Modeling their system on that of France, they introduced a series of reforms that led to more efficiency, increased revenue collection, a better military, and a decline of Church power and authority.

Soon after implementing their brand of enlightened despotism in Spain, the Bourbons turned their attention and policies to Spanish America. They created a Ministry of Marine and Indies, which assumed most of the functions of the Council of the Indies. The ministry became a royal agency for the issuance of new orders dealing with finance, commerce, and other colonial matters. Those orders neglected the more Christian and humanitarian aspects of earlier Spanish policies and emphasized stronger and more centralized control and greater efficiency in extracting wealth from Spanish America.

The Bourbon reforms that were introduced into the New World shook the foundation of colonial society. The Crown was primarily interested in tightening control over its empire, making it more efficient and productive, and increasing revenues for the depleted Spanish treasury. Because the monopoly of Cádiz had pushed prices up and fostered illegal trading and smuggling, the Bourbons opened all Spanish ports to commerce between Spain and its colonies. Commercial traffic tripled, commerce and industry prospered, and revenues soared. Yet, trade with Spanish America remained a Spanish monopoly. The colonies were still prohibited access to world markets, which limited their economic potential. The various duties or even prohibition in favor of Spanish goods curtailed the development of local manufacturing.

Aware that the job of organizing New Spain required a strong and loyal administrator, the Crown sent José de Gálvez as visitor general in 1765. Able, devoted, and thorough, Galvez traveled widely throughout the colony making recommendations to the king. Supported by the viceroy Marques de Croix, Gálvez introduced a series of profound changes. Taxes and tariffs were lowered, and quicksilver was made more easily available to miners. The fleet system was abandoned, and a colonial militia was created that was composed of Indians and mestizos and led by Creoles and *peninsulares.* The corrupt and inefficient system of *corregidores* and *alcaldes* was swept away and replaced by the *intendencia.* The colony was divided into twelve territories, each of which was under the control of an *intendente.*

These officials controlled finances, justice, and war. More carefully chosen and honest, this new bureaucracy tightened control over the collection of taxes and revenue, supervised royal monopolies, strengthened defense, reduced smuggling and banditry, and engaged in a massive construction program. New silver mines were discovered, and old ones became more productive. Sugar production increased. Tobacco became an important export crop, as did hides and cochineal. By the beginning of the nineteenth century, New Spain was the most productive and important Spanish colony, the envy of Europe, and the proud possession of Spain.

Gálvez paid particular attention to the defense of Spanish settlements, especially in northern Mexico. Spain perceived the growing power of England and its expanding empire in North America as a threat to Spain's colonial possessions. Northern Mexico had been settled primarily by missionaries. During the seventeenth century, Father Kino, a Jesuit, settled and worked among the Indians of Arizona and Baja California; Fray Antonio de Olivares and others established missions in Texas in the first decades of the eighteenth century; and the Franciscan Father Junípero Serra founded missions in California toward the later half of the century. These vulnerable, sparsely populated settlements could become tempting prey for European powers, particularly England and Russia. Spain was determined to keep them as part of its possessions.

After he returned to Spain and was appointed minister of the Indies, Gálvez implemented his plan to defend the northern territories. He created a new territorial organization, the Provincias Internas, which included the northern states of present-day Mexico, Texas, Arizona, New Mexico, and California. Under the military control of a commandant general, new frontier forts *(presidios)* were established, and Spain reasserted its authority. Yet, little Spanish population moved into this area. The lack of mineral wealth and labor, and the attraction of the existing wealth in and around Mexico City, kept the Spanish away from the more remote and hostile northern territories. While foreign threats never developed, Spain had to deal continuously with Indian resistance and opposition to Spanish control.

Administrative, territorial, and economic reforms paralleled religious reforms. The Bourbons were concerned and suspicious of Church power. Their objective was to reassert royal control, while reducing the Church's economic, social, and educational influence. Clerical meddling in government affairs was eliminated, and financial support for the Church was reduced. Yet, the biggest losers of the Bourbon anticlerical reforms were the Jesuits (the Society of Jesus).

The Jesuits were expelled from Spain and all its colonies, and their properties were confiscated in 1767. The reasons for the expulsion are many. First, it was part of a European movement directed at the society. They had previously been expelled from Portugal and Brazil in 1761. The Jesuits had become too powerful, too wealthy, and too independent. In New Spain, they controlled great numbers of Indians, numerous urban properties, and vast rural territories—as well as most educational institutions. Finally, because the Crown suspected the continuous allegiance of the society to the pope, it feared that the Jesuits might spread dangerous ideas that were not officially sanctioned by the Crown.

Reaction to the expulsion was violent. Initial shock and disbelief soon gave way to riots and demonstrations. In various towns, public officials were insulted and stoned; mobs roamed the streets chanting "death to the Spaniards," "down with the *gachupines.*" Gálvez reacted swiftly. He mobilized the army and crushed the rebellion. Gálvez set up special courts and dealt out summary justice—eighty-five men were executed, and almost a thousand were either jailed or banished, all of whom were Indian or mestizo.

The expulsion of the Jesuits had other implications besides Indian discontent. Jesuit plantations, some of the more productive and best run enterprises in New Spain, were seized and either abandoned or divided. The efficiency and productivity of the Jesuits were now lost. Indians were left to fend for themselves, often protected by neither Church nor state. Many Jesuit schools were closed or declined in quality. While the Franciscans took over some, they were not equipped to replace the Jesuits.

The expulsion and the continuous pressure exerted against the Church alienated many, particularly Church officials whose power and wealth were curtailed. Priests communicated their discontent to parishioners. Spaniards, Creoles, mestizos, and Indians all were subjected to the grumblings of an institution they respected and supported. When the Crown took over the Church's huge charitable fund in 1804, Church-state relations further deteriorated.

The impact of the Bourbon reforms were profound and far-reaching. They produced a degree of economic recovery and allowed for freer economic play. Naturally, these types of adjustments and change benefited some and hurt others. Businessmen who now enjoyed newfound prosperity demanded freer trade and more freedom. Smugglers and importers of non-Spanish goods suffered and grew dissatisfied with change. Both disliked increased taxation and the effectiveness of the Bourbon officials in collecting taxes. The creation of Crown monopolies hurt many producers. The tobacco monopoly, for example, displaced many involved in growing and producing tobacco and forced others to accept the new system imposed by Spain.

The great masses of the population, however, benefited little from the reforms. Prosperity was reserved for the *peninsulares* and Creoles. Indians and mestizos continued to live in poverty; some were indebted for life to the hacienda, others were abused and oppressed in the *obrajes;* still others were semienslaved in the mines. Seeing conditions in

Mexico, the Bishop of Valladolid lamented that in Mexico there were only two classes—"those who had everything and those who had nothing."

Despite the profound differences between rich and poor, a new middle class developed during colonial times. Composed of lawyers, accountants, small merchants, and planters, this new class, mostly criollos and some mestizos, exerted increasing influence toward the beginning of the nineteenth century. Many of them, educated by the Jesuits, rejected the prevailing scholasticism and participated in enlightened institutions, such as the Mining Seminary and the Botanical Gardens, which were devoted to the study of scientific changes. They founded several newspapers, such as *El Mercurio Volante* and the *Gaceta de Literatura* to foster the economic modernization of Mexico. Evenutally, they began to see themselves as different and separate from the mother country. This budding nationalism increased, as more Spaniards were sent to the colony to implement the Bourbon reforms and as prosperity attracted greater numbers of immigrants to Mexico.

The administrative reforms that protected the colony, made the system more efficient, and allowed for an increase in revenues for the Crown created significant resentment. The reassertion of political control by Spanish officials deepened the divisions in society between Creoles and *peninsulares*. Any hope the Creoles had of achieving power was shattered by the extensive and suffocating bureaucracy coming to Mexico.

CHAPTER 7

INDEPENDENCE
OR REVOLUTION

The Bourbon reforms awakened a society that had been partially dormant for two centuries. The changes introduced by Spain touched almost everyone in the colony. The emphasis on administrative efficiency, the territorial reorganizations, the increased taxation, and the expulsion of the Jesuits all induced disruptions that accentuated differences and that created conditions, if not for independence, then for civil war and violence among the various sectors of society.

The reforms spared very few. The Indians and mestizos were now required to work harder and produce more for the revived economy and the demanding mother country. Without the protection of the Jesuits and with a weakened Church, they fell prey to the excesses of merchants, hacendados, and Spanish officials. As Indian and mestizo unhappiness increased, so did mutinies and rebellions.

Unhappiness was not reserved to the lower ranks of society. Creole discontent increased with the new Spanish bureaucracy coming to Mexico. The Creoles saw the possibility for upward political and economic mobility curtailed by Spanish policies. The distinction between themselves and the new immigrants from Spain was greatly accentuated, as Spaniards controlled the higher governmental positions and benefited most from Spanish economic policies.

Although it is difficult to establish a causal connection between economic discontent and a desire for independence, it is clear that, when the conditions for independence developed, many groups seized the opportunity either to protect their interests or to take revenge on rival groups. The hatreds, jealousies, and antagonisms simmering for decades all emerged during the early 1800s. When Bourbon power collapsed in Spain, and the monarchy was taken over temporarily by Napoleon's French armies, civil war broke out: clericals versus anticlericals, conservatives versus liberals, Creoles versus *peninsulares,* and Indians and mestizos against all.

By the early ninteenth century, the Creoles had also developed a love for their birthplace. Mexico's beauty and wealth was a source of pride. Poetry and prose now began to praise the land and people as a unique society with its own charm and character. While it is difficult to pinpoint an exact date, a national spirit seems to have developed, and many in Mexico felt a separate and distinct identity—a consciousness of being American.

Worldwide changes also exerted significant influence on the course of events in Mexico. In North America, the English colonists rose in rebellion against the mother country in 1776 and established an independent republic. In Paris, mobs of revolutionaries decapitated the French monarch Louis XVI and established a republic embracing liberty, equality, and fraternity. In the Caribbean, Haitian masses of black slaves rose in rebellion, massacred their white, French masters, burned their plantations, declared independence, and proclaimed Haiti as the first black republic in the world in 1804. Such monumental changes sent shock waves through Spain and its empire in the New World and encouraged those who advocated either significant change in the relationship between Spain and its colonies or outright independence for Mexico.

The advocates for change were also affected by the ideological and intellectual climate in Europe. The Enlightenment with its criticism of society, especially religious and political institutions, exerted great influence on the Creoles in Mexico. Some responded to the ideas of the Enlightenment by emphasizing reason and experimentation as means of acquiring new knowledge. They advocated reforms but failed to question the fundamental nature of the system. Their energy was directed at improving the economic conditions of their birthplace. They joined economic societies, founded newspapers and literary gazettes, and improved education. They were antischolastic but not anticlerical. They remained Catholic in conviction and supported monarchy and authoritarianism to govern Mexico. They feared the more radical aspects of the French revolution, its antimonarchical and anti-Catholic aspects. But perhaps they feared even more the possibility that the masses of Indians and mestizos would rise and overthrow the existing order. Although they wanted equality with the *peninsulares,* they certainly did not advocate equality for the colored masses of Mexico. If independence were to come, their model would be the American, not the French, revolution. They preferred the American experiment, which eliminated the colonial power while preserving the social order—a relatively peaceful aristocratic and conservative revolution that kept the masses in their place.

A more radical group of Creoles received the impact of the Enlightenment directly from its English and French sources. Despite the Inquisition, books and pamphlets with the ideas of Newton, Voltaire, Rousseau, Montesquieu, Locke, and others circulated throughout New Spain. These Creoles advocated a more profound revolution—one that would eliminate the caste system as well as social and economic inequalities. Many of them longed for an independent Mexico in which the power of the Church would be curtailed. Certainly, they were a minority and they could be regarded as the precursors of the independence movement in Mexico.

Two Creole priests who led the movement for independence—Miguel Hidalgo and José María Morelos—belonged to this group. Born on May 8, 1753, Hidalgo was educated first by the Jesuits and later in the diocesan College of San Nicolás in Valladolid. There he would remain as part of the faculty and finally as rector. By the 1790s he had earned a bachelor's degree from the University of Mexico and had been ordained a priest. Because of his controversial ideas and mismanagement of funds, he was forced to resign from San Nicolás. After several tours in small parishes, he was assigned to the parish of Dolores in 1803, where he devoted himself to promoting local craft industries to benefit the Indians. It was also in Dolores that he joined a Creole conspiracy to expel the Spaniards from Mexico. As a result of his great speaking ability and charisma, Hidalgo rose to lead the movement.

The Spaniards soon discovered the conspiracy. In a dramatic pronouncement, the Grito de Dolores, on September 16, 1810, Hidalgo called for the end to bad government and abuses and the removal of the *peninsulares* from power. Short of calling for independence, he expressed support for the Church and the deposed King Ferdinand VII and opposed the French occupation of Spain. Indians and mestizos joined the rebellion. Although it was disorganized and had few weapons, this human mass, numbering approximately one hundred thousand took several small towns, massacred the Spanish defenders, looted the stores and government offices, and marched on Mexico City.

The Spanish government responded quickly. It publicized the violence and horror of this social and racial revolution unleashed by

A forerunner of Mexico's War for Independence, the Creole priest Miguel Hidalgo lead a social and racial rebellion of Indians and mestizos against Spanish control in 1810. He abolished Indian tribute and black slavery, and ordered lands restored to Indian communities. He was captured and executed by the Spaniards a year later. *Library of Congress*

Hidalgo. Many Creoles fearfully defected from his movement; Hidalgo hesitated and finally retreated to Guadalajara without attacking Mexico City. There, he issued edicts abolishing Indian tribute and black slavery. He ordered lands restored to Indian communities and called for the end of state monopolies.

Meanwhile, a large, well-trained Spanish army advanced on Guadalajara. In the ensuing battle, the rebel army was soundly defeated. Hidalgo fled north but was captured, tried, and sentenced to death. Before his execution in 1811, he repented and reaffirmed his loyalty to the Spanish monarchy.

Hidalgo's poorly organized uprising was followed by a more profound and methodical revolutionary movement led by José María Morelos, a mestizo parish priest follower of Hidalgo. Morelos possessed those qualities that Hidalgo lacked. Statesmanlike, disciplined, and capable, he organized a well-trained army and launched a campaign in southern Mexico that culminated in the capture of two strategic cities—Oaxaca and Acapulco. In the territories under his control, Morelos confiscated Spanish lands and wealth and abolished slavery and tribute.

In 1813, Morelos called the Congress of Chilpancingo, composed of representatives of the territories under his control, to consider his social and economic program. It called for Mexican independence and the abolition of all class distinctions, slavery, and tribute. Sovereignty would be vested in the people, and laws would be issued by a representative congress. It also called for republican institutions, a strong executive, and respect for property. It opposed the compulsory collection of Church taxes and even hinted at the distribution of Church lands. Morelos wanted not only independence but also the creation of a unique nation without discrimination. His proposals were far-reaching and laid the foundations for later reformers well into the twentieth century.

Morelos's vision for Mexico would have to wait. Bitter rivalries within his movement, mounting opposition from fearful conservative *peninsulares* and Creoles, and Spanish military efficiency and superiority doomed the rebellion. Morelos was captured, tried, and executed in 1815. Although two of his lieutenants, Guadalupe Victoria and Vicente Guerrero, continued guerrilla warfare, it was left to the conservative Creole aristocrat Col. Agustín de Iturbide to lead Mexico into independence.

Events in Spain precipitated the independence of Mexico. In 1820, a liberal movement forced the autocratic Spanish King Ferdinand VII to reinstate the liberal constitution of 1812 and to install a constitutional monarchy in Spain. The new government was controlled by liberal anticlerical elements determined to establish a reformist, constitutional government with guarantees of the rights of men, freedom of the press, representative government, and a parliamentary system.

The changes in Spain were welcomed in Mexico by liberal, anticleri-

A mestizo parish priest, José María Morelos was a visionary leader of the early Mexican struggle for independence. He organized a massive opposition to Spain and developed a social and economic program calling for independence and abolition of all class distinctions, slavery, and tribute. His program was far-reaching and laid the foundation for later reform.
Library of Congress

cal, and separatist Creoles as well as the remnants of the insurgent armies. Yet, the possibility that Spain might impose such a system in Mexico struck terror among *peninsulares,* conservative Creoles, and the Church hierarchy. For them, an independent Mexico, which could suppress and control the masses of Indians and mestizos and could protect their own interests as well as those of the Church, seemed preferable to remaining under the uncertain control of a liberal Spain.

They turned to one of their own—Agustín de Iturbide—a Creole aristocrat who had risen quickly in the militia and acquired a reputation for bravery and toughness. He fought on the royalist side against the insurgent armies, while amassing a personal fortune through bribery and intimidation. In a bold move, Iturbide convinced Guerrero, one of the remaining insurgent leaders, to join him in declaring Mexico's independence. On February 24, 1821, they issued the Plan of Iguala, which delineated a conservative program based on the three guarantees of religion, independence, and equal treatment for the *peninsulares* and Creoles. To secure these three guarantees, the army was called upon as protector and safekeeper of the new order.

The new realignment of forces led to the quick expulsion of Spain and the establishment of an independent Mexico. Iturbide's objective, however, was to create an independent Mexico with himself as monarch, while preserving Creole and Church privileges. Soon after independence, Iturbide fulfilled his own ambitions. On July 21, 1822, amid elaborate pageantry, he was crowned Emperor Agustín I. The new Mexican monarch created all the trappings of an elaborate court. He spent lavishly, reorganized the Church and asserted his authority to appoint church officials, and launched an invasion southward into Central America in a futile attempt to annex the newly independent countries of the region. Mismanagement, corruption, and waste flourished.

Iturbide also faced some difficulties with the United States. He hoped for diplomatic recognition as well as for a loan to assist his government. President James Monroe, however, hesitated, as he was unhappy that Mexico had established a monarchy and hoped that republican forces would eventually emerge victorious. He dispatched Joel Roberts Poinsett on a fact-finding mission to Mexico. Poinsett interviewed numerous Mexicans including Iturbide himself. "In a society not remarkable for strict morals," wrote Poinsett, "Iturbide was distinguished for his immorality. He is not scrupulous about the means he employs to obtain his ends."

Before Monroe could ponder Poinsett's reservations, Iturbide dispatched Manuel Zozaya as Mexican minister to Washington. Iturbide hoped that the reception of Zozaya would be a de facto recognition of the Mexican empire. Concerned that rejecting Zozaya would hurt U.S.-Mexican relations and would antagonize U.S. business interests eager for trade with Mexico, President Monroe recognized the Mexican government and appointed Poinsett as minister to Mexico in January 1823.

Despite this diplomatic victory, Iturbide's authoritarian rule and extravagant spending alienated most sectors of Mexico's society. The anticlericals resented his clericalism. The republicans despised his monarchical charade. The old insurgents, the unemployed rebels, and the ambitious and disappointed army officers opposed his policies and his flamboyant, wasteful style, hoping perhaps to obtain for themselves some of the spoils of office. By December 1822, opposition turned into full rebellion. The old insurgent generals Guadalupe Victoria and Vicente Guerrero and a young, ambitious, and unscrupulous officer, Antonio López de Santa Anna, who was commandant of the port of Veracruz, joined forces and pronounced against Iturbide. They issued the Plan of Casa Mata, which called for the abolition of the empire, the end of Iturbide's rule, and the establishment of a federal constitutional republic. Iturbide escaped into exile only to return several months later to lead a counterrebellion. He was arrested, tried, and executed in 1824. He died proclaiming his love for Mexico and the Catholic religion.

The independence of Mexico had started as an Indian-mestizo mutiny led by the Creoles against the *peninsulares*. It lacked a defined objective short of deposing the Spaniards from power. In its initial stages, it was a seminationalistic mass movement asserting freedom from French control. As it evolved, it developed a profound revolutionary ideology that emphasized, in addition to independence from Spain, agrarian reform, equality for the poorer elements of society, and anticlericalism. Yet, it ended as a conservative Creole reaction to the liberalism of Spain and as an attempt to maintain the power and privilege of the white minority. It was a minor change at the top with a continuation of the social and economic system implanted by the class-conscious Spaniards; the difference was that now the system was controlled by class-conscious conservative Creoles. Yet, independence unleashed uncontrollable forces for change. The seed of revolution had been planted. It began to grow in the nineteenth century and blossomed fully in the twentieth century. Mexicans had learned about dangerous Indian uprisings and about overthrowing oppressive political rulers. These lessons would be repeated often in Mexican history.

CHAPTER 8

THE AGE OF
SANTA ANNA

Numerous problems accompanied the emergence of Mexico as an independent republic. The years of warfare destroyed the economy, increased social and political tensions, and caused enormous suffering and misery. Of a population of seven million, an estimated half a million died during the wars for independence. Devastation in the countryside and in the cities left thousands unemployed. Disease, banditry, and violence were rampant.

The first president of Mexico, Guadalupe Victoria, inherited an empty treasury and a devastated economy. Because most of the fighting occurred in the mining areas, many silver mines were either closed or destroyed. Agricultural production was at a standstill, because many farms and haciendas had been destroyed or abandoned. Banditry increased as armed groups roamed the countryside, and looting, killing, and lawlessness were common.

In the urban areas, conditions were not much better. Many cities remained isolated from the rural areas owing to poor transportation or cut off by rebels and bandits. Few goods and products were moving. With few shipments of raw cotton, the prosperous textile industry ground to a halt. *Obrajes* closed. Laborers, particularly Indians and mestizos, sank to new levels of poverty.

Conditions were further aggravated by the flight of the *peninsulares*. During the wars, many had escaped the wrath of the insurgents by settling in Mexico City. Now that independence had been achieved, many moved back to Spain, because they were unwilling to return to their destroyed mines or haciendas, and with them went their capital and expertise. The anti-Spanish policies of the new government increased apprehension among the few *peninsulares* left in the country. Finally, in 1825, the Mexican government accused them of conspiring with Spain to regain its lost colony and expelled all Spaniards from Mexico.

The inexperience, bickering, and corruption of the new governing elites aggravated the already precarious economic conditions. The Creoles inherited power with little or no experience in government. They faced a divided nation riddled with regionalism and localism. Local military commanders exerted control over rural areas and were unwilling to submit to central control. These local caudillos or political bosses promoted the idea of a loose federal confederacy for Mexico. Yet others, fearing the breakup of the country into small fiefdoms, advocated a strong central government able to impose order and unite the nation.

Differences also existed concerning the role of the military. This institution now emerged as the most powerful in the country, and many feared that the rise of militarism would curtail freedom and suppress hard-won rights. Others saw the military as an institution to be used to advance their political and economic objectives. In most instances, the military became the tool of unscrupulous military as well as civilian leaders intent on using force to promote their own narrow interests. This pattern persisted through the century.

While the great masses of Indians and mestizos seemed uninterested in the political process and were primarily concerned with eking out an existence, deep ideological and political divisions existed in the upper echelons of society. Although the issue of republicanism versus monarchical rule had been resolved in favor of the former, many still longed for a monarchical type of government as the most suitable for Mexico. The proper role of the Church and the anticlerical feelings still simmering remained as a thorny, unresolved issue. Liberals and conservatives disagreed about the proper role of the Church in Mexican society. While the liberals supported the guiding role of the state over the Church, the conservatives advocated a Church that would guide the destinies of the nation.

The leading liberal theoretician during this period was José María Luis Mora. He advocated individual as opposed to communal property rights. He attacked the *fueros* or special privileges of corporate entities such as the Church and the army, because he believed that these *fueros* prevented economic growth. Mora advocated a federalist form of government and a limited democracy for Mexico. On the conservative side, the most important figure was Lucas Alamán. A statesman and historian, he is best known for his *Historia de Mejico,* a proclerical, conservative history of his country. Lucas Alamán admired the Spanish past, advocated a strong central government and Catholic Church, and supported corporate ownership in mining and industry. For the first fifty years of republican life, Mexico wavered between these two opposing ideological poles. The struggle, as these two leaders clearly envisioned, would shape the national character and define the type of nation Mexico would be. The conservatives wanted a strong unified Mexico under Church influence even at the expense of freedom. The liberals wanted a decentralized Mexico with an emasculated Church even at the expense of a fragile nation.

Amidst this chaotic situation, Mexico's political elite called for elections for a constitutional assembly. The Constitution of 1824 was partially modeled on the United States Constitution. Mexico was organized as a federal republic composed of nineteen states and four territories. A division of powers between executive, judicial, and legislative was established. The legislature was made bicameral, and each state was represented by two senators and one deputy for every eighty thousand citizens. The states were granted even stronger powers than those of the United States. The president and vice president were to be elected not by popular vote or an electoral college but by the state legislature for a four-year term. The Catholic religion was made the official religion, and the president was granted extraordinary powers in emergency situations, which was a provision often used by later leaders to assume dictatorial powers.

For the next fifty years, constitutions and laws hardly mattered. Constitutions were merely statements of objectives, and laws were made to violate them. Violence and instability permeated the political process. Violence came to be accepted as the legitimate means of promoting change, which is not to say that profound economic or social change occurred. On the contrary, most of the changes were at the top of the political spectrum. Leaders replaced one another advocating liberal or conservative causes, while the basic structure of society remained little changed.

During this period, thirty different individuals occupied the presidency. No president, except the first one, lasted for more than two consecutive years. Rebellions and coups occurred almost annually. Such internal chaos and instability invited foreign intervention and led to conflicts with France and the United States. A short war with France in

1838, a larger war with the United States from 1846 to 1848, and a war of liberation against the French and their Emperor Maximilian from 1862 to 1867 cost thousands of lives and further ruined a nation already in miserable conditions.

Of the earlier powers involved in Mexico, Great Britain became the most important. The British saw Mexico as a large and profitable market for their growing textile industry, among others. When the Holy Alliance offered Spain help in reconquering its colonies in Spanish America, the British threatened to use their navy to defend the newly established republics. Fearing American influence, the British were quick to recognize the independence of Mexico, as well as the rest of Latin America, and dispatched commercial and trade missions to the region.

As Mexico's economy floundered, the British were also eager to loan money to the new nation. These loans, each consisting of more than three million pounds, were floated in the London stock exchange. Yet, the fees and discount rates demanded by the London bankers were so high that only about half the money reached the Mexican treasury. These, as well as other loans from other European powers, remained a burden to the Mexican economy and resulted in European intervention.

The British and the Europeans were also successful during those early years in penetrating the Mexican market. British capital invested in the mining industry. A large proportion of Mexican trade was with England. Other nations joined in the perceived bonanza of Mexico. German and French capital entered the country.

U.S. ships also appeared frequently on Mexican ports. The Americans, however, found themselves at a disadvantage. The Mexicans seemed suspicious of their northern neighbor and of its Manifest Destiny, which was a situation encouraged by the British. The first American representative in Mexico, Joel Poinsett, did not help matters. A cultured and perhaps well-intentioned but tactless diplomat, he meddled continuously in the internal affairs of the country. Poinsett was strongly anti-Spanish and sided with the liberals in helping them to organize a Masonic lodge, which they hoped would become the leading center of radical thought. Poinsett's actions in part helped the British to advance their interests. The United States would have to wait until the last decades of the century to exercise great influence in the economic and political affairs of its southern neighbor.

Throughout this early period, one figure dominated Mexican politics: Antonio López de Santa Anna. Born in Veracruz, from a well-to-do business family, Santa Anna was sent to the military academy. He grad-

An ambitious and erratic leader, Antonio López de Santa Anna ruled Mexico for a quarter of a century, serving as president six times. He defeated the Texans at the Alamo and fought wars against France and the United States. Santa Anna was both the cause and the product of Mexican instability during the early years of the republic. *Library of Congress*

uated in time to join the royalist army against independence leaders. In 1821, he defected to the proindependence forces of Iturbide, and received the rank of colonel and later general. He soon turned against Iturbide's short-lived empire and supported the republican forces.

An ambitious, flamboyant, and erratic leader, Santa Anna ruled Mexican politics for a quarter of a century and served as president six times. He shifted political allegiances and ideologies to suit his own objectives. He started as a champion of the liberal-republican forces against the Iturbide empire and ended as a conservative defender of Church power and privilege. When a conservative anti–Guadalupe Victoria rebellion erupted, Santa Anna suppressed the uprising. During the late 1820s, he supported the insurgent leader Vicente Guerrero for the presidency and, although Guerrero lost the election, Santa Anna installed him in office with the support of the military.

In 1829, Santa Anna was catapulted to national prominence when he defeated a Spanish army that was attempting to reconquer Mexico. Spain had never recognized Mexican independence and longed for an opportunity to reestablish power over its former colony. The weakness of Mexico's government invited Spanish intervention and, in 1829, a Spanish army left Cuba for the Mexican coast. Santa Anna met the invaders in Tampico, routing the hungry, ill-prepared, and yellow fever–ridden Spanish forces.

The defeat of the Spanish army not only increased Santa Anna's popularity but also consolidated the independence of the new Mexican republic. It also helped to formulate what later became the major tenets of Mexico's foreign policy—self-determination, nonintervention, and Latin American solidarity. Prominent Mexican writers and intellectuals such as Francisco Azcárate, foreign minister under Iturbide, had advocated these principles as the basis for the foreign policy of an emerging Mexico. Azcárate warned about U.S. expansionist ambitions in the southwest, calling for closer integration with other Latin American countries and for strict adherence to the ideas of self-determination and nonintervention.

Santa Anna returned victorious and now extremely popular to Mexico City. In 1833, the grateful state legislatures elected the "savior of the nation" as president. As vice president, Santa Anna selected Valentín Gómez Farías, a distinguished writer and intellectual and a strong advocate of liberalism. Yet, Santa Anna had no sooner been elected than he returned to his estate in Veracruz. He tired quickly of the daily presidential routine and preferred to leave governing to his vice president.

The liberal administration of Gómez Farías introduced several antimilitary, anticlerical reforms. The size of the army was reduced, and military officers would now be subjected, for the first time, to civilian, instead of military, tribunals. The attack on the Church was more profound. Clergymen would be allowed to preach only about religious matters. All education from now on would become secular. Because of the large number of priests, the University of Mexico was closed down. The government, not the Church or the pope, would make all clerical appointments, and nuns and priests were allowed to forswear their vows. Finally, the payment of mandatory taxes to support the Church was abolished.

Reaction was swift. The Church, the army, and conservative elements banded together to oppose the regime. Rebellion and violence erupted all over the country. Smelling a popular cause, Santa Anna reversed his traditional support for the liberals, joined the conservative elements, overthrew his vice president, and marched victorious on Mexico City.

The reinstated president now undid what his vice president had done. He abolished all of Gómez Farías's reforms and established a Catholic, centralist dictatorship. He eliminated the Constitution of 1824 and replaced it with a new document, known as the Siete Leyes (Seven Laws) or Constitution of 1836. The states were converted into military departments that were commanded by army officers who had been appointed by Santa Anna. The right to hold public office was reserved to those with property and income, and the right to vote was restricted. The new regime and constitution dealt a death blow to the federalist experiment and instituted a centralized dictatorship led by the military.

Santa Anna's attention, however, shifted rapidly from domestic to international affairs. Significant numbers of U.S. citizens had entered Texas during the early nineteenth century. The Mexicans granted the Austin family from the United States permission to settle approximately three hundred Catholic families in the region. Yet, many more came in. Most were not Catholic. The Mexican government became alarmed and, in 1829, issued an emancipation proclamation, in hopes that the abolition of slavery would deter further U.S. immigration. The abolition was not enforced, and U.S. settlers continued to enter Texas. In 1830, Mexico prohibited all migration from the United States. It advocated better trade relations between Texas and Mexico and an increase in Mexican colonization of this otherwise sparsely populated Mexican territory.

The official ending of U.S. migration was but one of the grievances of the U.S. Texans. They felt unrepresented in the state legislature and were unhappy with Mexico's legal system. Political, religious, cultural, ethnic, and language differences accentuated tension with Mexican settlers. The Mexican government's insistence on integrating and exercising greater control over Texas increased resentments. When Santa

Anna abolished the federalist constitution and imposed a centralist state, some Mexican liberals opposed to Santa Anna helped the Texans establish the Lone Star Republic and choose David Burnet as president.

The stage was now set for open conflict. Santa Anna organized an army of approximately six thousand men and marched into Texas. On March 6, 1836, at the "battle of El Alamo," as is known in Mexican history or the "massacre at the Alamo" as is known in U.S. history, the Mexicans routed the Texans, killing all of the defenders of El Alamo. Opposition to Mexican "brutality" increased in the United States, along with sympathy for the Texans' cause. With renewed support and weapons from the North, the Texans reorganized under the leadership of Sam Houston. An opportunistic drunk, Houston had recently arrived in Texas and viewed the independence movement as a chance for fame and wealth. "Big Drunk," as the Cherokees used to call him, organized an army and prepared to confront the Mexicans. One month later, Houston forces surprised Santa Anna's army. At the battle of San Jacinto and under the cry of "remember the Alamo," the Mexicans were soundly defeated, Santa Anna was captured, and Texas became independent.

With uncanny ability, Santa Anna extricated himself from a difficult and embarrassing situation. He promised the Texans never again to use force against them and to help with the Mexican Congress in obtaining the recognition of the independence of the Lone Star Republic. The Texans sent him to Washington to meet with President Andrew Jackson for a brief discussion on the future of Texas and on U.S.-Mexican relations. In 1837, Santa Anna returned to Veracruz and insisted that the promises he had made while a prisoner should not be honored and that Texan independence should not be recognized. For the next eight years, the Texas Republic remained a thorny issue in U.S.-Mexican relations. The Mexicans refused to recognize the independence of Texas, and the United States refused to admit Texas into the Union.

Even more urgent was a short war with France. French businessmen in Mexico had filed numerous claims against the Mexican government as their properties had been damaged or destroyed during Mexico's unending civil strife. One of those claims was from a French owner of a pastry shop, whose store had been ransacked by Mexican army soldiers. When the king of France failed to receive any compensation for the claims, a French naval force blockaded and bombarded Veracruz on April 16, 1838.

The Pastry War, as this conflict became known, ended quickly, after the Mexicans expelled the French from Veracruz. Leading the Mexican forces was no other than General Santa Anna. He personally commanded the troops in Veracruz that expelled the French. During the fighting, a cannon burst wounded his leg, which had to be partially amputated. With great ceremony and fanfare, the "hero against France" buried his leg at his estate, but disinterred it in 1842 and placed it at the national cemetery in an urn atop a specially constructed stone pillar. Santa Anna returned victorious to Mexico amid clamor that he had saved the fatherland's honor. He soon retired to his estate and left the chores of governing to others. Yet, he never allowed the Mexicans to forget either his leg or his sacrifice in defending the fatherland.

This brave and energetic yet irresponsible, corrupt, and egotistical nineteenth-century military caudillo reflected the worst of Mexico's early years. In a sense, he was both the product and the cause of Mexican instability. The deep divisions within society, the weakness of political institutions except for the military, and the ambitions and, at times, lack of principles of many political leaders made the age of Santa Anna a disastrous period in Mexican history. Economically in ruins and about to lose a significant chunk of territory, Mexico floundered. Santa Anna was about to play his last, and probably worst, act in the Mexican tragedy—as leader of a war with the United States.

CHAPTER 9

THE U.S.–MEXICAN WAR

In 1846 the United States went to war with its southern neighbor. This conflict, the first U.S. war fought in a foreign land, profoundly affected both countries. The war divided U.S. citizens over the issues of slavery and the wisdom of U.S. expansionism, and it perpetuated the political instability of the Mexican state. Yet, the United States emerged revitalized from the fighting, while Mexico was physically and psychologically defeated.

There were many reasons for the war. The United States and Mexico had a long-standing border dispute, which included the annexation of Texas. Mexico had refused to pay the United States a debt owed for the mistreatment of U.S. citizens and for property either confiscated or destroyed in Mexico. More important, however, there was a belief within prominent sectors of the American political establishment that the whole of the North American continent must eventually be controlled by the United States. Combining land grabbing with political idealism, these expansionists proclaimed that it was the manifest destiny of the United States to extend the benefits of democracy and the American way of life wherever possible.

The issue of boundary disputes centered on the North American involvement in Texas. The Americans had coveted Texas since the turn of the nineteenth century. Men such as Aaron Burr supported expeditions against the Mexicans to gain control of Texas, and President

Andrew Jackson in 1829 offered Mexico five million dollars in exchange for this vast but mostly underpopulated land.

In 1835, the territory of Texas sought independence from Mexican control after Mexico refused Texas's bid to join the Mexican union. The dispute between Texas and Mexico arose over Mexico's arbitrary handling of the issue of further immigration from the United States to the territory. Originally, Mexico had encouraged settlement of Texas by all groups with enticements of free land, as Mexico never had the resources to settle properly its northern territory. The wars of independence had left Mexico financially and physically ruined. High mountains and disease-infested plains isolated many areas from the centralized control of Mexico City. Furthermore, the rampant political instability and frequent changes of government leadership and policies encouraged secessionist movements throughout the northern and southern states of Mexico.

By the early 1830s, however, U.S. settlers were quickly outnumbering the Mexican nationals. Compounding the problem was Mexico City's worry over U.S. expansionism throughout the West, especially in the New Mexico and California regions. The ruling elites in Mexico City made the decision to close the border to all further immigration. This move angered the Texans. Led by Stephen Austin, the settlers of Texas petitioned the Mexican state to be given equal status as Mexican nationals. When its bid for statehood failed, Texas declared its independence from Mexico. Subsequently, the Texans achieved their independence after defeating Santa Anna at the battle of San Jacinto in 1836.

Although U.S. citizens had enthusiastically supported Texas's fight for independence, the political atmosphere in the United States prevented the annexation of Texas. The problem of annexation centered on the issue of slavery. Northern congressmen feared that if Texas were permitted into the Union, it would enter as a slave state. Unwilling to create political turmoil in the United States, President Andrew Jackson recognized Texas's independence in 1837, instead of offering it statehood. Therefore, any potential confrontation with Mexico over Texas was sidestepped for ten years.

For the time being, Texas remained an independent republic. With an exuberant self-confidence, some of the Texans began now to consider a western expansion, which would make their nation a strong and leading power in North America. Yet, they had few resources with which to achieve their objectives. During the presidency of Mirabeau

Bonaparte Lamar (1838–1842) Texas incurred a heavy debt, mostly owed to the United States. An unsuccessful attempt by a Texas military expedition to capture Santa Fe destroyed whatever chance there had been of securing Mexican recognition.

In 1842, Houston succeeded Lamar and sought help from European powers. Either France or England should guarantee Texas's independence in return for economic concessions. Texas was even willing to abolish slavery in return for British support. As Houston probably had calculated, these proposals caused considerable consternation in the United States. If Texas were to become a political and economic dependency of a European power, it would violate the 1823 Monroe Doctrine and would be contrary to U.S. foreign policy, which emphasized no new colonization by European powers and no transfer of territories in the New World among those powers. As enunciated in the Monroe Doctrine, the United States preferred for the Western Hemisphere to remain isolated from Europe. If diplomacy failed, the only option open to the United States would be to incorporate Texas into the Union.

Meanwhile, Mexico staunchly refused to recognize Texas's independence even after being encouraged by the British to do so. The British recognized the independence of Texas and tried to influence Mexico's policy. They realized that Mexico could not regain control over its lost territory and believed that the British could impede the westward expansion of the United States by creating a separate nation along its border.

In Mexico, the loss of Texas infuriated the Mexican people, who demanded that their leaders recover it, by force, if necessary. The Mexican political leadership reacted in two ways: first, it encouraged border raids by Mexican troops into Texas; and then it warned the U.S. government that any attempt to annex Texas would create a state of war between the two countries. President José Joaquín Herrera—who had succeeded Santa Anna as president in 1844, after Santa Anna was exiled—went so far as to ask the Mexican congress for a declaration of war to take effect if the United States annexed or invaded Texas.

With the election of James Polk to the presidency in 1844, the United States initiated formal annexation procedures for Texas. President Polk had run for the presidency on a platform advocating westward expansion and that the territories of Texas and Oregon be added to the United States. His election was considered to be a mandate from the American people on these issues. Therefore, on March 1, 1845, Texas was formally offered annexation by the United States. Thirty days later, Mexico responded by severing diplomatic ties with the United States.

Further aggravating the situation was the fact that the United States now claimed its southern border at the Rio Grande River, which infuriated the Mexicans, who considered the border to be at the Nueces River.

The second factor leading to war between the United States and Mexico was the concept of Manifest Destiny. This belief among the American people was in part related to the issue of Texas, and it had a major impact on Polk's electoral platform concerning U.S. expansionism. The term "manifest destiny" was coined in 1845 by John L. O'Sullivan, editor of the *Democratic Review,* to describe the U.S. destiny to conquer and occupy North America. This belief, however, was not new to the country. Thomas Jefferson and others had spoken about the hope and need for the citizens of the United States to control all of the Americas. Although there were Americans who objected to this sense of superiority and even racism toward other cultures, President Polk's election signified a victory for those who dreamed of U.S. rule from coast to coast. Furthermore, President Polk did not even try to conceal this wish to incorporate the western part of the continent into the United States. Unfortunately, Mexico was in the way of the expansionists' dreams; Texas became the battleground.

Proponents of Manifest Destiny over Texas argued that it was the U.S. mission to seize the territory because Mexico was unworthy to possess it. Newspapers editorialized about this duty to save the land from "the lazy, immoral, and corrupt Mexicans." Some even argued for the outright annexation of Mexico. These attitudes among the North Americans only fueled the atmosphere of crisis over Texas and, perhaps, impeded attempts at settling the dispute peacefully.

The dispute over Mexico's failure to pay recompense for its treatment of U.S. citizens and their property aggravated an already charged situation. President Polk used it as one of his reasons for requesting a declaration of war against Mexico. On May 11, 1846, he told the U.S. Congress that "the grievous wrongs perpetrated by Mexico upon our citizens for a long period of years remains unredressed; and solemn treaties have being disregarded. . . . In the meantime we have tried every effort at reconciliation. The cup of forbearance has been exhausted, even before Mexico passed the boundary of the United States, invaded our territory, and shed American blood upon American soil."

The conflict over Mexico's failure to pay restitution to the United States concerned damages suffered by U.S. citizens on Mexican soil. The years of political turmoil in Mexico had caused lawlessness to prevail throughout the country. Unfortunately, U.S. citizens and their property were sometimes the target of this anarchy. The U.S. government demanded compensation for the injuries suffered by its citizens. An International Tribunal was created to settle the dispute, and in 1841, it awarded the United States two million dollars. Yet, Mexico would not or could not pay because of its chaotic financial situation.

The issue of compensation, however, was not the most critical factor in determining the U.S. willingness to go to war. In 1845, President Polk was willing to exchange the amount due for the Mexican recognition of the U.S. border at the Rio Grande and the right of the United States to purchase New Mexico and California. Mexico perceived the offer as a threat to its nationhood and rejected Polk's suggestion. As a result of Mexico's response, President Polk ordered Gen. Zachary Taylor to move the U.S. Army to Corpus Christi, Texas.

Yet, President Polk still did not consider war with Mexico as inevitable. In 1845, he sent John Slidell, a Democratic politician from Louisiana, to Mexico to try to resolve the dispute over the annexation of Texas and the U.S. claim of the Rio Grande River as the border. Slidell was also instructed to try to buy California. The political chaos in Mexico prevented Slidell from reaching an agreement with any Mexican government official. He was even denied an audience with the Mexican president. Because he was in a weak and insecure position, President José Herrera did not wish to jeopardize his presidency by being accused of selling out to the Americans. The failure of Slidell's mission prompted President Polk to order General Taylor's troops moved to the Rio Grande. Mexico perceived Taylor's advance as an act of war, and the Mexican government ordered Taylor to retreat to the Nueces River.

Awaiting orders from Polk, General Taylor ignored the Mexican warning, precipitating the start of armed conflict. On April 25, 1846, the first shots of the war were fired, when the Mexican cavalry attacked a group of U.S. soldiers, killing or wounding several. Mexican troops laid siege to the U.S. fort at the Rio Grande. The siege, however, did not last long because General Taylor brought reinforcements and defeated the Mexicans at the battles of Palo Alto and Resaca de la Palma. Outgunned and plagued by desertions and poor leadership, the Mexican troops withdrew, abandoning Matamoros to General Taylor.

Meanwhile, on May 13, 1846, the United States Congress declared war on Mexico, and President Polk called for fifty thousand volunteers to join the U.S. military. Caught up in the patriotic fervor sweeping the country, thousands of young men heeded the president's call to arms. Yet, the American people were far from unanimous in supporting the war. There was strong opposition in the Northeast, where many believed that the expansionist demands came mostly from cotton growers whose purpose for the war was to acquire territories for slavery. The war was most popular in the West, and most of the army volunteers came from the Mississippi Valley.

After obtaining a declaration of war, President Polk ordered Col. Stephen Kearney to form the Army of the West and to march to New Mexico and California. He also ordered Commodore Charles Stockton, commander of the Pacific fleet, to seize California. Polk hoped that, if the United States occupied these territories during the war, the Mexicans would have to view it as a fait accompli, and cede the territories to the United States at the end of the hostilities.

In August, Commodore Stockton conquered Los Angeles, and Colonel Kearney occupied Santa Fe. Although Mexican loyalists retook Los Angeles, both Stockton and Kearney would control San Diego and Los Angeles by early January 1847. This eliminated all effective resistance to the United States in the West for the duration of the war.

While the war was being fought in the West, Santa Anna returned to Mexico with the help of the United States. He had convinced President Polk that he could end the war on American terms, if he were allowed to return to Mexico. Santa Anna quickly realized that the Mexican people wanted to resist the Americans, so that capitulation to the Americans would be politically impossible. He assumed control over the military once again and moved his troops from San Luis Potosí to engage Taylor's forces. The two armies clashed at the battle of Buena Vista in February 1847. The actual fighting ended in a draw, but Santa Anna was forced to retreat after suffering heavy casualties.

Although Taylor's army had advanced about two hundred miles across the Rio Grande, he was ordered to remain on the defensive, partly because the American military lacked confidence in his ability and partly because his popularity at home would make him a possible opposition presidential candidate in the upcoming elections. Polk did not want to make Taylor a greater hero. The main military operation of the war took the form of an invasion by way of the Gulf of Mexico under Gen. Winfield Scott to capture Mexico City.

In March 1847, General Scott landed his troops at Veracruz. Twenty days later, the city surrendered to the invading Americans. The quick successes of Taylor's and Scott's troops encouraged Polk to try to find an immediate solution to the fighting. He appointed Nicholas Trist as chief peace negotiator. His mission was to go to Mexico to find a peace acceptable to the Mexicans, but Trist found the same problems that

Gen. Winfield Scott's entrance into Mexico City. In the era of Manifest Destiny, the United States and Mexico fought a costly war (1846–1848) that ended in Mexico's defeat and loss of half of its territory. *Library of Congress*

Slidell had earlier. The unstable political leadership and nationalist feelings of the Mexican people impeded Trist's attempts to reach an accord.

While Trist was trying to arrange an armistice with the Mexicans, General Scott was marching on Mexico City. He defeated Santa Anna at the mountain pass of Cerro Gordo, after a spectacular drive by the American troops that bypassed the entrenched Mexican position and attacked them from the rear. The way to Mexico City was now left open. Santa Anna's men tried to halt Scott's advance by engaging his troops at Contreras and Churubusco, but they were defeated. Then, on September 13, the historic battle at Chapultepec Castle in Mexico City was fought.

Displaying unparalleled bravery, General Scott's troops overwhelmed the seemingly impenetrable fortress within a day. The castle was defended by approximately one thousand troops and the cadets of the Military Academy, the *Niños Héroes,* or heroic children, many of whom died rather than surrender. After the battle, the citizens of Mexico City forced Santa Anna and his men out of the city and surrendered it to General Scott's forces. Santa Anna resigned both the presidency and his position as the commander of the military and fled. The battle of Chapultepec ended the war, and U.S. representatives prepared to negotiate a tough peace agreement.

On February 2, 1848, after months of indecision and procrastination by the Mexicans—because no one wanted to be identified with defeat—a peace agreement was signed. The Treaty of Guadalupe-Hidalgo was soon ratified by the U.S. Congress on March 10. The treaty stipulated the Rio Grande as the boundary between the United States and Mexico. Mexico recognized the U.S. annexation of Texas and ceded the California and New Mexico territories. In return, Mexico accepted compensation of fifteen million dollars. The war was finally over.

The United States had little difficulty in defeating the Mexicans. The U.S. soldiers were better trained and more enthusiastic, their generals were more competent, and their guns and equipment were far superior. The Mexican army was ten times as large as that of the United States, but it consisted mostly of underfed, poorly trained, and poorly motivated Indian conscripts who had been equipped with old weapons purchased from Great Britain two decades earlier. The jealousies, divisions, and bickering within the Mexican military also contributed to its defeat.

Although more than thirteen thousand U.S. soldiers died in Mexico, in the United States, the war became nothing more than a footnote, soon overshadowed by the issue of slavery and the Civil War. The same

U.S. forces storming Chapultepec Castle in Mexico City during the last battle of the Mexican War. The defenders included cadets of the Military Academy—the *Niños Héroes,* or heroic children—many of whom died rather than surrender. *Library of Congress*

cannot be said of the Mexicans. The war left a legacy of hatred and hostility toward the United States. It created a lasting phobia in Mexican consciousness toward any act that could be perceived as interventionist. In Mexican schools, children recite tales of the valiant struggle against the U.S. invader. The battle at Chapultepec has become a memorial to the boy cadets who committed suicide rather than surrender the Mexican flag to the Americans. The war is not referred to as the Mexican-American war, but as the war of the North American invasion.

After the war, the defeat and loss of over half of its national territory left Mexico in chaos, poor, and disunited. Pessimism and doubt about their ability to govern themselves gripped the thinking of writers and intellectuals. Some even advocated a foreign ruler, such as a European prince, who could unite and pacify their defeated nation.

Both the liberals and the conservatives blamed one another for the defeat and national humiliation. The conservatives claimed that Mexico needed to revive the monarchy, to reinstill aristocratic values among the people, and to restore the glory of the Catholic Church. The liberals, for their part, blamed the Church, the army, and regional caciques for Mexico's failure. They argued that these institutions should be destroyed because they had prevented the Mexican people from uniting as one nation. They believed that economic and political stability was needed to ensure the survival of the Mexican state; hence, the old pillars of Mexican society had to be crushed. The aftermath of the conflict would lead Mexico to anarchy, civil war, and French intervention.

CHAPTER 10

PRELUDE TO REVOLUTION: LA REFORMA

The war with the United States had a profound impact on Mexico. Not only did the country lose half of its territory, but future generations would grow up fearing and hating the Colossus of the North. The country was humiliated and disillusioned. Commerce was at a standstill. The forces for decentralization were strong, and Mexico seemed to be falling apart.

For the last time, Santa Anna would take power. In 1853, at sixty years of age, he was made perpetual dictator of Mexico. With the conservative leader Lucas Alamán as head of his cabinet, Santa Anna embarked on a program of economic development. New roads and telegraphs were built, and unoccupied lands were colonized. Unfortunately, Alamán died soon after taking office, and without his restraining influence, Santa Anna's excesses became notorious. He increased the size of the army, and Spanish and Prussian officers were brought to Mexico to improve and discipline it. Most liberals were either repressed or sent into exile. Santa Anna spent lavishly and borrowed heavily to keep his flamboyant dictatorship alive.

Ironically, he turned to Mexico's nemesis—the United States—for financial relief. The U.S. government wanted the Mesilla Valley (a chunk of land in present-day southern New Mexico and Arizona) to build a railroad to California. Santa Anna negotiated the sale of this territory to the United States for ten million dollars. Known as the Gadsden purchase, this transaction was received with anger and skepticism in Mexico. Santa Anna's lavish spending and increased taxation rallied internal opposition. To make matters worse, bubonic plague spread throughout the country.

In the south, the center of old liberalism, a new generation was emerging that was prepared to challenge the existing order. Fiery and nationalistic, this generation had been educated in the secular schools established since independence. Although most of them were mestizos, they included some Indians who rose to prominence in the politics and administration of the provinces, primarily Michoacán and Oaxaca. They rejected the Hispanic Catholic tradition and advocated subordinating the Church and the army to civil authorities, representative democracy, federalism, and a nation of small landholders. While they feared their northern neighbor, they admired U.S. institutions and economic development and longed for a prosperous and united Mexico without anarchy and corruption.

The leader of this new generation—a man who would dominate Mexican history for the next two decades—was Benito Juárez. A pureblooded Zapotec Indian, Juárez was born in Oaxaca in 1806. Orphaned at an early age and unable to speak Spanish until the age of twelve, he left his family's adobe hut and moved to Mexico City to work as a household servant. His philanthropic master provided him with a limited education and encouraged him to become a priest. Juárez, however, was more interested in law and, after much hardship, graduated as a lawyer.

Law soon gave way to politics. He was elected to the national Congress in Mexico and served as provisional governor of his state. As governor, he refused Santa Anna's request for refuge in Oaxaca after the U.S.–Mexican war. Juárez considered Santa Anna a disgrace for Mexico and wanted nothing to do with the opportunistic caudillo.

In 1848, Juárez was elected for a full term as governor. His administration was honest and progressive. Although he failed to introduce major revolutionary changes, he constructed rural schools, developed the port of Huatulco, which encouraged trade and commerce for the state, and reduced the large bureaucracy. By the time he left office, the state was on a sound fiscal footing, and Indians had a greater stake in the administration of this state.

Soon after his governorship, Juárez faced Santa Anna. The dictator

A pure-blooded Indian, Benito Juárez rose to power in the mid-nineteenth century as a leader of the Reforma, a profoundly liberal movement that opposed church power and called for the redistribution of land and the destruction of Mexican society's feudalistic organization. Juárez helped draft the 1857 liberal constitution, served as president on various occasions, and led the struggle against French occupation. *Library of Congress*

remembered Juárez's refusal to allow him to seek refugee in Oaxaca and feared the growing power of the liberal forces and of this righteous and determined Indian. Juárez was arrested and, after several months in jail, was exiled to New Orleans, where he joined other exiled Mexicans plotting the overthrow of Santa Anna. He met Melchor Ocampo, one of the brightest ideologues of the liberal cause, who influenced him profoundly. In 1854, they all joined forces and began supporting Gen. Juan Alvarez, an old liberal guerrilla chieftain, then leading an antigovernment rebellion in the state of Guerrero. From exile, Ocampo and Juárez drafted a general statement of principles, which later became known as the Plan of Ayutla. This broad plan outlined grievances against Santa Anna and advoated a temporary dictatorship, led by the liberals and followed by the election of a constitutional convention, which would establish a republican representative government.

The rebellion spread throughout the country. Although Santa Anna's armies were better equipped and trained, they were unable to crush the liberal forces. While the rebels had no organized army but only ill-trained bands of guerrillas, they commanded significant popular support. The Plan of Ayutla and the anticlerical, constitutional ideas of the liberals captured the imagination of a population tired of dictatorship, corruption, and militarism. In August 1855, sensing that the end of his regime was near, Santa Anna galloped off to Veracruz and exile for the last time. Seventeen years later, he was allowed to return to Mexico, where he died poor and forgotten in 1876.

With Santa Anna out of the picture, the stage was set for the bitter conservative-liberal struggle that followed. The Reform, as this period was known, lasted several years, cost many lives, produced the Constitution of 1857, and culminated in a bizarre episode—the French intervention and the establishment of the Maximilian empire in Mexico.

The aims of the reform were clearly a social, political, and economic revolution that would transform Mexico. The liberals wanted to destroy society's feudalistic organization, to establish constitutional government, to destroy the powers and privileges of both the Church and the army, to develop the economy by distributing and making productive the properties and lands of the Church, and to create a nation of small property owners.

Yet, above all, the role of the Church was the issue that captivated the liberals. For them, an all-powerful institution, usually above the law and controlling much of the wealth of Mexico, was intolerable. The pro-Spanish, promonarchical attitude of the church during and immediately after independence was still bitterly recalled.

The reform period brought to the forefront Indian and mestizo leadership. It seemed, for a brief moment, a repetition of the events of the independence period during the early nineteenth century, when Hidalgo and Morelos led the masses of Indians in a social and racial revolution against the Spaniards in Mexico. For now, in the middle of the century, the presence of Indians and mestizos in leadership roles, as well as in the ranks of the liberal forces, gave the struggle the partial appearance of a racial as well as a socioeconomic rebellion. It was not that all Indians and mestizos supported the liberal cause, but a significant number did. Those who followed Alvarez, Juárez, and Ocampo wanted a new and different Mexico without a powerful Church and a strong Spanish heritage. They had begun to study their indigenous past and had found a glory that seemed to have been denied by the Spanish conquest and civilization. A budding *indigenismo* was taking root during this confused and violent period.

In 1855, the liberals took power; dressed in black, in a black carriage, and surrounded by Indian masses, Benito Juárez rode into Mexico City. Although initially Alvarez was appointed provisional president and was later replaced by Ignacio Comonfort, a moderate colonel in the insurgent forces, the moment belonged to the more revolutionary elements within the liberals. Melchor Ocampo became secretary of the treasury; Miguel Lerdo de Tejada, secretary of development; Juárez, secretary of justice. The new government set out to dismantle the institutional structures underpinning the conservative state.

The first important piece of legislation that emerged was the Ley Juárez. This law abolished the military and ecclesiastical *fueros,* which were the special privileges that exempted soldiers and clerics from being tried in civil courts. It restricted the jurisdiction of ecclesiastical courts to only ecclesiastical cases.

The second major piece of legislation was the Ley Lerdo, which prohibited corporations such as the Church or civil communities from owning land not directly used in day-to-day operations. The aim of the Ley Lerdo were to destroy the economic power of the Church, raise revenues for the state, and create a new class of small proprietors by breaking up communal holdings of Indian villages. Although the Church would be allowed to retain buildings and schools that were being used for religious purposes, they would lose most of their rural and urban properties. The massive real estate holdings that the Church had accumulated since colonial times were now to be put up for sale at public auction.

The Ley Lerdo brought unexpectedly negative results. It partially destroyed the economic foundations of the country. Church properties were mostly well managed, and overseers of these properties, generally, treated the mestizo and Indian workers reasonably well. These enterprises, furthermore, supported charities as well as educational institutions. Once auctioned, they were not distributed among the poor but fell into the hands of speculators, many of whom were foreigners. Wealthy Catholics refused to bid for expropriated Church properties, which resulted in wealthy speculators, most of whom were not interested in productivity but only in quick profits, benefiting most from these auctioned properties.

The destruction of communal lands did not produce a country of small landholders. The Indians had neither money nor any conception of private property. They also lacked the proper tools, credit, fertilizers, and expertise to make their land productive. The ancient *ejidos,* or communal land holdings, were bought up at a fraction of their value by speculators, mostly mestizos, caciques, and hacendados. Instead of increasing support for the liberals, the Ley Lerdo alienated entire Indian tribes who failed to comprehend this attack on their traditional way of life.

Other less significant laws followed. The power of registering births, marriages, and deaths was taken away from the Church and given to the state. Cemeteries also were placed under state control. The Church was prohibited from charging high fees for administering the sacraments. The poor would not have to pay, and those who could afford to pay would be charged only a modest fee.

As advocated in the Plan of Ayutla, the government now called a constitutional convention to draft a new constitution. Influenced by liberals, the Constitution of 1857 incorporated laws issued during the previous months, including the Ley Juárez and the Ley Lerdo. The constitution set up a democratic, representative government of a single house; it retained the federal system, but attempted to control its excesses by providing Congress with the power to remove state officials. While the liberals disliked the earlier excessive concentration of power in the hands of the executive, they also feared regionalism. They attempted, therefore, to create a balance between the old, traditional congressional subservience and executive preeminence, which provided for greater congressional power.

The constitution also provided for a comprehensive bill of rights, which included freedom of speech, the press, petition, assembly, and the mail. It voided all compulsory service and titles of nobility and provided the right of habeas corpus. Finally, it established secular education and tacitly recognized freedom of worship by not mentioning it.

The constitution was important in other practical aspects. It provided for the establishment of a federal supreme court whose responsibilities included, among others, enforcing the constitution and guaranteeing individual rights. A new procedure called the *amparo* was also introduced into the constitution. It permitted any individual whose rights were threatened by any authority to appeal directly to the supreme court for protection. Essentially, the constitution was establishing the principle of legal equality for all classes. While the Church suffered discrimination and was prevented from owning property, the constitution went a long way toward creating a more egalitarian society that provided protection for the less privileged sectors of society.

The tremendous reaction stirred up against the constitution by the enemies of reform made its enforcement impossible. Individual rights and free elections remained ideals to be implemented later. Yet, the seed of a more egalitarian society in the future was being planted in the confusion and violence of nineteenth-century Mexico. It would require a violent revolution in the twentieth century to consolidate the partial victories of the reform and to fulfill many of the provisions of the 1857 constitution.

Debate on the constitution had barely ended before the pope injected himself into the internal affairs of Mexico. In a shocking and extraordinary act, the pope denounced the reform program and declared null and void the laws and the constitution. The Church further criticized those who had obeyed the liberal government, calling them "sacrilegious men, full of avarice, who are preparing mourning, bloodshed and devastation for Mexico and will complete our ruin if Divine Providence does not watch over good Mexicans."

The war of words soon degenerated into a war of bullets. From 1858 to 1861, the War of the Reform engulfed Mexico. As in other previous conflicts, this one began with a plan and a pronouncement. Conservative General Félix Zuloaga issued the Plan of Tacubaya, dissolved Congress, and arrested Juárez. A nationwide conspiracy led by the Directorio Conservador, a conservative group, staged a series of successful uprisings against the liberal government. While President Comonfort attempted to mediate, the lines were being drawn. Liberals in the provinces supported the constitution; conservatives in Mexico City proclaimed Zuloaga president. Juárez managed to escape to Querétaro, where his supporters proclaimed him president.

Mexico now had two presidents and the makings of a horrible civil war. The liberals, with Juárez at the helm, established their government in Veracruz, where they controlled customs receipts and received military aid from abroad. Juárez issued a series of decrees implementing the constitution and including complete separation of Church and state, secularization of all male religious orders, reduction of the number of official religious holidays, suppression of all religious corporations, limitation of religious processions, and confiscation of Church property.

Meanwhile, in Mexico City, the conservatives were furthering their own agenda. Zuloaga declared the Reform Laws null and void, swore allegiance to the pope, and prepared to destroy the heathen liberal. He also secured recognition from Washington and the major European powers. While France, England, and particularly Spain offered their support to the conservative cause, Washington began to waver and, before long, switched its support to the liberals. In desperate financial need, Juárez welcomed Washington support.

War raged on. In a series of initial skirmishes the conservative armies defeated the liberal forces. Yet, they were unable to win the war. The conflict dragged on until 1860. With money collected from the port of Veracruz, the liberals were able to organize a well-trained and equipped army. Internal rivalries, poor finances, and weak morale undermined the conservatives. By the end of that year, the liberals reconquered several states and defeated the now outnumbered conservative armies. In

January 1861, the victorious liberal army entered Mexico City. Soon thereafter, Juárez entered the city in his traditional black carriage and black suit. The stubborn determination and persistence of this Indian leader had triumphed. Yet, Juárez was not smiling, for he realized that he now had to govern a prostrate nation, which had been divided and bloodied by years of civil war.

Perhaps he also knew that the reforms he so dearly espoused had not been totally successful. Feudalism was only partially destroyed; regionalism and decentralization were still strong; property was not radically redistributed; the Indians were not rescued from peonage; militarism was a growing and menacing force. Although the conservative elements had been defeated, they had not been crushed. They now conspired with foreign monarchs to establish their rule over Mexico. In a desperate and cynical gamble to save their power, their property, and their Church, they were willing to turn over their country to a foreign power.

CHAPTER 11

MAXIMILIAN AND FOREIGN INTERVENTION

The end of the War of the Reform was followed by a difficult period. Although the country needed tranquillity, peace was nowhere to be found. The scars of war were too deep; the needs and hatreds of the warring factions were overwhelming. Disgruntled conservative and liberal generals and soldiers roamed the countryside, private armies pillaged and plundered the partly destroyed haciendas, highways in disrepair became even more dangerous, and commerce was at a standstill.

The years of war had produced a profound cleavage in society. While some advocated forgiveness and reconciliation, others called for justice and vengeance. Changes in the Juárez cabinet were frequent, debate in the Congress was tumultuous, and speeches were fiery. In the streets, mobs stoned bishops, sacked churches, and destroyed church libraries and buildings; they stole valuable jewels and artwork. To placate the more radical elements, the government expelled a number of bishops, the Spanish ambassador, the papal nuncio, and other foreign envoys whose sympathies were with the conservative forces during the war. The army was reduced considerably; conservative officers were expelled; some were arrested, and a few were executed.

Neither revenge was one-sided. Liberal leaders in the provinces were hunted down and killed by conservative officers who still commanded troops and roamed the countryside. One of these shot and killed three important liberal leaders, including Melchor Ocampo. Despite Juárez's attempts at conciliation through numerous amnesties and pardons, the level of violence continued unabated. Conventional war between armies gave way to a disorganized, sporadic, and guerrilla type of warfare. Pacifying Mexico seemed an almost impossible task.

Governing was difficult with little money in the treasury and a bankrupt country. The income from the sale of expropriated Church properties was much less than had been anticipated, as many were sold at a fraction of their true value. The greater part of the revenue from customs was pledged to foreign debtors. Internal revenue from commerce and industry was negligible. Borrowing from abroad seemed the only way to finance government operations. Mexico, however, already owed plenty, and European powers were more interested in collecting their old debts than in lending fresh money. In 1861, Juárez declared a two-year moratorium on the payment of Mexico's foreign debt. Although he stressed that this was not a repudiation but simply an attempt to gain time to put Mexico's economic house in order, Europeans protested bitterly.

For a while, European powers had been contemplating intervention in Mexico. England, France, and Spain studied the possibility of occupying Mexico to impose peace and collect their debts. The U.S. policy since President Monroe's proclamation in 1823 helped to restrain European desires for intervention. More important, however, were the rivalries and jealousies among European monarchs and their differing views of the civil war in Mexico. While England seemed inclined to favor the liberals, Spain supported the conservative, proclerical groups. The French had other, grander ambitions.

Opportunity arrived in 1861. While the United States was occupied with its own civil war, European powers decided to act. On October 31, 1861, representatives of Spain, France, and England signed the Convention of London. They agreed upon a joint occupation of the Mexican ports until their money was repaid. They further agreed that they would not acquire any Mexican territory or interfere in the internal affairs of the Mexican government.

France, however, had other ideas. Under the rule of Louis Napoleon III, nephew of Napoleon I, France had embarked on an aggressive foreign policy. Napoleon III aimed at emulating his uncle and establishing French hegemony over large and distant lands. He founded colonies in West Africa, established a protectorate over Indochina, landed troops in the Middle East, and staked his claim in Algeria.

He also coveted a spot in the New World. He still remembered Haiti's wealth as a French colony during the eighteenth century, when the island had become the world's largest sugar producer. The real or imagined wealth of Mexico tempted his expansionist desires. Supporting the Church and the Catholic elements in Mexico also played well to French internal politics.

The numerous Mexican exiles living in Paris encouraged the monarch's ambitions. In particular, a young, dazzling Mexican diplomat, José Manuel Hidalgo, charmed and befriended Empress Eugénie. A conservative landholder, Hidalgo had lost his lands in Mexico and wanted revenge against the liberals. The empress had introduced him and other Mexican refugees to Napoleon. The emperor listened attentively to the Mexicans' tales of their homeland's wealth and of the desire of the Mexican masses for a foreign prince to come to impose order and religion. Napoleon was convinced. He would restore monarchical rule in Mexico and establish a French empire in America.

During late 1861 and early 1862, the occupation of Mexico began. Spanish, English, and French troops landed in Veracruz. It soon became apparent to the Spanish and English that France was intent on collecting more than payment for debt. After a series of meetings among representatives of the three nations and exchanges of not overly diplomatic notes, the English and Spanish withdrew from Veracruz.

With the other powers out of the way, France's intentions became clear. The French army marched inland toward Puebla. Juárez ordered his army, commanded by Ignacio Zaragoza, to resist the French invader until death. The battle for Puebla cost both sides dearly, but a young Mexican officer, Porfirio Díaz, distinguished himself helping to repel the invaders, many of whom had been weakened by disease and heat exhaustion. The French army retreated to await reinforcements.

The news of the French defeat at Puebla infuriated Napoleon. He ordered thirty thousand troops to Mexico. With such numerical superiority, the French easily overran Puebla and marched on Mexico City. Sensing that the defense of the city would be futile, Juárez, his cabinet, and his depleted army fled into the mountains to conduct guerrilla warfare against the French army of occupation.

Meanwhile, in Europe, Napoleon and his advisers had settled on an unemployed prince to rule Mexico—Maximilian Hapsburg. Younger brother of Austro-Hungarian emperor, Franz Joseph, Maximilian had the background and polish of the best of the European nobility. He was well educated, had traveled extensively, and had commanded the imperial fleet. In 1857, the same year that the Mexican liberals issued their

A liberal European prince, Maximilian of Hapsburg hoped to become the beloved monarch of Mexico. Supported by Napoleon III's troops, he landed in Mexico in 1861 and established a French empire. *Library of Congress*

constitution, Maximilian married Princess Charlotte Amalie, daughter of the king of Belgium. Soon thereafter, he moved into his castle in Miramar near Trieste to await a royal assignment.

Representatives of Napoleon and of the Mexican conservatives visited him in Miramar to offer him the Mexican throne. Maximilian, who was in his early thirties, was eager to accept. His only condition was that the Mexicans approve his tenure. A rigged plebiscite was soon arranged in Mexico under the supervision of the French army. The Mexicans "voted overwhelmingly" for their new monarch. Maximilian was informed, and preparations followed for the royal voyage to Veracruz.

Maximilian and his wife, who had been renamed Carlota, arrived in Veracruz in May 1864. Instead of the warm welcome Maximilian had expected, the Mexicans were somewhat curious about, but mostly disdainful of, their new ruler. The port was a hot, muggy, dirty, and fly-infested place, which contrasted sharply with the clean and beautiful European courts and palaces that the young couple had frequented. The trip to Mexico City was long and tedious but gave the new monarch an opportunity to see the country he was about to rule. He settled at the refurbished Castle of Chapultepec on the outskirts of the city and began to organize his government.

If the conservatives had hoped for a proclerical, reactionary monarch they were quickly and sadly disappointed. Maximilian was eager to help the poor and the oppressed and to abolish injustices. A romantic idealist, he was ideologically closer to the liberals. He was proud of his Hapsburg ancestry, wanted to do well for Mexico, and wished to be a beloved ruler in his new empire. His strong-willed wife wanted her husband to achieve the glory that he deserved or, at least, that she expected.

Maximilian soon alienated his conservative supporters. He refused to abolish the laws of the reform, to return confiscated Church properties, or to reestablish the Catholic religion to the exclusion of all others. He declared a free press, proclaimed a general amnesty, and appointed a moderate liberal as secretary of foreign affairs. He also passed legislation that established a school system, abolished peonage, and regulated a Mexican navy, which he hoped to build. He also dreamed of a larger empire, which would include all of Central America southward to Panama.

Maximilian seemed to love Mexico and to enjoy his role as monarch. He wore Mexican clothes and spoke of "we Mexicans." He praised the leaders of Mexican independence. He traveled widely and enjoyed rid-

Empress Carlota, the wife of Emperor Maximilian. When the liberal forces led by Benito Juárez defeated the French armies, she went to Europe to seek support for her husband. Rejected by Napoleon III, she became mentally ill and died in Belgium. *Library of Congress*

ing in the mountains to the flower gardens of Cuernavaca. He marveled at the Mexican vegetation and the climatic variations among different zones of the country.

Evidently, Maximilian had hoped to be the monarch of all Mexicans. He hoped to attract liberal support and to inspire confidence among the liberal elements through his efforts. Yet, most liberals wanted nothing to do with him. Although some joined his administration, more from economic need than from conviction, a hard core led by Juárez and Lerdo de Tejado swore revenge and continued guerrilla warfare from the northern mountains. "I shall never yield to a foreign enemy," Juárez proclaimed. "I shall wage the war that the whole nation has accepted until Maximilian recognizes the justice of our cause."

Defeating the liberals proved an impossible task. Europeans were unaccustomed to guerrilla warfare and were fighting in unknown terrain. The liberals found refuge and support from local chieftains and from poor Indians and mestizos. The war dragged on. Maximilian instituted the death penalty for the Juáristas and attempted in vain to pacify the country.

Two events proved decisive for Juárez and his supporters. Prussia's successful wars against Denmark and Austria increased Napoleon's apprehension. Defending France became his urgent priority. Opposition to the Mexican adventure was also increasing at home. After all, this was not the fast and sweet conquest of a Francophile people that he had expected, but a long and costly war. In an interview with the British minister to Mexico, Sir Charles Wyke, Napoleon confessed his mistake. "I realize I got myself into a tight place," he told Wyke; "the affair has to be liquidated . . . but in France it is no longer permissible to make mistakes." In 1866, Napoleon instructed his generals in Mexico to crush the rebels and prepare to return to France. He hoped that Maximilian would also leave with the French army.

The second event was the end of the U.S. civil war. The United States watched with concern and consternation happenings south of the border. The U.S. government opposed French intervention in Mexico, as a violation of the Monroe Doctrine, and feared French expansionist objectives in the region. A nation at war could do very little to oppose the mighty French empire, however. President Lincoln protested mildly to the French, refused to recognize Maximilian, and instead maintained recognition of the Juárez government. In 1864, the U.S. House of Representatives passed a resolution proclaiming that it was not U.S. policy to view with inaction the establishment of monarchical governments, backed by European powers, on the ruins of republican ones. Some aid and weapons began to flow to the rebels.

The end of the U.S. civil war accelerated this support as well as increased U.S. diplomatic pressure on the French. Weapons began to flow freely to the rebels, and several thousand Union veterans joined the Juárista army. President Andrew Johnson and Secretary of State William Seward now urged Napoleon to leave Mexico. The mood in the United States was turning ugly. Some even called for a U.S. military intervention in Mexico to expel the French. With about forty thousand troops along the Rio Grande, Gen. Ulysses S. Grant argued for an armed expedition. Calmer heads prevailed and war fever gave way to forceful diplomacy. Finally, Napoleon blinked and set up dates for evacuating his army.

Maximilian should have seen the writing on the wall and returned to Europe. Yet, he was a proud prince married to a proud princess. He refused to leave and pleaded unsuccessfully with Napoleon to reconsider and keep the French army in Mexico. Carlota traveled to Europe and appealed directly to Napoleon and then to the pope. Both rejected her pleas, with the latter still complaining about Maximilian's refusal to return Church properties in Mexico. Carlota became mentally ill, was hospitalized, and later died in Belgium.

Meanwhile, Maximilian wavered from abdicating the throne and leaving Mexico to fighting on for his empire. The terrible news about his wife depressed him deeply. Believing that abdicating would blemish the Hapsburg honor and that his wife's sacrifice would have been, therefore, in vain, he opted to stay. He appointed a conservative cabinet and prepared to lead his troops personally. With the French army in retreat and with a reduced number of soldiers, Maximilian faced the more numerous and better organized Juárez army. At the colonial city of Querétaro, Maximilian's army was routed and the emperor was forced to surrender.

Juárez immediately decided Maximilian's fate. He must suffer the fate that he had inflicted on others, he explained. The emperor was court-martialed and sentenced to death. Despite pleas of clemency from European monarchs and Latin American presidents, Maximilian, along with several conservative officers, was executed in the outskirts of Querétaro on June 19, 1867.

What a tragic ending to the French intervention! Napoleon gambled in Mexico and lost. His intervention was born of greed and ignorance. Little did he understand the reality of the land of Juárez. Before listening to the Mexican conservatives in Paris, he should have heeded Machiavelli's advice in *The Prince* "to never trust exiles, because they will tell you what they want you to hear and lead you astray." But, Napoleon heard what he wanted to hear. The exiles' words fitted his dreams of glory and power. His Mexican ambitions in ruins and his chosen prince dead, he soon forgot the New World to concentrate on European affairs. While shocked at the "barbarous" Mexicans, Europeans also turned away from Mexico, never again to intervene militarily there.

Emperor Maximilian's last moments. Despite an overwhelming revolt against his rule, Maximilian decided to stay and fight for his Mexican empire. The Juárez forces captured, tried, and executed him in 1867, bringing the French occupation to a tragic end. *Library of Congress*

The conservative, proclerical elements in Mexico also learned a bitter lesson. Their desperate gamble to protect their power, Church, and property did not pay off. They were not only defeated but were now also identified as *vende patrias*—those who were willing to sell their nation to a foreign power. Beaten and discredited, some emigrated from Mexico. Most, however, stayed to witness the victory of the liberal forces and Juárez's return to power.

Juárez entered Mexico City on July 15, 1867, to a popular outburst of support and jubilation. The liberals were now identified with Mexico's sovereignty and national independence, and Juárez's popularity had reached its peak. He was soon elected president and began to consolidate the newly restored republic.

Governing Mexico was no easier now than it had been previously. While the liberal-conservative feud that had dominated political life seemed to have abated, rivalries persisted among liberal caudillos. Absorbing into the civilian sectors the thousands of soldiers who had fought against Maximilian and who were being discharged from the army was at best a difficult task. Juárez inherited a paralyzed economy, a burdensome foreign debt, and lawlessness and violence in the rural areas.

Yet, he tackled those problems forcefully and optimistically. With the help of his able secretary of the treasury, Matias Romero, he developed an economic program that advocated exploiting mineral resources by attracting foreign capital, improving transportation facilities, and organizing an efficient bureaucracy. The tax and tariff structures were revamped as incentives to foreign, as well as domestic, capital. Still, Mexico's instability failed to attract much foreign investment.

Romero's measures and the relative tranquillity that followed Juárez's rise to power helped the economy. Juárez organized a rural police force, the *rurales,* which imposed order in the countryside, making roads safer and commerce possible. To foster national unity and heal the wounds of the anti-Maximilian struggle, he pardoned and freed conservatives and pro-Maximilian elements. Mining activity was revived. Commerce flourished. A railroad between Mexico City and Veracruz, which had been started in 1837, was now completed with English help. It is possibly one of the most spectacular feats of railroad engineering of the times.

One of Juárez's priorities was to create a secular system of education that could foster national development while particularly helping his Indian brethren. The development of the system was entrusted to Gabino Barreda—a physician educated in France and a follower of the positivist philosophy of Auguste Comte. Positivism emphasized the study of mathematics, science, and the physical world, at times to the detriment of the humanities. Even more significant, Comtian positivism emphasized the doctrine of hierarchy and authority, which later became a justification for the long dictatorship of Porfirio Díaz (1876–1910).

In foreign affairs, Juárez fostered Mexico's prestige. He developed closer relations with the United States and publicly acknowledged U.S. support during the war against Maximilian. Secretary of State William Seward visited Mexico in 1869, and the two countries submitted pending claims to a mixed arbitration commission. Relations with Europe also improved but at a slower pace. Most Latin American countries supported Juárez and welcomed, with a sigh of relief, the expulsion of the French and the restoration of Mexican republicanism.

The presidential elections of 1871 tested the nascent Mexican democracy. Of the three candidates, Juárez, Lerdo de Tejada, and Porfirio Díaz, none received the required plurality of votes. The election was thrown to Congress, and Juárez was elected president. An ambitious and unscrupulous military leader, Díaz denounced Juárez and staged an unsuccessful insurrection. The discontented former officers and soldiers, the provincial political bosses, and the remnants of the defeated conservatives all joined in opposition to Juárez. They wanted power and were unwilling to wait much longer. They did not have to wait long. On July 18, 1872, Juárez suffered a heart attack and died in office.

CHAPTER 12

THE PORFIRIATO

After more than fifty years of violence, bloodshed, and misery, Mexico seemed ready for a period of tranquillity. The conservatives and proclerical elements had been defeated, and their daring gamble with a foreign prince had failed. The ideological divisions that plagued Mexican society for a half a century disappeared or at least were buried beneath the surface. While regionalism and localism still flourished, and the forces for decentralization were still strong, Mexico emerged from the anti-French crusade more unified and proud of having defeated and expelled a mighty invader. There seemed to be a feeling of exhaustion accompanying the numerous civil wars and killings. The victorious liberals set out to pacify the country and to develop a modern economy.

A new generation was also emerging that clamored for peace and prosperity. They looked with envious eyes to their northern neighbor. While Mexico floundered in instability and poverty, the United States was leaving behind its civil war and growing into a unified and prosperous nation. This new Mexican elite was concerned less with ideas and more with action. They wanted to bring order from the existing chaos. The central government had to have the power and authority to bring about the political control and the economic transformation of the country. Local caudillos had to be subjugated, the army had to be modernized and reduced, and a new, efficient, and professional bureaucracy had to be organized.

This new group rallied around an unusual and unlikely leader, Porfirio Díaz. Born in Oaxaca in 1830, Díaz came from a poor Indian family with some Spanish blood. His father died when he was three, and the young Porfirio had to work to help his struggling mother. He studied first for the priesthood but never finished. Then he tried law, but again dropped out. During the 1850s, he joined the army and fought on the liberal side during the War of the Reform. At thirty-two, he achieved the rank of brigadier general. A ruthless and daring leader, Díaz gained national fame fighting the French and defeating them in several critical battles. From the military, he turned to politics. He ran unsuccessfully for governor of Morelos and then for federal deputy. Finally, he was elected deputy in 1868. His experience in the Mexican Congress seems to have been disastrous. With a very limited education and few ideas to offer, Díaz's impact was negligible. He broke with the popular Juárez and joined the opposition ranks. Bored with parliament and politics and unable to influence that body, he soon abandoned his seat and retired to Oaxaca. In 1871, he ran unsuccessfully for president against Juárez and Lerdo de Tejada. He surpassed Lerdo in popular voting but was unable to defeat Juárez, who was elected president.

What he failed to achieve through ballots, Díaz achieved through bullets. In 1871, he rebelled against Juárez's reelection. In the Plan de la Noria, he proclaimed that reelection of the president was contrary to the principles of the liberal revolution and the 1857 constitution. His rebellion was quickly crushed. While a few local caudillos supported his movement, most of the country wanted nothing to do with rebellion, especially against the still popular Juárez.

Defeated and disillusioned, Díaz retired to Veracruz to await a more propitious occasion. After the death of Juárez, Lerdo de Tejada assumed the presidency temporarily. In the next election, Díaz opposed Lerdo but was again soundly defeated.

The Lerdo presidency provided a welcome period for Díaz to organize his followers. Lerdo concentrated on improving the condition of the country. He constructed a railroad line from Mexico City to the U.S. border and expanded telegraph lines. He accelerated the construction of schools and continued the educational program initiated by Juárez. In an attempt to pacify the country, he offered an amnesty to the defeated Porfiristas.

Despite these accomplishments, Lerdo failed either to unify the country or to create a solid base of support. Within a couple of years, he had lost most of his popularity. He certainly was no Juárez, lacking the charisma and mystique of the now departed liberal leader. As an intellectual, Lerdo experienced difficulty communicating with the masses of Indians. His attempts at centralization met with stiff resistance from regional caudillos. The unemployed army officers and soldiers were restless and seeking new leaders.

When Lerdo announced in 1876 that he proposed to seek reelection, all of these forces coalesced in opposition. Díaz became their leader. Launching a nationwide rebellion, he proclaimed the Plan of Tuxtepec, which charged Lerdo with violating state rights, wasting public funds, and reducing elections to a farce. The plan called for no reelection of the president and state governors. The Porfirista army, swelled by disgruntled soldiers, easily defeated the pro-Lerdo forces. On November 21, 1876, Lerdo escaped to the United States and Díaz occupied Mexico City.

For the next third of a century, Díaz either directly or indirectly controlled the destinies of Mexico. No single man had ever wielded so much power for such a long time in Mexican history. By then, Mexicans were ready to accept peace, and hopefully prosperity, almost at any price. Porfirio Díaz would create an efficient despotism that reached into every level of society. *Pan o palo* was his slogan. Bread for the army and bureaucrats, for the capitalist and the foreigner, even for the Church. The stick for his enemies, for the poor masses, and even for the local caudillos who did not accept his total control.

The first task for Díaz was the pacification of the country. He knew well that to attract foreign and domestic investors and to retain power himself, he needed to cripple any opposition to his rule. Rebellions were still occurring in various parts of the country. Exiles in Texas supported clandestine organizations in Mexico. Unhappy officers plotted against Díaz.

His pacification was swift and brutal. The army was split into smaller units and scattered throughout the country. The *rurales,* the rural police force, were improved. They received better salaries, weapons, and the authority to shoot on sight enemies of the Porfiristas. Opponents were arrested or shot, using an effective method called the *ley de fuga.* This was not a law, but the practice of killing opponents "while trying to escape." On one occasion, when a governor telegraphed Díaz asking what to do with a number of prisoners, Díaz responded, *"matalos en caliente"* ("Kill them while you can, at once").

Díaz's pacification encouraged trade and commerce. Smuggling along the border with the United States was discouraged through stiff penalties for smugglers. New Mexican consulates to stimulate trade with the United States were opened along U.S. border towns. The government bureaucracy was reduced and made more efficient, although still corrupt. Manufacturing and agriculture flourished. Minerals began to flow north to feed expanding U.S. industry. Mexican coffee, bananas, sugar, and henequen began to be exported, primarily to the United States.

Relations expanded with Western Europe and Latin America. Although these countries recognized the Díaz administration, the United States withheld recognition until mid-1877. Problems relating to compensation for American properties in Mexico that had been destroyed or confiscated and continuous border crossings by Mexican bandits and cattle rustlers strained relations. Díaz finally agreed to the almost four million dollars in reparations decided by a mixed claims commission. He also reinforced the border so as to prevent further raids and tensions in the area. For the next three decades, U.S.–Mexican commercial and diplomatic relations flourished, and the United States maintained close and friendly relations with Mexico. The neighbor to the south became a favorite place for U.S. investments.

As his first presidential four-year term ended, Díaz announced that he would not seek reelection. Instead, he threw his support to Manuel González, a young military leader and his secretary of war. González had fought with Díaz against Lerdo and was trusted to keep the presidential seat warm for the return of Díaz in four years.

González won the election by a large majority. His administration was characterized by significant economic development coupled with major corruption. Concessions were provided to American railroad builders, usually after significant "donations" to government officials. Real estate corporations were permitted to survey public lands, keep part of the surveyed land, and sell part to generals and foreign investors. Indians were again subjected to abuses as their lands and *ejidos* (communal holdings) were taken, usually without any legal pretense or compensation.

A new mining code was issued, which modified old Spanish laws. Spanish law had traditionally established that the subsoil rights belonged to the state. The new code vested ownership of coal, oil, and other mineral rights on the owners of the surface, so that in providing concessions for land cultivation, the government was also providing ownership of valuable subsoil rights. This would become a major issue of contention between the United States and Mexico during the Mexican revolution in the early twentieth century, when U.S. oil properties were confiscated by the Mexican revolutionary regime.

By the end of his term, the González government was on the verge of financial collapse, riddled with graft, and carrying an enlarged foreign debt. There had been significant economic growth, which was pri-

Porfirio Díaz was a ruthless dictator who ruled Mexico for over thirty years at the turn of the century. He created an efficient despotism, pacified and unified the country, and brought prosperity to the upper classes, while Indians and mestizos sank into abject poverty. He encouraged foreign investments, particularly in petroleum and railroads, and by the end of his administration, Mexico had excellent credit abroad. His rule masked the seeds of discontent that grew into the Mexican revolution of 1910. *Library of Congress*

marily the result of foreign investments. González's popularity was dwindling, and many clamored for the return of Díaz.

Don Porfirio was elected to a new four-year term. This time, he had no intention of relinquishing power or abiding by his earlier promises of effective suffrage and no reelection. While out of power, he had married Carmen Romero Rubio, the daughter of a Lerdista statesman and member of the Creole upper class. She was eighteen and he was fifty-one. They traveled widely, primarily in the United States. Díaz changed profoundly. Instead of the crass and ill-mannered guerrilla leader, he was now a refined and mannerly gentleman who dressed in stylish European clothing and hosted lavish parties for his newly acquired upper-class and business friends.

Díaz also entered into a close relationship with the Church. Through the good auspices of his devout Catholic wife, he met the leadership of the Mexican Church and agreed to ignore the laws of the reform. Religious schools were permitted to flourish. Monasteries and nunneries were established. The Church prospered, and its ranks were swelled by Spanish, Italian, and French priests. In return, the Church used its influence to preach obedience to the regime. Clerical appointments, furthermore, were submitted to the dictator for his approval. The Church became, as in the past, an instrument of the status quo, ignoring the less privileged sectors of society and joining forces with the wealthy and powerful of Mexico.

Díaz made state and federal governments the tools of his wishes. Elections became a mere formality, and the federal Congress consisted of Díaz nominees. He referred to them as his "herd of horses," and even made his dentist a member of Congress. Díaz appointed all twenty-seven state governors and provided them with concessions to run gambling, prostitution, and liquor monopolies. He generously rewarded loyalty and harshly punished betrayal. To modernize the country, Díaz turned to a group of young and bright Mexican economists. Led by José Limantour, the son of a French immigrant, members of this group became known as the *científicos*. They believed that Mexico was not ready for democracy and that a dictatorship was the only suitable form of government for their country. Strongly imbued with positivist ideas, mostly of the Comtian variety, they advocated order and progress, which meant for them less politics and more management.

Managing the economy was what they did best. Duties were lowered on many imports. A series of loans at low interest rates were secured in

Europe. Railroad, telegraph, and telephone lines were expanded. Harbors were enlarged and modernized. The administrative machinery was overhauled, making it more efficient and less corrupt. Mining, in particular, boomed as a result of foreign capital and technology. Silver and gold production rose significantly. Old mines became productive again, and new ones were developed.

The United States invested heavily in Mexico, primarily in mining, land, and oil. The Guggenheim interests owned silver and gold mines in northern Mexico. Edward Doheny, an American oil developer from California, purchased Mexican lands and became one of the major oil explorers and producers. His Mexican Petroleum Company, together with El Aguila Company, a British consortium, controlled the Mexican oil business and made Mexico in the early twentieth century one of the largest producers in the world.

Commerce and manufacturing also flourished during the Porfiriato. The volume of manufactured goods doubled. Europeans invested heavily in Mexican industries. Breweries, cement, textile, cigar, and cigarette factories were established. Monterrey, in particular, became an industrial center. Attracted by its proximity to the United States, excellent climate, and communication facilities, as well as by generous tax exemptions for industries, foreign and domestic capital poured into the area.

Land throughout Mexico was thrown open to colonization, primarily by foreigners. About one fifth of the entire area of the country was sold at below-market prices to speculators and foreign investors. Even the remaining lands of the Indian communities were open to settlement. When the Mayas and Yaquis protested and rebelled, the Díaz forces brutally suppressed them, and thousands of Indian prisoners were transferred to work as slave laborers in plantations and haciendas. The worst features of colonial Mexico's debt peonage now reappeared with malevolent force under Díaz.

For the *científicos* and for the Porfiriato leadership, the Indians were considered inferior. They felt that the nation could expect very little from the indigenous population. They lacked education and good health and were the poorest sector of society. Yet, because these conditions were considered to be the result of lack of ambition or intelligence or both, it was believed that the state should not concentrate its resources in helping them. The *científicos* encouraged European immigration in part because Europeans were considered better workers. While millions of immigrants came to the United States and Latin America, primarily Argentina, Chile, and Uruguay, only about one hundred thousand entered Mexico. For the European, the less populated southern cone, with its availability of empty land and without the social, racial, and antiforeign attitude of Mexico, seemed more attractive.

This is not to say that all *científicos* considered the Indians to be inferior. Voices crying in their behalf were often heard. Yet, positivist thinkers such as Limantour and the historians Francisco Bulnes and Justo Sierra—editor of the newspaper *La Libertad* and secretary of education under Díaz—viewed the Indians as the least important sector of society. As a group, they were hopelessly condemned to a lower status and unworthy of redemption.

By the turn of the century, Mexico was a relatively prosperous and peaceful nation enjoying excellent credit and reputation abroad, but this prosperity and peace had a price. Below the sea of tranquillity brewed the sources of violent instability. Masses of Indians were oppressed and abandoned. An expanding working class, which had developed with industrialization and economic growth, had neither unions nor rights and was brutally repressed whenever it attempted to assert its demands. There was a growing and nationalistic middle class that resented the power and wealth of the upper classes and foreigners. Finally, there was a frustrated intelligentsia that longed for freedom and change, which had been influenced by socialist, anarchist, and various other foreign ideas.

The main event that unleashed these forces was an interview granted by Díaz and published in the United States in *Pearson's Magazine.* In 1908, Porfirio told James Creelman, an American newspaperman, that he would not seek reelection in 1910. Intended for a U.S. audience, the news spread like wildfire throughout Mexico and ignited the flames of hope and opposition.

Two books critical of Díaz's regime soon appeared. The Mexican sociologist Andrés Molina Enríquez published *Los grandes problemas nacionales* (*The Grave National Problems*), which was a stinging indictment of the dictatorship. It advocated profound reforms, especially in the rural areas. A wealthy landholder, Francisco I. Madero, wrote a more popular and influential work, *La sucesión presidencial en 1910* (*The Presidential Succession in 1910*). In it, Madero explained that the problems of Mexico were political and called for free and honest elections and the formation of an antireelection party dedicated to the principles of the 1857 constitution.

Madero traveled throughout the country advocating honest elections and no reelection. His popularity increased as great numbers cheered his speeches. By mid-1910, the antireelection movement had developed to such an extent that it held a convention in Mexico City and nominated Madero for the presidency. Sensing Madero's growing popularity and the widespread discontent, Díaz reacted harshly by arresting Madero and numerous supporters. He also announced that the fatherland still needed him, and that he would run for president again. When the elections were held, very few doubted the result. Díaz was reelected for another term.

Yet, times were different now. From within the administration, various groups that had hoped to succeed Díaz saw their hopes and aspirations shattered. Madero was eventually released and traveled to Texas. There, he drafted the Plan of San Luis Potosí, declared the recent elections illegal, appointed himself provisional president, and called on all Mexicans to rise in arms to overthrow the Díaz dictatorship.

His call was heeded throughout Mexico. In the north, Pascual Orozco—a storekeeper—and his friend Doroteo Arango, better known as Pancho Villa—a cattle rustler and guerrilla fighter—rose in rebellion and organized an army. In the south, Emiliano Zapata, a horse trainer and small landholder, called on the Indians to rebel and to reclaim their lands. To the cry of "death to the hacendados," Indians and mestizos rose in arms against their masters as well as against the Díaz army. Rebellion spread throughout the countryside. Bands of guerrillas captured first small towns and then larger ones. In Mexico City, the otherwise obedient Congress called for Díaz's resignation. Without consulting the dictator, Limantour negotiated with the rebels and agreed to Díaz's resignation. A new government with a provisional president would be set up, which would be followed by popular elections.

When the news of Limantour's agreement spread, mobs roamed the streets looting and rioting and asking for Díaz's resignation. Troops deserted to the rebel ranks. On May 23, 1911, after a bloody clash in Mexico City where several hundred were killed or wounded, Díaz resigned and left for exile in Europe. With his departure, his thirty-five-year dictatorship crumbled. He left behind a more modern and unified country. Yet, the country longed for both change and a more egalitarian society. The mantle of power was now passing to a younger generation that was destined to lead Mexico into a new period of violence, turmoil, and finally revolution.

CHAPTER 13

THE MEXICAN REVOLUTION

During the first century after independence, Mexico's political system had been permeated by instability and violence. Most local and national caudillos ruled the country with little regard for the masses of Indians. Except under a few leaders such as Juárez, the Indians suffered neglect and sank to new levels of poverty and despair. The conflict between Church and state sapped the resources of the nation and consumed the efforts of the population. No well-organized or long-lasting political parties appeared during this period; the Mexicans preferred to follow leaders. *Personalismo* was strong, and political groups—the Juaristas, Lerdistas, or Porfiristas—were identified by their leaders.

Throughout these years, regionalism and localism helped shape the country's identities. Regions and their leaders forged relationships with foreign powers and the world economy. Unification of the nation was delayed until a powerful central state emerged during the late nineteenth century, which was supported by the railroads, modern communications, and a brutal centralizing dictatorship.

The seeds of nationalism, democracy, and electoralism were planted during the century after independence, but they flourished only occasionally. The rise of the military, the propensity toward violence, the firmly rooted social and economic conflicts, the unwillingness of leaders to accept electoral results and the legitimacy of the electoral process all contributed to weakening the growth of democratic institutions.

Nationalism manifested itself primarily in opposition to the United States and foreign intervention. The U.S. war with Mexico and the Maximilian empire fostered a xenophobic mentality among the Mexicans. They feared and distrusted foreigners, while admiring and welcoming their economic contributions to the modernization of the country.

These conflicts surfaced in 1910. Underneath the apparent tranquillity and relative prosperity of the Díaz regime, forces for change were brewing: a frustrated middle class; a local business community indignant at the arrogance and control of foreign capital; urban youth longing for freedom; a working class in constant protest and influenced by socialist and anarchist ideas; an Indian peasantry in a state of serfdom, oppressed by the hacendados, and ready to rebel to recover its dignity and lands; and a group of theorists of change questioning the existing order and calling for a more egalitarian and just Mexico.

All of these forces coalesced after the overthrow of the Díaz regime. What started as a political rebellion to unseat the dictator acquired the characteristics of a major revolution that would shape and influence Mexican society until the present. The new revolutionary leadership that emerged after 1910 considered itself the heir of the Juaristas as well as of Morelos, Hidalgo, and the precursors of the independence movement. It aimed to overthrow the Creole landowners, the *científicos,* and their foreign allies, and to complete the work left unfinished by the War of Independence and La Reforma. For these leaders, nationalism, the redemption of the Indians, the recovery of the national resources, and a more independent, anti-American posture in foreign affairs were the basic tenets of the revolution.

They differed significantly, however, from the earlier leadership. Laissez faire liberalism was now abandoned, and the interests of the state were placed above those of groups and individuals. The strengthened central government would guide the nation's destiny, and rival institutions would be weakened. A unified political party would emerge as the dominant political institution, which would attempt to represent most sectors of society.

The revolution that developed was principally experimental, piecemeal, and pragmatic. As the first major revolution of the twentieth century, it had no models, but even if it had, the Mexicans wanted to find Mexican solutions to Mexican problems and were unwilling to import ideological models. As a matter of fact, the revolution lacked a clear, defined ideology and, for the first decades, was essentially an agrarian revolution.

When Madero entered Mexico City in June 1911, he was hailed with greater enthusiasm than any previous victorious political leader. This small man, with a high-pitched voice and nervous mannerisms, was seen as the rescuer of Mexico from the long and sinister dictatorship. He was soon elected president by an overwhelming majority. Madero felt that people wanted freedom more than bread. He allowed free speech and a free press and guaranteed the right of assembly. He proposed to restore the Constitution of 1857 and return the lands illegally taken from the Indians. Yet, he had no economic program, and, what was worse, he had no talent for governing at such a crucial and difficult time. While he preached freedom and love, his brother organized a brutal secret police and wielded real power. Nepotism and corruption flourished. The president quickly began to lose popularity and, when he refused to return Indian lands, rebellion seemed inevitable.

The leader of the movement was Emiliano Zapata. Disillusioned with the Madero regime and its failure to fulfill its agrarian promises, he called his people to arms and issued his Plan of Ayala. The plan called for the immediate restoration of the lands illegally taken and the

A wealthy landowner with little political experience, Francisco Madero opposed the Díaz dictatorship and called for honest elections. When Díaz was overthrown, Madero was catapulted to national power and elected president. He presided over the beginning of the Mexican revolution but was unable to control the forces unleashed by the end of the dictatorship. He was assassinated in 1913. *Library of Congress*

Seated here in the middle, Emiliano Zapata was the leader of the landless Indian masses who waged guerrilla warfare in southern Mexico. A brave and unselfish revolutionary, he became a national hero and, together with Pancho Villa, occupied Mexico City in 1914. Zapata was assassinated in 1919. *Library of Congress*

seizure of one third of the lands of the hacendados. Waging guerrilla warfare as he had previously, Zapata began distributing lands in Puebla and Morelos. Despite attempts at negotiation, followed by military attacks, the Zapatistas continued to fight, Zapata's reputation grew, and his followers multiplied.

Discontent was not reserved to the agrarian sector. Ambitious military leaders still loyal to the old regime and generals promoted by Madero plotted to overthrow him. Bernardo Reyes, an ex-Porfirian general, attempted to organize the remnants of the Porfirian army to stage a counterrevolution. He failed and was arrested, but while in jail he continued to plot. Felix Díaz, Porfirio's nephew, headed an abortive rebellion to install his uncle's style of regime with himself at the helm. He was also arrested. Pascual Orozco, an ex-Maderista general, accused the president of selling out to the United States and landed elements and of betraying the interests of the working class. His uprising was quickly crushed, and Orozco escaped to Arizona.

Madero also incurred the displeasure of Henry Lane Wilson, the U.S. ambassador to Mexico. While President William Howard Taft was initially sympathetic to Madero, he feared that the Mexican president could neither keep order nor protect U.S. properties. An aggressive and arrogant diplomat, Ambassador Wilson was associated with the Guggenheim business ventures, which were in competition with those of the Madero family. He became a bitter enemy of the Mexican government and reported to Washington that Mexico was seething with discontent. He threatened Madero with U.S. intervention and meddled constantly in the internal affairs of the country.

By early 1913, military leaders were ready to act against Madero. Elements of the army released Díaz and Reyes from prison and marched on the presidential palace. Forces there remained loyal to Madero, and, when Reyes and his men reached the gates, they were met with a burst of fire that killed Reyes and numerous innocent people on their way to Mass. Madero then made the fatal mistake of appointing Gen. Victoriano Huerta as head of the palace guard. A drunkard whom Madero had dismissed earlier from the military because of graft, Huerta was an unscrupulous, ambitious, and brutal general. Huerta's loyalty was only to himself. He longed for the elimination of Madero so that he could assume the presidency. For the next few days in February, "the tragic ten days," Huerta and Díaz blasted each other with artillery, which killed more innocent bystanders than troops from either side.

The U.S. ambassador saw an opportunity to influence events. Wilson arranged a secret meeting with the warring generals, and an agreement was struck. Huerta would become provisional president, to be succeeded by Díaz after elections could be held. Madero and his vice president would be exiled to the United States. Once the Pact of the Embassy, as the agreement became known, was finalized, Huerta arrested Madero, and Wilson introduced Huerta to the diplomatic corps as the savior of Mexico and urged them to recognize him as the new head of Mexico.

Huerta's pledges of safe-conduct for Madero were not honored. Madero's brother was delivered to soldiers who tortured him to death. The president and vice president were mysteriously killed while being transferred from one prison to another. The shocked world watched the events in Mexico and lamented the brutality of Mexican politics.

The "tragic ten days" caught the government in Washington by surprise, which placed it in an uneasy position. Taft and the Republicans were leaving power, and Woodrow Wilson and the Democrats were coming in. The new president immediately recalled Henry Lane Wilson and refused either to appoint a successor or to recognize Huerta. "I will not," he said, "recognize a government of butchers."

He issued a policy on recognition that differed from earlier U.S. policies. Since Jefferson's time, the United States had recognized any government in control of its territory and people. Wilson declared now that recognition was "possible only when supported at every turn by the orderly process of just government based upon law, not upon arbitrary or irregular force . . . just governments rest always upon the consent of the governed, and that there can be no freedom without order based upon law and upon the public conscience and approval."

President Wilson made his nonrecognition policy of Mexico a general policy for all of Latin America. He hoped that a policy of nonrecognition of governments that subverted the liberties of their people would put pressure on Mexico and force the ouster of Huerta.

Little did he understand the dynamics of Mexican politics. Huerta threw most of the members of Congress in jail and inaugurated a savage military dictatorship. He also initiated a mild program of reforms. He built new schools, increased the education budget, and broke with the *científico* tradition. The regime even initiated a modest agrarian reform program, providing free seeds to the Indian communities and restoring some *ejidos* to the Yaqui and Maya Indians. Yet, Huerta had no real social program, and he relied heavily on the military to suppress opposition. His year and a half in power consisted of an orgy of corruption, drunkness, and repression.

President Wilson, however, was determined to oust Huerta and teach the Mexicans a lesson. He first attempted diplomacy by enlisting British support. He told the British that "he was going to teach the South American republics to elect good men," and that he would work to establish in Mexico a government where foreign contracts and concessions would be safe. Britain withdrew recognition of Huerta and awaited U.S. policy initiatives. Frustrated at the failure of diplomacy, Wilson opened U.S. borders for shipments of weapons to Huerta's opponents.

One of these was an uneducated, orphaned peasant named Pancho Villa. A horse trader and thief, Villa opposed the Díaz regime and joined the Madero forces. Because of his skills as a guerrilla fighter and organizer, he was given the rank of colonel. Imprisoned for defending the Madero regime, he was able to escape to the United States, where he organized his followers and entered northern Mexico to fight Huerta. By 1913, he commanded a large army in the north and had became a leader of the people. He imposed a primitive reform program in the territories he controlled. He gave land to the peons and built schools. Yet, he imparted justice through the barrel of a gun, and he was never seen without a weapon on his belt. He was cruel toward his enemies

A villain and a bandit to many Americans, Pancho Villa became a popular folk hero to his countrymen, who sang his praises in songs ridiculing the gringos. He was mysteriously assassinated in 1924. *Library of Congress*

and generous with his friends. A brutal and vulgar figure, Villa became a folk hero to some and an opportunistic bandit to others.

On April 9, 1914, the Tampico incident occurred, and the U.S. air was filled with calls for war with Mexico. A group of American sailors landed at that port and mistakenly entered a restricted area. The sailors were arrested and later released. The local commander apologized to the U.S. admiral in charge of the American naval squadron, but the admiral, with the backing of President Wilson, demanded a twenty-one-gun salute to the U.S. flag. On April 18, Wilson issued an ultimatum to Huerta to salute the flag or face the consequences, and upon learning that a German ship was near the port loaded with ammunition for Huerta, he ordered the U.S. Navy to occupy Veracruz. The marines soon captured the port and the city and lost nineteen men; the Mexicans suffered two hundred losses. The American intervention, which lasted until November 1914, was condemned by both the followers and opponents of Huerta. In Mexico City, congressmen criticized the United States while mobs looted American businesses and burned the American flag.

As the Tampico incident complicated Huerta's foreign relations, the internal situation continued to deteriorate. In the north, another

The "first chief" of the Mexican revolution, Venustiano Carranza presided over the drafting of the liberal constitution of 1917. His election to the presidency allowed for some land distribution to the poor and the organization of the first nationwide labor union. He was assassinated in 1921. *Library of Congress*

voice was raised to avenge Madero. General Venustiano Carranza, governor of Coahuila and leader of the anti-Huerta forces in the north, denounced the occupation as a violation of the Guadalupe-Hidalgo treaty. Carranza had supported the Madero regime but now organized an army to oppose Huerta. An elderly landowner, this tough, but not particularly brilliant, leader issued his Plan of Guadalupe. It called for the overthrow of Huerta and the establishment of a constitutional government. Carranza engineered an uneasy coalition that included Villa and Alvaro Obregón of Sonora, who was probably the most able and principled military chieftain of this troubled period. In the south, Zapata and his guerrilla forces were willing to join the anti-Huerta campaign and to accept Carranza as the "First Chief" of the revolution. A series of decisive victories followed, and, as the armies of the north moved south, Huerta resigned in August 1914 and fled to the United States.

The overthrow of Huerta did not bring peace; it merely ushered in another period of civil war and anarchy. The revolutionary factions now began fighting among themselves. Zapata and Villa struck an uneasy alliance to oppose Carranza and Obregón. The latter captured Mexico City only to relinquish it to the followers of Villa and Zapata. While Zapata's Indians begged for bread in the city, Villa's troops raped, murdered, and robbed the residents of Mexico.

In the northern states, Carranza and his followers issued decrees

After the assassination of Zapata, some of his supporters continued to roam the countryside, calling for land distribution and justice for the poor. *Library of Congress*

and proclamations advocating agrarian reform, labor rights, and the destruction of the army and the clerical elements. From this chaotic period of bloody civil war, which lasted until 1917, a revolutionary platform began to emerge. Carranza and Obregón began to expound this still amorphous yet profound revolutionary program that would transform Mexico.

In defeat, Villa made every effort to provoke the United States. Angered at the American refusal to continue to provide him with weapons, Villa began to murder Americans and then conducted a raid into New Mexico. The United States responded by sending Gen. John Pershing across the border to capture Villa. Unfamiliar with the terrain and weakened by heat and diseases, the U.S. expeditionary force was unable to capture the elusive Villa, who took refuge in his friendly mountain hideouts. Villa became a popular folk hero in *corridos,* which were Mexican songs that ridiculed the gringos and praised the exploits of their native hero.

The American expeditionary force stayed in Mexico through most of 1916. A Mexican-American commission met during the period preceding Wilson's reelection in the autumn of 1916 and was able to neutralize the tensions precipitated by U.S. intervention. The United States was about to become involved in World War I, so its need to secure a friendly country on the southern flank made it advisable to remove American troops from Mexico. The withdrawal was completed by February 1917, and the United States extended recognition to the Carranza regime and sent a new ambassador to Mexico, scarcely a month before the U.S. declaration of war against Germany.

Meanwhile, Carranza had called a constitutional convention in December 1916. The Constitution of 1917 was soon drafted and approved. It embodied the ideas and programs of the most radical elements of the revolutionary leadership such as Obregón and Francisco Mugica. The majority of the delegates were young writers, lawyers, and professionals, most of whom were from the middle class. For them, the constitution was a weapon that would ensure the success of the revolution. The document was based primarily on the Constitution of 1857, but it contained several provisions that departed drastically from the laissez-faire ideas of the nineteenth-century liberals. The new state would actively direct and control the economy; it would be a secular state free of clerical influence.

The constitution contained a series of anticlerical measures and three extremely important articles dealing with land tenure, education, and labor. The anticlerical measures sought to curtail the power of the Church. Marriage was declared a civil ceremony, worship outside churches was barred, religious organizations would enjoy no special legal status, and all priests had to be native born and were prohibited from forming political parties.

Article 27 was intended to reconquer all the land expropriated or sold in the past and granted exploitation rights only to Mexican nationals. Its object was the destruction of large landholdings and the hacendado class. The article required that lands seized illegally from the peasantry and Indians be restored. Private ownership was no longer considered to be an absolute right but a privilege. The state owned all the subsoil minerals, including petroleum, and these could be exploited only by Mexican nationals. This provision would cause significant consternation among foreign companies and remained a thorny issue in Mexico's foreign relations with the United States, England, and others.

Article 3 provided for free and compulsory primary education. Yet, the radicals' addition mandating that education be secular caused bitter resentment among conservative and clerical elements. Calling the Church "the most baneful and perverse enemy of Mexico," the radicals dealt a death blow to the influence and power of the Catholic Church and vindicated the nineteenth-century anticlerical struggle of La Reforma.

Article 123 became the covenant of Mexican labor. It recognized workers' rights to organize, strike, and bargain collectively, and to receive adequate compensation. It provided for an eight-hour workday and a six-day workweek. This article's objective was primarily to convert to the revolutionary family the growing labor movement and to ensure its loyalty.

Naturally, Carranza was the first president to be elected under the new constitution. His four-year presidency coincided with World War I. While many Latin Americans supported the United States, Mexico wavered. Opponents of Mexico's support for the United States argued that Germany had never landed troops on Mexican soil, stolen Mexican property, or intervened in the internal affairs of the country. Pro-German sentiment and Carranza's own indecision encouraged the Germans to approach Mexico. Carranza indirectly received a strange proposal from the German Foreign Secretary Arthur Zimmermann. In exchange for Mexico's support, Germany would return the lands the Mexicans lost to the United States in the nineteenth century. Carranza refused the offer and decided to remain strictly neutral during the war years.

The issues that consumed Carranza were mostly internal. He still had to contend with the possibilities of renewed military warfare. The Zapatistas in the south were still restless; they demanded land and the implementation of the constitution. When he was unable to defeat Zapata's followers through military means, Carranza plotted to eliminate him. In 1919, this brave and unselfish revolutionary was ambushed and assassinated by an army officer.

Carranza now turned to implement the constitution. A reluctant lib-

Alvaro Obregón and his bride. One of the most popular and astute leaders of the Mexican revolution, Obregón rose to the presidency in 1921. He pacified the country, improved education, allowed for labor and peasant organizations, and distributed some three million acres of land. He was murdered by a religious fanatic in 1928. *Library of Congress*

eral, he had no faith in its more radical provisions. He recovered more than thirty million acres of land. But the promise of land for the masses remained just a promise. During his administration, fewer than half a million acres were distributed. No wonder Zapata had complained to Carranza before his death that the president had betrayed the ideals of the revolution and that Carranza had used a revolution that was fought for the masses "to oppress and deceive."

Carranza's policy toward labor was no better. When workers protested low wages paid in worthless paper currency, Carranza ordered the army to suppress labor demands. Article 123 was forgotten. In 1918, however, a young labor leader, Luis Morones, seized the opportunity during a labor convention and organized the first nationwide union, the Confederación Regional de Obreros Mexicanos (CROM). Although labor made small gains during this earlier period, the creation of CROM provided an institutional framework for advancing future labor causes. A year later, CROM entered politics, organizing a Mexican Labor Party to sponsor Obregón's candidacy for the presidency.

Obregón seemed the obvious and popular successor to the presidency. Carranza, however, had no intention of backing Obregón. Forced to accept the slogan of no reelection, which had helped him come to power, he supported Ignacio Bonilla, Mexican ambassador to Washington but an unknown political figure in Mexico, unconnected to any of the revolutionary groups. With the backing of CROM, Obregón rebelled. A new army from the north marched once again on Mexico City. Carranza fled ahead of the advancing armies, but one of his own guards assassinated him.

Despite the continuous violence and Carranza's unwillingness to implement fully the constitution and effect major social change in Mexico, the revolution had advanced significantly. It had awakened a spirit of nationalism and hope that could not be suppressed. Indians and mestizos were now at the forefront of society. The supremacy of the Creole and the foreigner gone. Land distribution and labor organization had made a modest beginning. A constitution that embodied the ideals of the revolution was in place, awaiting for leadership to implement it. The years of struggle and bloodshed were beginning to pay off, for Mexico was now emerging as a proud and determined nation in a process of change that would accelerate in the coming decades.

CHAPTER 14

THE REVOLUTION
TAKES SHAPE

Obregón's rise to power initiated a period of economic reform and relative tranquillity. The preceding decade had witnessed the
dismantling of the Porfirian dictatorship, the development of a revolutionary program embodied in the Constitution of 1917, and a bitter
struggle for power among revolutionary leaders. The schism and violence of the early years decreased substantially, and the government
focused its efforts on the development of labor unions, agrarian reform
programs, and a widespread educational system. The revolution was
now becoming a more peaceful process to effect more orderly change.

A popular, astute, and powerful military leader, Obregón realized
very early that, to consolidate the revolution, workers and peasants had
to be incorporated into the revolutionary family. Obregón worked closely
with Morones and CROM. The labor organization received the blessing
as well as the monetary support of the government. Other labor organizations were either discouraged or absorbed. In turn, Morones supported Obregón and restrained the demands of the growing labor
movement. He prevented major strikes and refrained from attacking the capitalist system. By the end of the Obregón administration,
CROM enjoyed undisputed control over the labor movement, and
membership had increased to more than one million. The initial foundation on which the revolution would rest for the next decades and into
the present was firmly in place.

Co-opting peasant groups and organizations seemed more complicated. Their demand for land and for immediate restitution of the *ejidos* conflicted with Obregón's fear that this would lead to major disruptions and a reduction in agricultural productivity. He believed that Mexico was economically dependent on the hacienda and, therefore, proceeded cautiously. The government distributed approximately three million acres mostly to communal *ejidos*. More than three hundred million acres remained in private hands, primarily a few thousand hacendados. The followers of Zapata were allowed to organize, and, although land was not distributed as rapidly as expected, Obregón's policies introduced the foundation for a growing alliance between rural groups and the government.

Obregón next tackled the country's educational problems. He turned to José Vasconcelos, one of Mexico's most distinguished intellectuals, and appointed him secretary of education. With increased government funding, Vasconcelos initiated a literacy campaign in the rural areas and built approximately one thousand rural schools. These schools became not only agents of basic education but also centers of learning and culture. A legion of nationalistic, dedicated teachers resembled the priests of the colonial era in the task of educating the Indians, albeit in a secular fashion. Although he admired Spanish civilization and culture, Vasconcelos wanted to incorporate the Indians into the mainstream of society; he explained that his proposal was "contrary to the North American Protestant practice of approaching the teaching of the native as something special and separate from the rest of the population."

Vasconcelos also encouraged the arts. He hired Diego Rivera, David Alfaro Siqueiros, and José Clemente Orozco, Mexico's leading artists, to paint murals on public buildings. The murals depicted some of the themes of the revolution: nationalism, the glory of Indian civilization, Mexican historical events, and the struggle between capital and labor. Many of these murals still adorn public buildings throughout Mexico.

Mexico's artistic renaissance stimulated literary works. Although less dramatic than the murals and at the time less prominent, many of the new books depicting the problems of the revolution had a significant impact on later generations. A physician, Mariano Azuela, portrayed the Revolution in several novels. The best known, *Los de Abajo* (*The Underdogs*) described the sufferings and killings during the revolution. Martín Luis Guzmán wrote a masterful chronicle of the Revolution in *La águila y la serpiente* (*The Eagle and the Serpent*). Gregorio López y Fuentes described Indian life and suffering in *El Indio,* a novel that probed their deep suspicion of white society.

Music was also impacted by the revolution. A new nationalistic-

In this detail from a Diego Rivera mural, *Sunday Dream on the Alameda Central,* the Calavera (skeleton) takes the arm of José Guadalupe Posada, an earlier wood-cut artist who inspired many muralists, and holds the hand of the child Rivera. *Library of Congress*

nativistic movement was initiated by Manuel Ponce, a young pianist who rejected foreign melodies and emphasized the native folk tradition. This was continued by Carlos Chávez, Mexico's most distinguished musician of the 1930s and 1940s. Basing some of his music on Mexico's Indian heritage, he composed several popular works such as *Llamadas* (1934) and *Obertura republicana* (1935).

Relations with the United States remained tense throughout most of Obregón's administration. The United States refused to recognize Obregón's advocating an agreement that would protect American properties and rights in Mexico. Oil interests complained that Article 27 should not be applied retroactively. As the Mexican elections approached, Obregón was willing to compromise. He accepted that Article 27 would not be retroactive. Foreign claims for damages incurred during the revolution were allowed, and payments on foreign debts were resumed. On August 23, 1923, President Calvin Coolidge finally recognized Obregón.

As the Mexican elections approached, Obregón picked Plutarco Elías Calles, his secretary of the interior, to succeed him. Claiming that Obregón had betrayed the revolution, Gen. Adolfo de la Huerta rebelled. Tension increased when Pancho Villa was mysteriously assassinated. While many conservatives, hacendados, Catholic leaders, disgruntled army officers, and even some disillusioned revolutionary figures supported Huerta, the rebellion was brutally crushed. Several thousand died in the fighting before the government was able to impose order and hold elections. Calles was easily elected.

The Calles presidency coincided with the years of prosperity that preceded the Depression of the 1930s. Increasing quantities of Mexican raw materials were exported to the United States and Europe. Commerce and industry flourished. To increase agricultural productivity, the government initiated a series of irrigation projects and extended credit to small farmers and the *ejidos*. The tempo of land distribution

This engraving of Emiliano Zapata is one of the strongest graphic images of the Mexican revolution. Its authorship is disputed. *Library of Congress*

also accelerated. Approximately eight million acres of land were parceled out, primarily to the *ejidos.*

Calles continued Obregón's labor and educational policies. The alliance between labor and government was enhanced with the appointment of Morones as labor secretary. CROM continued to expand, and new unions, under the watchful eye of CROM and Morones, were organized.

In the educational field, Calles continued the dynamic policies of Vasconcelos. Thousands of new schools were added, mostly in the rural areas. Teaching Spanish was emphasized as a means of integrating remote villages of Indians into society. The government also built modern roads, which reduced the isolation of many rural areas and enabled sanitation and health programs.

Although Calles accelerated social reforms and was more eager to enforce the provisions of the 1917 constitution than his predecessor, he had none of Obregón's tolerance and intelligence. He concentrated power in the office of the president and grew increasingly dictatorial as time passed. To the *ley de fuga,* he now added the *ley del suicidio.* Many of his opponents "committed suicide" while in jail. Repression and violations of human rights were commonplace.

Calles generously rewarded his allies. Most of his cabinet members grew rich. The president himself became a wealthy landowner. Under the protective umbrella of the government, businessmen received lucrative contracts, mostly in construction and consumption industries. Labor leaders also benefited, and Morones became a very wealthy "proletariat." A pattern of graft and corruption permeated society.

The most serious challenge to the Calles regime came from the Catholic Church and the clergy. Calles's anticlerical statements and the unhappiness among conservative, clerical elements finally surfaced in 1926, when the president was attacked in the conservative press. Calles retaliated by deporting approximately two hundred priests and nuns and by closing all religious schools. Religious services ceased. In the states of Jalisco and Michoacán, a violent rebellion broke out. Known as the Cristero War, this bloody uprising was brutally suppressed. For the last time now, the heirs of the anti-Juárez, pro-Maximilian tradition were to test and challenge the power of the new Mexican state.

Conflict also developed with the United States, especially over oil rights. Calles announced that oil companies would have to exchange their land rights for fifty-year leases. Oil companies protested, and relations with the United States deteriorated rapidly. The appointment of Dwight Morrow as United States ambassador, however, greatly improved relations. Morrow demonstrated a genuine interest in Mexican culture and generally showed great respect for Mexican traditions and the social changes taking place. Through his ability and congeniality, Morrow established a good working relationship with Calles and soothed Mexican ill will and suspicion of the United States. Mexican courts finally decided that oil companies had to apply for new concessions, but that they would not expire in fifty years.

As the election of 1928 approached, the constitution was modified to provide for a six-year presidential term and the possibility of reelection, if it were not consecutive. Obregón naturally became Calles's candidate. Although he was duly elected, he never assumed office, for he was murdered by a religious fanatic in 1928.

During the next six years, Calles ruled from behind the scene. To consolidate his power and institutionalize the revolutionary process, he organized in 1928 the Partido Nacional Revolucionario (PNR), (National Revolutionary Party). This "official single party" became a cartel, which included labor and peasant leaders, the military, elements of the growing state bureaucracy, and Calles's allies and cronies. It was supported, in part, by taking a percentage of the salaries of all government employees, except the military. In 1937, it became the Partido de la Revolución Mexicana (PRM, Party of the Mexican Revolution); and in 1945, it was transformed into the Partido Revolucionario Institucional (PRI, Institutional Revolutionary Party), the current ruling party.

Unable to succeed himself to the presidency, Calles ruled now through puppet presidents (Emilio Portes Gil, 1928–1930; Pascual Ortíz Rubio, 1930–1932; Abelardo Rodríguez, 1932–1934). Although elections were held, the PNR candidate always won, which became the norm from the Calles era. Since that time, no opposition candidate has been able to win the presidency in Mexico. As Calles and his allies became wealthy, they also became more conservative. Many bought fancy homes in Cuernavaca, near their boss on a neighborhood labeled "the street of the forty thieves." Social reforms were neglected and the tempo of revolution slowed considerably. Fearing the growing power of CROM, Calles encouraged independent unions and virtually destroyed the large labor confederation. The small and unimportant Communist Party suffered a similar fate. Fearing any form of anti-Calles radicalism or opposition, the government persecuted and imprisoned its leaders. The party itself was divided into factions and was weakened by the expulsion of the Trotskyites.

Although Communists and fellow-travelers occupied positions in government, they never determined policies and exerted only minor

influence in society. Through bribes and intimidation, the revolutionary leadership ensured that the more radical elements both of the left
and of the right would exert limited influence in the Mexican political
process. By monopolizing the rhetoric of revolution, espousing popular
causes, and catering to labor and peasant groups, the revolutionary
leadership undermined and weakened the Communist appeal. The
Mexicans also refused to import foreign ideologies and were determined to develop a revolution devoid of doctrinaire excesses or ideological straitjackets. Anti-Communist feelings also ran strong, and Gold
Shirts, who were groups of fascist thugs, were organized to intimidate
Communists and Jews.

By 1934, the winds of change again blew Mexico's way. The Great
Depression caused significant economic problems, as exports declined,
industry suffered, and capital fled the country. Unemployment increased. A restless generation questioned the purpose and achievements of the revolution and longed for new, honest leadership. Many
were discontented with the slow pace of agrarian reform as well as the
weakness of the labor movement.

By this time, however, instead of the customary external rebellions,
differences and conflicts were being fought within the party. A left
wing, strongly influenced by Marxist and Socialist ideas, pushed for a
renewed revolutionary momentum. The PNR responded to the growing pressures by issuing the Six-Year Plan. The plan called for accel-
eration of land distribution, protection of labor rights, conquest of
illiteracy, and economic independence.

The Callistas had no desire to relinquish power but recognized the
need to propose a reformist candidate for the approaching elections.
They settled on Lázaro Cárdenas, governor of Michoacán. Army general, cabinet member, and former supporter of Obregón, Cárdenas had
won a reputation for honesty and devotion to reform while governor of
his state. Having pacified the left by providing a plan and a candidate,
Calles hoped for another obedient president who would follow his
wishes. Cárdenas was elected in July 1934.

Calles soon discovered that Cárdenas was no puppet. The new president believed in the Six-Year Plan and had traveled before his election
throughout the country to campaign for reform and social change. With
a sharp instinct for politics, Cárdenas realized that, before he could
implement his program, he had to rid the country of Calles and his
millionaire friends who had subverted the revolution. He built a solid
following with labor by allowing strikes and supporting their causes, he
closed the gambling houses that had enriched Calles and his friends,

President of Mexico from 1934 to 1940, Lázaro Cárdenas implemented a strongly reformist program. He distributed some forty-nine million acres of land, built up communal land holdings, improved education, organized labor and peasant groups, and nationalized foreign-owned oil and railroad companies. A popular leader, Cárdenas rekindled the flames of nationalism and national sovereignty. *Library of Congress*

and he actively cultivated younger army officers. He raised salaries for the military and supported a system of schools within the army. Two years into his administration Cárdenas was ready for a showdown with Calles. When Calles began to fight back and criticized the president publicly, Cárdenas exiled Calles and a group of supporters to the United States, warning them not to return to Mexico.

For the next four years, Cárdenas implemented a profoundly reformist program. He took over the PNR, purged Calles's followers, reorganized it, and renamed it the Party of the Mexican Revolution, PRM. His reorganization did not produce a more open or democratic institution but strengthened instead its authoritarian corporate characteristics. Cárdenas embarked on a major reform program. He distributed about forty-nine million acres of land, more than had been distributed in all the years since the revolution. About one third of the Mexican population received land under the agrarian reform program, most of which went to the communal *ejidos*.

The most important project of the Cárdenas administration was the Laguna cotton *ejido* on the Coahuila-Durango border. Approximately eight million acres in size and with thirty thousand families working the land, the *ejido* produced primarily cotton but also a variety of foodstuffs for commercial sale. Most of the families were also provided with small plots to raise their own animals and crops. In addition to distributing land, the government provided education, social services, and finances. The need for capital in this and other *ejidos* established by the government prompted the Cárdenas administration to create the Banco de Credito Ejidal, which was a state banking institution that provided credit to the *ejidos* throughout the rural areas.

The strongest support for the Cárdenas regime came from labor. The president fostered the creation of a new labor organization, La Confederación de Trabajadores de Mexico (CTM, Mexican Labor Confederation), under the leadership of Vicente Lombardo Toledano, who was an instructor of philosophy at the national university and a Marxist intellectual. With the backing of Cárdenas, CTM grew into the most influential labor group in the country and soon supplanted CROM. CTM improved the wage structure and obtained a minimum salary for all workers. It sponsored health and recreational programs. Toledano also organized working-class militias to back his friend Cárdenas and provided an important basis of support to the president by balancing the power of the military. The CTM motto was "for a classless society" and, a few years later, Lombardo Toledano explained that the federation had been guided by socialism. He emphasized that labor was "in agreement with Cárdenas. There will come a time when the proletariat of Mexico will not need to agree with anyone." In reality, CTM submitted to the government. Even today, a close relationship exists with the government that influences labor decisions; labor, in turn, supports PRI policies and activities.

Parallel to the CTM, Cárdenas promoted the creation of a Confederación Nacional de Campesinos (CNC, National Peasant Confederation). Collective agrarian communities, *ejidos,* and other rural groups were joined into leagues and the leagues formed a central confederation. Through membership in the leagues and the confederation, peasants and poorer elements now had a voice, albeit minor, in the party and its decisions. Cárdenas's policies went a long way to ensure the continuous support of labor and peasants for the party—a coalition that still survives today.

This broad power base allowed Cárdenas to institutionalize the gains of the revolution and to accelerate the tempo of social change. His agrarian reform program significantly weakened the hacienda system that had dominated rural agriculture since colonial times. In addition, although the *ejido* and the cooperative system of agriculture that developed were not the economic panacea that the government expected, they increased support for the party and partially satisfied the rising expectations of this poor sector, which had been neglected for centuries. Cárdenas developed an impressive program of rural education, reorganized the labor movement, and avoided conflict with the Church. His talent for persuasion and negotiation enabled profound changes to be made in an orderly fashion without major violence.

Cárdenas's policy toward the Spanish Civil War and the U.S. oil companies in Mexico, however, created much controversy. He and the CTM supported the Spanish Republic during the Spanish Civil War and permitted refugees from the war to settle in Mexico. Many Mexicans condemned Cárdenas as Communist, and conservative elements vociferously criticized the president. Yet, Mexico was enriched by the many intellectuals, scientists, writers, and artists who refused to return to Franco's Spain and settled permanently in the country. Although ideologically to the left of the Mexican political spectrum, these refugees reinvigorated Mexican cultural life.

The most dramatic event of the Cárdenas administration was the nationalization of the oil companies. A labor dispute and a strike over wages were arbitrated by a board, and its decision to increase workers' salaries was upheld by the Mexican Supreme Court. When the companies refused to obey the court order, President Cárdenas lamented that

they had violated Mexican sovereignty and signed a decree nationaliz-
ing the holdings of seventeen oil companies on March 18, 1938. Earlier,
he had nationalized the railroads. After a brief period of labor management, Cárdenas incorporated the railroads as an autonomous unit
under state control.

By then United States policy toward Latin America had changed
considerably, and U.S.–Mexican relations were friendly and cooperative. The Roosevelt administration was somewhat sympathetic toward
the Cárdenas reforms and was buying considerable quantities of silver
from Mexico. The U.S. objective at the time was to develop hemispheric unity against the threat of Axis aggression. Both the Hoover
and Roosevelt administrations rejected the earlier big stick policy and
pledged U.S. nonintervention in the affairs of the American republics.
The "good neighbor policy" of the United States was reaffirmed at the
Buenos Aires Conference in 1936, and President Roosevelt journeyed to
Argentina to open the conference in person. The United States joined
in a Declaration of Principles of Inter-American Solidarity and Cooperation in which the signatories "proclaim their absolute juridical sovereignty, their unqualified respect for these respective sovereignties and
the existence of a common democracy throughout America."

Although the nationalizations were condemned in the United States
with calls for intervention and reprisals, Roosevelt refused to budge. A
mixed claims commission was created that awarded the companies
compensation, albeit a considerably smaller amount than expected.
Relations eventually returned to normal, although U.S. foreign investment in Mexico suffered a major setback. It would be years before U.S.
businesses would renew large-scale investments in the country.

The nationalization caused a significant impact on the domestic
economy. The government had made no preparations to administer the
oil industry and had to create a government oil company, Petróleos
Mexicanos (PEMEX), for that purpose. With little capital, technology
and management production declined. Because other exports lagged
and foreign investments decreased, the national debt rose and the cost
of living soared.

Despite mounting economic problems, Cárdenas retained great popularity and respect. He had significantly advanced the social gains of
the revolution and had rekindled the flames of nationalism and national
sovereignty. He was the last of the great populist caudillos of the revolution. By 1940, the party was a well-oiled machine confident of its power
and control. None of the presidents who followed Cárdenas were identified with the violent period of the revolution, nor did they appear to

have a desire to move the revolution ideologically closer to the left. In fact, they viewed their immediate tasks as the consolidation of recent gains and the modernization of their country. Although they continued to pay lip service to "the Revolution," they were much more conventional bureaucrats and technocrats than revolutionary caudillos.

CHAPTER 15

POLITICAL
STABILITY AND
UNEVEN GROWTH

The first three decades of the revolution had produced significant changes in Mexico. A new nationalistic and ethnically different generation reached power after 1910. It considered its responsibility was to rescue the nation from dependency on foreign investors; to emphasize the "good" values of the past, such as the legacy of an idealized glorious Aztec civilization; to break the backbone of the Church and the hacienda; to contain militarism; and to incorporate labor and peasant groups into the revolutionary family.

By 1940 much had been accomplished. Railroads and oil companies were under state control, and economic nationalism had become an ideological cornerstone of the revolution; the Church was weakened and subdued, and the military had been forced to accept civilian leadership. Unlike in the rest of Latin America, from this time on, the military refrained from open intervention in the political process. It became an institutional pillar of the government and the party and a force for authoritarian control. The participation of the military leadership in decision making at high levels seemed to have been a factor in preventing the pattern of political instability and militarism prevalent in other countries of the area.

Although the hacienda system had not been completely obliterated, millions of acres had been distributed, and the *ejidos* were reinvigorated. The CTM and peasant groups became integrated components of the party machinery and obediently followed the wishes of the Mexican president. Education advanced greatly, though illiteracy, poor schooling facilities, and ill-trained teachers remained a major problem. Health care also improved somewhat, but a major gap existed between health delivery systems in the rural and urban areas, with the latter faring better. Although living conditions had not improved significantly, and poverty persisted as a major problem, the great masses of the population had hope and faith in the revolutionary leadership and expected a brighter future.

The revolution, however, was not conducted without human suffering and sacrifice. Thousands of Mexicans had either died or left their country for exile, as a result of the three decades of turmoil. Numerous injustices were committed. Many lost their properties and hard-earned savings, usually without compensation. Political violence, while decreasing by 1940, continued unabated during the early years, and major leaders of the revolution, such as Madero, Carranza, Obregón, Zapata, and Villa, were all assassinated. Repression and violations of civil rights were common.

The economy also suffered during this period. The three decades are best characterized as a period of limited and sporadic economic growth. The value of mining, for example, the most important sector of Mexican exports under Díaz, did not return to its 1910 level until well into the 1940s. Agricultural and livestock output were half of what they had been in the latter years of the Porfiriato. Petroleum was the single exception in this difficult economic picture. Production rose sixfold and, by the 1940s, Mexico became an important oil exporter. Economic growth in general, however, proceeded slowly throughout this period; Mexico remained a poor country whose more backward rural regions and expanding metropolitan areas, primarily Mexico City, contrasted sharply.

As the presidential elections of 1940 approached, advocates of continued, accelerated change were outnumbered by those who believed that the revolution had gone too far, too fast, and that the achievements of the past decade had to be consolidated. The war in Europe and the economic conditions at home also convinced many that it was time to slow down. Cárdenas himself belonged to this group. He settled on his Secretary of Defense Manuel Avila Camacho to lead a new period of political stability and economic growth.

Little known outside military circles, Avila Camacho was a generally conservative, church-going Catholic. Commonly referred to as the "unknown soldier," he was "overwhelmingly" elected. A recently created conservative party—the Partido de Acción Nacional (PAN, National Action Party)—nominated its own opposition candidate, Juan A. Almazán, a wealthy Catholic landowner. Yet, as expected, no administration candidate could or would be allowed to be defeated, and Avila Camacho became the new president.

The new regime lived up to its promises, and the pendulum of change immediately swung back toward the middle. Avila Camacho's rise to power actually ended the violent, accelerated period of social and economic reforms. Although political leaders continued to spout revolutionary propaganda and professed allegiance to the revolutionary principles, in practice, Mexico became more moderate. The changes of the last three decades were not reversed, but new emphasis was placed on economic growth based on more productivity and less on distribution of wealth. Although the state continued to guide development, private enterprise was welcomed and protected. Foreign investors were encouraged, and capitalists' methods and policies were followed in modernizing Mexico.

The presidency of Avila Camacho also witnessed the arrival of a generation of extremely pragmatic leaders. Each succeeding president has applied practical solutions to the problems of Mexico. They have refused to rely on either imported ideologies or dogmatic solutions, and it is this pragmatism that has inspired and characterized Mexico until the present.

Avila Camacho's administration coincided with World War II. Although some elements in Mexico advocated neutrality, the government's position was clearly pro-Allied. Mexico broke diplomatic relations with the Axis powers after Japan attacked Pearl Harbor, and the German sinking of several Mexican merchant ships accelerated Mexico's entrance into the war. In May 1942, Mexico declared war and provided a small military contingent to the Allied war effort.

More important than the manpower contribution, however, were the strategic minerals that Mexico provided to the United States. The Mexican government imposed price controls to prevent exporters from gouging the American war machinery at a time of increased demand for Mexican minerals. The United States and Mexico also agreed to allow Mexican laborers to enter the United States to provide much-needed manpower in the agricultural sector. Although the bracero program, as it was known, solved the immediate U.S. need for agricultural workers, it also created numerous problems because Mexican labor was abused and many encountered racial prejudice and even hostility. The bracero program also accelerated the migratory trend of Mexicans into the United States, which was the impetus for major immigration conflict in the postwar period.

The war had a significant impact on Mexico's internal economic development. Although land distribution did not stop, it slowed considerably. Avila Camacho distributed about ten million acres, most of which went to individual families. In part because of the low productivity of communal landholding, emphasis was now placed on individual ownership rather than the *ejido*. A social security system was inaugurated in 1943, but only a small number of workers were initially covered. Labor received far less support from the government, and Lombardo Toledano was replaced as head of CTM by the more conservative Fidel Velázquez.

Faced with war shortages and a reduction of imported goods, the administration emphasized industrialization. New industries received tax exemptions, and a government bank, the Nacional Financiera, was created as a lender to industrial enterprises. Foreign investment was encouraged, although the government prohibited foreigners from owning more than forty-nine percent of the stock of any Mexican corporation, which was a frequently waived or violated requirement.

Such measures, along with the impact of U.S. purchases, stimulated industrial growth. While consumer industries such as food processing and textiles continued to expand, new chemical, cement, metallurgical, and beer industries were established. American capital rushed into Mexico for many of these and other industries; U.S. and international banks and organizations provided credits for industrial development. In early 1943, presidents Roosevelt and Avila Camacho met in Monterrey—the first visit by a U.S. president to Mexico—inaugurating an era of good feelings and cooperation.

The war boom also had other less benign results, such as uncontrolled inflation, the development of a new class of rich and powerful industrialists and businessmen, and the erosion of workers' and peasants' purchasing power because of inflation. Mexico City continued its rapid growth to the detriment of less urbanized areas. Corruption increased among an ever-expanding bureaucracy. Ideals of social justice and economic nationalism seemed somewhat diminished in an atmosphere of accelerated capitalism and industrialization.

The 1946 election clearly indicated that the policies of Avila Camacho would be continued. Just before the election, the Partido Revolucionario Institucional or PRI was established as the official ruling party.

The PRI nominated Interior Secretary Miguel Alemán, who pledged to foster economic growth and major industrialization as his principal policies. The election, which was free of violence, was interesting because of the large opposition vote. While Alemán was elected with almost two million votes, opposition candidate and former foreign minister Ezequiel Padilla received almost a half million votes.

A colorful and dynamic leader, Alemán led a business like administration devoted to economic development. As the first civilian president since Juárez to complete his term in office, he had not played a role in the revolution and was devoid of the revolutionary rhetoric and baggage. He reduced the military budget and engaged in a major public works program, which included the National University and several important dams and hydroelectric stations. Thousands of acres of arable lands were, therefore, added to the agricultural base of the country. Alemán modernized the railroad system and completed the Mexican segment of the Pan American highway, which facilitated road travel from the United States through Mexico to Guatemala. He also initiated the construction of a major highway between Mexico City and the Pacific resort of Acapulco. Tourism boomed, which provided a major source of revenue, while trade with the United States and American investments in Mexico also increased.

Relations with the United States continued to improve. Alemán became the first twentieth-century Mexican president to visit Washington, and U.S. President Harry S Truman reciprocated by visiting Mexico in 1947. The United States provided credits for Mexico and welcomed the political and economic policies of the last decade.

Mexico joined in creating the Organization of American States (OAS) in 1948. It considered the organization an essential element in securing Latin American sovereignty and in fostering closer relations among nations in the region. Mexico's views on the peaceful resolution of conflicts were included in the OAS Charter, and Mexico adhered to a policy of nonintervention and self-determination for states. Mexico also joined the United Nations and actively participated in issues dealing with disarmament, maritime rights, the codification of international law, and nonintervention.

Although superficially Mexican politics appeared stable and peaceful, currents of dissatisfaction ran deep among certain sectors. Conservative, right-wing, and Catholic groups distrusted the government. Some opposed the pro-U.S. policies of the Avila Camacho and Alemán administrations. During the Cárdenas administration, they had formed an organization—the Union Nación al Sinarquista. Its ideology was similar to that of the Spanish Falange—God, Church, and family. They emphasized *hispanismo,* the unity of the Hispanic world in opposition to Anglo-Saxon materialism, called for obedience and loyalty to the Catholic Church, and admired Franco's Spain. Partly a result of frustration at being marginalized from the Mexican political process, the movement grew substantially during the next decade. Sinarquistas frequently demonstrated and rioted, and their newspaper vociferously criticized the government. Driven underground by government repression, they reemerged in the city of León, Guanajuato, in 1946, and vigorously campaigned against the PRI candidate. When the Sinarquistas advocated violence and demonstrations throughout the city, the military responded. In the ensuing clash, several Sinarquistas were killed and hundreds were wounded and arrested. The "León massacre" caused such commotion that Alemán was forced to call off the troops. The Sinarquistas won the state election, the first counterrevolutionary government since 1910.

As an organized movement, Sinarquismo disappeared after the 1950s. Many of its supporters joined the Partido de Acción Nacional (PAN). Others were somewhat placated by the government's more conciliatory policies during the next decades toward the Church. Most remained unhappy by their virtual disenfranchisement from the political process and their limited influence in post–World War II Mexico.

As the PRI leadership pondered the successor to Alemán, the one issue that became paramount in their considerations was the need to reinvigorate confidence in the party by selecting a candidate of unquestioned integrity and efficiency. By then, major corruption had become a national ill. They settled on Adolfo Ruiz Cortines. Alemán's secretary of the interior and former governor of Veracruz, Ruíz Cortines had gained a reputation for party loyalty and integrity. He had run his state efficiently and had eliminated widespread graft and waste.

Elected in 1952, Ruíz Cortines proceeded to implement generally expected policies. He initiated a cleaning of the bureaucracy by firing corrupt officials, demanding honesty and efficiency, and even confiscating some of the ill-gotten gains of several members of Alemán's inner circle. Responding to women's organizations that were clamoring for the women's right to vote, he successfully promoted a bill in Congress fully enfranchising woman. Although he distributed some land primarily toward the end of his administration, Ruíz Cortines encouraged private ownership and induced the population to move to the central plateau, where land had been developed through major irrigation projects. Unlike his predecessor, he did not engage in major public works, but completed many already begun by Alemán. He emphasized hospital and school construction, primarily in the rural areas, and expanded social security coverage in both rural and urban areas.

Industrial expansion continued strongly under Ruíz Cortines. He devalued the peso, which temporarily helped to stabilize the economy, contain inflation, and encourage foreign investment. As U.S. capital and products continued to pour into Mexico, the country became a favorite destination for American visitors.

By 1958, the pendulum of Mexican politics had moved significantly to the right. Social progress was sacrificed for economic progress. While industrialization and modernization—primarily of Mexico City and other major urban areas—had advanced significantly, land distribution, health, and educational programs lagged behind. Poverty remained as a major problem, and the gap between rich and poor seemed as wide as ever. Peasant and student unrest and demonstrations increased. Business worried about a deteriorating economic climate. Both the left and the right criticized the PRI as undemocratic and unrepresentative.

Sensing the growing popular dissatisfaction and the need to maintain support for the PRI, the party nominated Adolfo López Mateos as its presidential candidate. A well-educated and astute political leader, López Mateos had served as secretary of labor under the previous administration. Much younger than his predecessor, López Mateos was a charismatic and dynamic leader well liked by labor and peasant organizations and by Mexico's youth. He seemed the ideal candidate to swing Mexican politics back toward a more populist course.

And swing Mexico's political pendulum to the left he did. During his six years in office, López Mateos distributed approximately thirty million acres of land to both individual owners and collective enterprises. He also opened up new lands for agriculture in the south, which was an extremely poor area of increasing social tension and concern. He initiated massive housing projects, primarily in Mexico City, to cope with the vexing problems of mass migration from rural to urban areas and to accommodate rising birth rates. Rents were modest, and schools and nurseries were added to attract low-income renters. For the first time, a Mexican administration acknowledged the problem of population explosion and tried to cope with its housing needs. Although it was impossible to deal quickly with such difficult problems, at least he made a start.

López Mateos revised the laissez-faire policies of the earlier administrations, and his government participated actively in directing and managing the economy. The government expanded the public sector by purchasing controlling stock in numerous foreign companies, particularly in the electric, telephone, and motion picture industries. In 1962, it created the Comisión Nacional para el Reparto de Utilidades, which was a special commission organized to implement an almost forgotten article of the 1917 Constitution that called for labor to share in the profits of enterprises.

Social programs were expanded. Public health campaigns were initiated in rural areas, which significantly reduced tuberculosis and polio rates. Medical care and sanitation projects were vastly expanded, and diseases such as malaria were almost eradicated. Social security and old age pensions were also expanded, primarily in the rural areas.

In the educational field, López Mateos also emphasized the needs of rural Mexico. He made education the largest single item in the budget and initiated a program of low-cost school construction. With Indian communities providing the labor and the government furnishing the construction materials, thousands of schools were built. Teachers received special incentives for working in the rural areas. Not only was formal education expanded, but adult education and literacy campaigns were also initiated. López Mateos's decision, however, to adopt government-approved textbooks issued by the state created significant controversy. The textbooks, while prepared in consultation with leading authorities in the country, emphasized the positive aspects of the Mexican revolution and neglected many of its shortcomings. Although both the right and the left criticized the textbooks, they were adopted and distributed widely throughout the country.

In foreign affairs, López Mateos maintained friendly relations with the United States while opposing American policy toward Cuba. The López Mateos administration coincided with the rise of Fidel Castro in Cuba and the subsequent establishment there of a Communist system that was closely allied with the Soviet Union. Invoking the Estrada doctrine, Mexico refused to break relations with Cuba during the early 1960s, at a time when most of Latin America isolated the Castro regime. The Estrada doctrine issued in 1930 by Mexico called for the recognition of governments on a de facto rather than a de jure basis. The doctrine stated that the establishment of a government was each nation's internal affair, and diplomatic relations between Mexico and other countries would continue regardless of the regime, provided such relations did not violate Mexico's national interest. This doctrine became the cornerstone of Mexican foreign policy and has been applied consistently with the exceptions of Spain and Chile, where Mexico refused to recognize the Franco and Pinochet regimes.

To reaffirm Mexico's independent foreign policy, López Mateos visited Poland, Yugoslavia, India, and several North African countries, and hosted French President Charles de Gaulle and other foreign dignitaries in Mexico. President John F. Kennedy also visited Mexico in 1961 and was warmly received. This new Mexican activism in foreign policy was dictated also in part by the economic need to expand Mexico's foreign markets. In 1962, when the Soviets surreptitiously introduced nuclear missiles in Cuba, Mexico condemned the Soviet Union and supported the U.S. naval blockade of the island.

One of López Mateos's foreign policy coups was his agreement with the United States over the Chamizal. A change in the course of the Rio Grande had left a piece of Mexican land on the U.S. side of the border. For nearly a century, this controversy remained a thorny issue in U.S.–Mexican relations. Finally, in 1963, the Kennedy administration agreed to return the disputed territory to Mexico and to compensate El Paso residents for their real estate losses. In September 1964, Lyndon Johnson, who became president after Kennedy's assassination, visited López Mateos at the Chamizal and formalized the agreement for the return of the approximately six hundred acres. The resolution of this dispute greatly improved U.S.–Mexican relations.

In 1964, Gustavo Díaz Ordaz, former secretary of interior under López Mateos, was elected president. A conservative Catholic and hard-line political leader, Díaz Ordaz represented a pendulum swing back to the right in Mexican politics. He was probably the most conservative president to have been elected since 1910. During his tenure as secretary of the interior, he had jailed the Communist muralist David Alfaro Siqueiros and had vigorously applied laws against dissenters and opponents of the PRI government. Díaz Ordaz now faced a Congress that contained many members of the rightist Partido de Acción Nacional as well as from the leftist Partido Popular. The new composition was the result of electoral legislation introduced by the López Mateos administration's opening up the political process.

Díaz Ordaz's real problems came not from a Congress with more opposition leaders but from Mexican youth in general and university students in particular. During the 1960s, worldwide student demonstrations and discontent affected Mexican students. The Cuban revolution, U.S. involvement in Vietnam, and Soviet expansionist policies contributed to student protest and activism. The ideological impact of

Castroism, particularly its commitment to violence, anti-Americanism, and internationalism, found receptive ears in Mexico, as well as in many parts of Latin America. The Argentine-born guerrilla fighter Che Guevara was idolized throughout the developing world.

Not that Mexican youth needed external elements to accentuate their discontent. Domestic sources of unhappiness included a decreasing faith in the PRI and its leadership, as well as increasing dissatisfaction with an economic model that, despite significant growth, had failed to resolve the problems of poverty, the imbalances between rural and urban areas, or the widespread illiteracy. Mexico's youth, as well as other sectors of society, questioned the country's political and economic model. They criticized the corruption and their politicians' lack of leadership and vision. Mexican students, similar to students in many countries, lashed out at their political system but failed to provide a clear model with which to replace it.

This political and economic malaise reached its peak in Mexico City's Tlatelolco Plaza in 1968. A series of student demonstrations had shaken the Díaz Ordaz administration, as it prepared Mexico for the 1968 Olympic Games. During September, the government occupied the National University and threw several hundred students and demonstrators in jail. The students called for a massive demonstration at the Tlatelolco Plaza in the center of Mexico City on October 2. The army moved in and surrounded the plaza. When shots were fired, the army responded. Several hundred students and bystanders were killed or wounded; thousands were arrested.

The massacre at Tlatelolco, as this event became known, profoundly affected subsequent Mexican developments. Writers and intellectuals openly and vociferously criticized the president and the political system. Although previously, most intellectuals supported the PRI and its leaders, now many took a more independent, critical position. The massacre also encouraged the growth of opposition from both the left and the right. PAN grew in membership, and leftist politicians raised their voices against PRI rule. Within the party itself, a profound debate began concerning the best political and economic model for Mexico. Self-doubt, disillusionment, and self-criticism increased. Years later, this internal rift led to a major defection by Cuauhtémoc Cárdenas, son of the former president, the creation of the Partido Revolucionario Democrático (PRD), and the most serious challenge to the PRI's undisputed monopoly of power.

The massacre also encouraged the opening of the political process. Criticism was more readily tolerated. Effective suffrage and increased

participation of opposition in the political process became more accepted. Decentralization of political authority increased, and the states
assumed a more important role. Finally, while many clamored for
greater state intervention in the economy and more populist policies,
the economic model of Mexico in the next quarter of a century evi-
denced a decline of state involvement in the economy with greater privatization and foreign investment. The emphasis was on modernization
and competition, particularly in international markets.

Díaz Ordaz himself promoted several important economic and social
programs. Expenditures for education reached over 26 percent of the
national budget, one of the largest in the world. The tourist industry
continued to expand, and industrialization projects multiplied.

Luis Echeverría, the newly elected president, assumed office in 1970
in an atmosphere of greater political tension and uncertainty than had
existed in Mexico for decades. An emerging guerrilla and terrorist
movement, given impetus by the events of 1968, had developed. Two
decades of industrialization and import substitution policies, which
depended heavily on imported capital goods and foreign technology,
had failed to foster a self-sustaining economic growth. A negative trade
balance, an alarming and increasing trade deficit, and continued high
unemployment, underemployment, and income maldistribution contributed to the economic reality that Echeverría inherited. Worse yet,
Mexico's major trading partner, the United States, was also experiencing difficulties. The Nixon administration imposed a 10 percent tax on
all imports. Mexico appealed unsuccessfully for exemption from this
tax on its exports.

Echeverría's authority and credibility to tackle these problems were
weakened further by the fact that he had been secretary of the interior
during the Tlatelolco massacre and many blamed him for the brutal
army repression. Because he had a reputation for toughness and inflexi-
bility, it did not seem that he would foster a climate of reconciliation.

During the first eighteen months of his administration, violence
increased. Urban terrorism was led by the Movimiento de Acción Rev-
olucionaria (MAR), which was a Maoist group sympathetic to Cuba and
China. The rural guerrilla movement was located in the mountains in
the state of Guerrero, which threatened the growing tourist industry in
Acapulco. A wave of bank robberies and kidnappings of important businessmen and political leaders swept the country, as guerrillas sought
ways to finance their activities.

To deal with the growing unrest, Echeverría used the traditional PRI
strategy of co-opting the opposition through dialogue. This democratic

"opening" did little to appease the left and increased opposition from the right. A conservative demonstration on the feast of Corpus Christi on June 10, 1971, clashed with a radical student march. In the ensuing battle, eleven students were killed, and several hundred were wounded.

While publicly calling for reconciliation, Echeverría privately took a strong stand. Security forces were modernized and improved, and repression of terrorist groups increased, as approximately ten thousand troops were sent to Guerrero to destroy the guerrillas. Although it took the army a year to end the guerrilla *foco*, the leadership was eventually eliminated and the area was pacified. In March 1971, Echeverría expelled from Mexico five Soviet Embassy personnel for allegedly helping to train Mexican guerrillas in North Korea. Some also suspected that the Cubans were involved with Mexican guerrillas and terrorists.

Echeverría made significant attempts to co-opt the youth and the left. In early 1971, he released a majority of students jailed as a result of the Tlatelolco events. He brought young people into important positions in government. The voting age was lowered to eighteen; the age for holding a Senate seat was lowered from thirty-five to thirty, and for membership in the Chamber of Deputies from thirty to twenty-one. Echeverría also nationalized the telephone and tobacco industries and announced the need to restrain industrialization. He expanded state-owned enterprises and encouraged oil exploration and the growth of PEMEX, the state-owned petroleum monopoly. He placed great emphasis on extending the rural road system and rural electrification. As he faced increasing inflation, he tried to minimize its impact on the poor and the middle class by instituting tight price controls and taxing luxury items.

Echeverría also sought to use foreign policy to build a constituency at home, primarily among the left. The president began a series of foreign trips that took him to thirty-six countries in six years. He established diplomatic and commercial relations with sixty-two governments and signed a hundred bilateral agreements and international accords, which included not only economic and commercial accords, but also cooperative projects in the technical, scientific, and cultural fields. He dramatically improved relations with the Soviet Union, and his visit to Moscow in 1973 was the first by a Mexican president. He allowed hundreds of exiles from Chile to settle in Mexico, after the overthrow of the Allende regime, and refused to establish relations with the Pinochet government in Chile, the Franco regime in Spain, and the apartheid administration in South Africa. Violating Mexico's own Estrada doctrine, Echeverría explained that Mexico would not resume relations with

those countries until they had reestablished "democratic principles."
Meanwhile, Echeverría continued to maintain close relations with Castro's Cuba and increased collaboration with the regime in Havana.

This foreign policy activism catapulted Echeverría into a prominent
position in the developing world. He became a leading spokesman for a
united stand to pressure developed countries into making concessions
to poorer nations. Echeverría's foreign policy emphasized Latin American solidarity and political independence of U.S. positions and stressed
the concept of ideological pluralism and *tercermundismo*. His foremost
consideration was the expectation that such a foreign policy would generate support from the left in Mexico. Echeverría felt that he could
revitalize the economy by expanding Mexico's foreign markets and
reducing dependence on U.S. trade. A revived economy would also win
him support from national business and industrial sectors.

Interestingly, under Echeverría Mexico never joined OPEC or the
nonaligned movement. Echeverría was sufficiently pragmatic to understand that Mexico did not need to join OPEC to benefit from OPEC-
led oil prices. Joining OPEC would also antagonize the United States
and create unnecessary strains with its northern neighbor. Similarly,
membership in the nonaligned movement would have entangled Mexico's foreign policy agenda with that of other developing countries and
forced it to accept positions that would increase tensions with the
United States.

Yet, if Echeverría expected his foreign policy to benefit his country's
economy, he was sadly disappointed. By the end of his administration,
the economy was in shambles. Inflation was out of control. Mexico's
foreign debt had increased substantially, and imports surpassed exports
by almost $3.5 billion in 1975 alone. Industrial production had declined.
Concerns about the economy and a possible peso devaluation caused a
massive capital flight, as Mexicans exchanged their currency for dollars
and invested in the United States. Mexico's decision to vote in support
of a UN resolution equating Zionism with racism inflamed the Jewish
community in the United States and led to a Jewish tourist boycott of
Mexico. Although Mexico was forced to retreat from its position and
sent its foreign secretary to Israel to mend fences, the boycott cost
Mexico an estimated $200 million in revenue and hurt a hitherto flourishing industry. It also demonstrated how Mexico's economic weakness
and vulnerability imposed serious limits on the country's ability to pursue an independent foreign policy. Just before his departure, Echeverría
devalued the Mexican peso, which emphasized the country's economic
difficulties and the government's inability to respond to the crisis.

Echeverría's espousal of third world causes and his inability to deal effectively with the economy scared domestic and foreign investors. The economy grew by only 3.2 percent in 1976, which was half its usual rate, and unemployment rose sharply. Mexico was suffering its worst economic crisis in three decades. In an attempt to boost his populist image just before leaving office, Echeverría expropriated approximately two hundred thousand acres of rich farmland and distributed them to landless farmers.

The election of Echeverría's Secretary of Finance José López Portillo to the presidency in 1976 seemed to allay, at least temporarily, the fears of Mexico's business community. The president implemented the International Monetary Fund's prescribed austerity program, reducing imports and public-sector spending. He capped wages, but not prices, and instituted a program to stimulate exports.

López Portillo also moved to improve relations with the United States. In 1977, the Mexican president visited President Jimmy Carter. Migration of Mexican workers, reduction of U.S. barriers to Mexican agriculture and manufactured goods, and U.S. purchases of oil and natural gas dominated the discussions. López Portillo proposed to build a gas pipeline up to the Texan border, and the two countries created a joint commission to hold discussion on trade, energy, and migration. He called on Carter to use U.S. leadership to create "a more reasonable world order" and to grant the Panamanians sovereignty over the Panama Canal. López Portillo made statements emphasizing Mexico's role as a spokesman for regional and third world causes and expressed his desire to see the Castro regime reintegrated into the hemispheric community by offering Mexico's good offices to mediate the normalization of U.S.–Cuban relations.

López Portillo's statements combined with internal pressures in the United States forced the Carter administration into a tense relation with Mexico. President Carter announced tighter U.S. border policies and refused to reduce protectionist barriers for Mexican products. The U.S. refusal both to approve a gas deal with PEMEX because it considered the price inflationary and to sell Mexico U.S. F-5 supersonic fighters increased Mexican unhappiness. The Mexicans complained about the U.S. lack of sensitivity to the impact that American decisions often have on Mexico. Carter's visit to Mexico in 1979 did little to improve relations, especially after the Mexicans reacted bitterly to an innocent remark made by Carter regarding "Montezuma's revenge." The failure of the two countries to achieve any tangible results during Carter's visit left Mexican–U.S. relations strained.

While López Portillo seemed intent on improving U.S.–Mexican relations, he was also committed to building upon and strengthening Echeverría's effort to make Mexico an influential actor in regional affairs. López Portillo was using Mexico's enormous oil wealth, estimated now at forty-three billion barrels, to underwrite his foreign policy. The rise of the Sandinistas in Nicaragua, the violent civil war in El Salvador, guerrilla fighting in Guatemala, Cuba's policies and actions, and U.S. intervention in Grenada provided the Mexican president with opportunities to reaffirm his policies, defy the United States, create leverage over U.S. policies, and project Mexico as an active regional power.

Central America became the initial testing ground. In June 1979, Mexico opposed a plan by the United States, Guatemala, El Salvador, and Nicaragua that advocated that the Central American Defense Council mediate a conflict between Somoza's Nicaragua and Costa Rica. After the Sandinistas' rise to power in Nicaragua in 1979, Mexico provided economic aid as well as emergency relief. Much to the chagrin of the United States, it praised the Sandinista revolution even after the establishment of a Marxist dictatorship. Mexican foreign policy was motivated by a desire to weaken Cuban influence; to preclude a further radicalization of the Nicaraguan revolution and the creation of an unfriendly regime in the region; to prevent the spread of political instability and guerrilla groups into El Salvador and Guatemala, which could threaten Mexico's stability and southern oil fields; to placate domestic leftist groups sympathetic to the Sandinistas; and to prevent a U.S. intervention, which could polarize the region and increase instability in the area.

By 1980, Mexico began to feel the impact of the Central American crisis, as hordes of Guatemalans, Salvadorans, and Nicaraguans began to escape the violence in their countries and seek refuge in Mexican territory. Leftist guerrilla groups, primarily from Guatemala, began to use Mexican territory as a staging ground for attacks on their country. Refugee camps along Mexico's southern border served both as a source of material and human support and a refuge for many of these groups. The refugee flow implied expenditures of limited resources and a strain on social services in one of Mexico's poorest regions.

As part of his approach to the region, López Portillo accepted Venezuela's invitation to participate in creating the Economic Cooperation Program for Central America (the San José accords), which provided low-cost oil to Central America and Caribbean nations. López Portillo actively supported the Castro regime and made a visible three-day trip to Havana during the Mariel boat lift in 1980, when 125,000 Cubans escaped to the United States. A joint Cuban-Mexican communiqué condemned the U.S. occupation of Guantánamo naval base, the economic boycott of the island, and human rights violations in El Salvador. It reaffirmed support for Nicaragua and warned against any possible U.S. action against Cuba. López Portillo expected a more conciliatory Cuban policy in Central America, which could effect a negotiated settlement to the Nicaraguan and Salvadorean conflicts and a tacit agreement that the Cubans would respect Mexican sovereignty and refrain from supporting insurgent groups in Mexico.

Although Mexico failed to achieve the former objective, it enjoyed more success with the latter. A settlement in Nicaragua took several years. A massive U.S. effort to support the contras—a guerrilla operation inside Nicaragua directed at destabilizing the Sandinista regime—and major pressure from the Soviet Union and other countries prompted the Sandinistas to hold elections in 1990. Surprisingly, the opposition coalition won, and the Sandinistas lost power, although they retained control of the military.

In El Salvador, Mexico's policies failed even more miserably. In a bizarre action, López Portillo announced in 1981 a joint Mexican-French recognition of the Salvadorean Marxist coalition, the FDR-FMLN, as a representative political force. The objective of López Portillo and of François Mitterrand, the recently elected Socialist president of France, was to force the inclusion of guerrilla representatives in the Salvadorean congressional elections of 1982. The United States and most countries of the region rejected the Franco-Mexican recognition because it provided legitimacy to Marxist insurgency in the area. In a massively concurred election, the U.S.-backed moderate Christian Democratic Party received 40 percent of the vote; an alliance of various rightist parties won control of Congress; and the FDR-FMLN proved to represent only a very small sector of Salvadoran society. Even the United States was surprised and somewhat embarrassed when the staunchly conservative Arena party, the largest of the rightist groups, was publicly legitimized by the elections.

For Mexico, the Salvadorean election represented a major defeat. López Portillo had always given the Christian Democrats a cold shoulder and had even excluded them from a Mexican-sponsored conference of Latin American political parties that was held in Mexico during 1981. Mexico now had little or no influence with either the Christian Democrats or the Arena party—the two groups that would rule El Salvador for the next decade and a half.

While Mexico dabbled in Central American politics, the United States maintained a hard line toward Cuba, the Sandinistas, and the Salvadorean guerrillas. Days before leaving office, in response to a Salvadorean major guerrilla offensive, President Carter resumed military aid to the Salvadorean government and authorized covert operations against the Sandinistas. This ushered in the hard-line commitment of the incoming Reagan administration, which sought to contain the Cubans and Sandinistas and to prevent another Nicaragua in Central America by using all of the diplomatic, economic, and military instruments available to the U.S. government.

Mexican–U.S. relations remained estranged throughout this period. Both the Mexican shenanigans in Central America and López Portillo's support for Cuba caused significant unhappiness in Washington. The Mexican initiatives were seen, at best, as ill-timed and counterproductive to U.S. interests and as security concerns. Although Washington understood the geopolitical and domestic concerns of Mexico, it worried that the confrontation in Central America was occurring in the broader context of Soviet-American rivalry, and that U.S. responses in the region would test the credibility of the United States worldwide. Mexico's narrower interests occasionally conflicted with U.S. policy.

Policymakers in the Reagan administration attempted to influence López Portillo. The United States finalized the sale of U.S. supersonic fighter jets to Mexico, which had been denied by the Carter administration, and sent Gen. Vernon Walters to Mexico to discuss Cuban-Nicaraguan military aid to the Salvadorean guerrillas. During 1981, Reagan also sent Secretary of State Alexander Haig to seek Mexican collaboration for his new initiative for a multinational effort to foster economic development in the Caribbean Basin and to entice Mexico into creating a North American common market, which was a project that was initially announced during Reagan's presidential campaign.

Mexico reacted coldly to U.S. initiatives. Whether the U.S. proposals came too late in the López Portillo administration, or the atmosphere in Mexico was not receptive, especially after two Mexican administrations that had emphasized Mexican nationalism, U.S. proposals had to wait for more receptive leadership.

By the end of the López Portillo *sexenio,* not only had Mexico failed to achieve any foreign policy successes, but the economy was deteriorating rapidly. After three consecutive years of rapid economic growth, fostered by historically high oil prices and production as well as access to external financial assistance, the Mexican inflation rate reached nearly 100 percent. Gross domestic product fell drastically and brought with it the value of the peso, which saw a devaluation of 176 percent in a year. Salaries fell, and the government deficit increased to 18 percent of GDP. Capital flight was estimated at twenty-two billion dollars.

López Portillo's response to the economic crisis was disastrous. He nationalized private banking and rigidly controlled exchange rates. In his last state of the nation address, he lashed out at the United States for not accepting the existence of the Castro regime, for not leaving Nicaragua in peace, and for continuing to impose its will on the region.

Neither his ill-timed and ill-conceived economic measures nor his appeal to anti-Americanism could rally internal support for López Portillo. His economic initiatives actually worsened the economic situation, which resulted in increasing political instability and a repudiation of the government by large sectors of Mexican society, especially the business sector. Charges of widespread corruption also marred López Portillo's last months in office. The president himself was widely accused of sending millions out of the country to invest in California real estate. Although various attempts to bring legal action against the president failed, he left office vilified and disgraced.

The election of López Portillo's appointed successor, Miguel de la Madrid (1982–1988), and of Carlos Salinas de Gortari (1988–1994) marked a significant turning point in Mexican history. Each made a concerted effort to repudiate both the anti-American, internationalist foreign policy and the statist concept of development espoused so vehemently by their two predecessors. Instead of confrontation with the United States, these two administrations sought cooperation and help from their neighbor to the north. Under Salinas, Mexico went as far as signing a free trade agreement, NAFTA, incorporating Canada, the United States, and Mexico into a potential major economic bloc that could rival the East Asian and European common markets.

The de la Madrid administration began the reversal of state control of the economy and a trend toward privatization, which accelerated under Salinas. By the end of the López Portillo administration, the state had become the leading economic entity in the developmental process—more significant than either private enterprise or market forces. Whereas during the 1960s, the Mexican state administered 259 enterprises, by 1982, there were 1,155 government-owned enterprises. These corporations represented one fifth of all investments, while their share of the Mexican debt was almost 50 percent. Mismanagement, inefficiency, corruption, and nepotism characterized these enterprises, which were stifling Mexican economic growth. The challenge to the de la Madrid administration was to introduce economic liberalization and privatization without embracing full-scale political reform. The changes would have to be carefully managed from above, so as not to weaken the PRI's control. The state would have to perform a balancing act to blend its continuous authoritarian rule with the need to transform the state-controlled economy.

De la Madrid's initial objective was to put Mexico's economic house in order. He introduced a stabilization plan known as the Programa Inmediato de Reordenación Económica (Urgent Program for Economic Restructuring) in 1983, a Pact of Economic Stability in 1987, and a Pact for Economic Stability and Growth in 1988. The programs restructured the public sector, reduced costs, increased honesty and efficiency, and generated revenues through fiscal reforms. The government also commenced the sale of state enterprises—a process that accelerated after 1985 when oil prices dropped and inflation grew—which exacerbated Mexico's fiscal crisis.

De la Madrid also initiated a vigorous anticorruption campaign. This included a major overhaul of the country's various security and police forces. A controller general was appointed to monitor expenditures in the public sector, and restrictions were imposed on nepotism, which was a widespread and firmly entrenched practice throughout the Mexican bureaucracy. PEMEX, the vast state oil monopoly, was streamlined, and several high officials, accused of corruption, were removed from office.

The de la Madrid administration realized that it needed U.S. help to lift Mexico from its deepening economic crisis. Even the López Portillo administration, in its final year, had offered an olive branch to the United States. During the Falklands-Malvinas War in 1982, when Great Britain and Argentina went to war over the Malvinas Islands in the South Atlantic, Mexico toned down the more radical Latin American resolutions at the OAS condemning U.S. support for Britain. The following year, when the United States intervened in Grenada to eliminate the Soviet-Cuban presence there and to protect American citizens, the de la Madrid government criticized the United States for violating the principle of nonintervention. But even this criticism was somewhat lukewarm and short-lived. Mexico was unwilling to make Grenada a major issue in U.S.–Mexican relations.

The Mexican economic crisis also worried the United States. A scenario of social and political instability on the U.S. southern border, together with the possibility of massive Mexican migration into the

United States, disturbed Washington policymakers. The economic impact of the crisis on U.S. banks and on American economic interests also loomed as a major disaster for the United States and potentially for the entire Western financial system.

The Reagan administration responded by leading an international bailout of the Mexican economy. The rescue effort consisted of a $1 billion agricultural credit, a $700 million U.S. federal reserve support of the peso, a $1 billion advance of Mexican oil sales for the U.S. strategic petroleum reserve, and an almost $7 billion combined public-private loan, albeit at substantial interest, from a consortium of U.S., Canadian, Japanese, and European banks. Little did anyone realize that a much more serious economic and financial crisis would shake Mexico and the world in late 1994 and 1995.

Meanwhile, the United States pressured de la Madrid into reaching an agreement with the IMF regarding a program of Mexican austerity. The government responded by lowering government expenditures, reducing the role of the state in the economy, and privatizing inefficient state enterprises. Unlike other Latin American countries, Mexico refused either to impose a moratorium on the payment of its debt or to join other nations in calling for the total repudiation of their foreign debt. More important, Mexico entered GATT, the General Agreement on Tariffs and Trade in 1985. The decision to enter GATT and to accept the other economic measures introduced by de la Madrid were partly the result of both the increasing competitiveness of Mexico's exports and the ultimate realization that the statist economic model had failed.

The crisis and the austerity measures imposed by the administration had a significant impact. Student riots broke out in Mexico City in 1983, which were followed by increased unrest in both urban and rural areas. Opposition groups became more vociferous in advocating freer elections and the democratization of the political process. In states such as Sonora and Chihuahua, the PRI was accused of election fraud, and local elections were contested.

The United States also called for democratization in Mexico. The U.S. press criticism of Mexican corruption and either its inability or unwillingness to reduce drug trafficking created tension between the two countries. Friction increased when the U.S. Congress passed a controversial immigration law imposing sanctions on employers who hired illegal workers, most of whom came from Mexico. Enforcement of this law would be inconsistent and lax.

By then, however, the de la Madrid administration had decided on a much needed cooperative relationship with the United States. Presidents Reagan and de la Madrid met on numerous occasions to resolve the two countries' differences. The United States provided significant aid during the devastating earthquake that hit Mexico in 1985. Even more significant, however, was that by then the Mexican government had toned down its criticism of the United States and seemed less concerned with foreign policy issues and more with its internal economic crisis. Relations with Nicaragua, Cuba, and Central American revolutionary groups cooled. De la Madrid continued to play a reduced, but still activist, foreign policy role, primarily in regional affairs and as a broker on East-West issues. He took a leadership role in Contadora, the process organized by Panama, Colombia, Venezuela, and Mexico, which sought a negotiated settlement of Central American conflicts. This process led to a broad peace settlement in Central America and to free elections in Nicaragua and El Salvador, which rejected radical left political leadership. Ballots were replacing guerillas and guns. Yet he discontinued previous efforts to play a leadership role among third world countries and on North-South issues. De la Madrid also curtailed foreign travel, and the trips he took abroad were intended to expand markets for Mexican products and to attract capital and technology rather than project Mexican political influence.

As the 1988 presidential election approached, a vigorous debate developed in Mexico over the direction of socioeconomic reforms in the country, the proper relationship with the United States, and the nomination process for the next president. A faction within PRI vehemently challenged the accelerated trend away from statism in the economy, the relative neglect of social projects, the growing U.S. influence in Mexico, and the increasingly pro-U.S. policies of the administration. The dissident movement, known as the Democratic Current, was led by Cuauhtémoc Cárdenas, a former state governor and son of the earlier revered President Lázaro Cárdenas. The Democratic Current campaigned for the democratization of decision making within the party and advocated that the presidential candidate be chosen by the rank-and-file members rather than by the incumbent president, as was the tradition in Mexican politics. Not surprisingly, Cárdenas aspired to his party's presidential nomination.

Cárdenas's considerable prestige, influence, and name recognition attracted a significant following from the more radical, leftist, and nationalist elements within the party and throughout society. Beset by economic difficulties, accusations of fraud, corruption, and a continuing power monopoly, and unable to dispense the usual economic favors to labor, peasant, and radical groups, the PRI was under siege. Yet, the party's establishment rejected Cárdenas's prescription for democratizing the PRI as well as his other political and economic demands. Cárdenas broke with the PRI and became a candidate for the Frente Democrático Nacional, which is a coalition that included much of the left.

The PRI selected Carlos Salinas de Gortari as its presidential candidate. The thirty-nine-year-old minister of budget and planning was trained in economics and had been educated at Harvard University. He was committed to economic development, modernization, and free enterprise. To the Mexican left and to nationalist and anti-American groups, he represented an even more radical tendency toward an economic liberalization that rejected state control of the economy, and sought a closer relationship with the United States. In the 1988 elections, Salinas de Gortari won with less than 52 percent of the vote amidst a major voter abstention. Cárdenas received 30 percent and the conservative PAN won 16 percent. Even though this percentage of victory was the lowest ever admitted by the PRI for a presidential candidate, charges of corruption and fraud flared. Cárdenas complained bitterly that he had been robbed of an electoral victory.

The Salinas administration was remarkable in several ways. The president undertook a major restructuring of the economy and advocated free trade and open-market policies that were designed to force the country's industry, long accustomed to protectionist policies, to become more efficient and enable it to compete in worldwide. He sold off 1,155 state companies—a full 85 percent of all state enterprises. The sale brought the government more than $21 billion, most of which was used to retire part of the national debt. He also opened the economy to competition and outside investment. By the end of his administration, inflation was reduced from a whopping 150 percent to about 12 percent annually.

The savings on debt payments enabled Mexico to spend more on social programs and to proceed with even bolder economic reforms. To raise his dwindling popular support, Salinas resorted to a program of public spending, particularly through the Program of National Solidarity (PRONASOL). The government made federal funds available directly to independently organized, local communities. PRONASOL's populist social program ensured social peace during the early years of the Salinas administration, which enabled the government to pursue economic restructuring in relative tranquillity without substantial political reform.

The crowning achievement of the Salinas administration was the North American Free Trade Agreement with Canada and the United States. The president threw the growing prestige of his presidency behind NAFTA in the hope that freer trade would increase Mexican exports to the United States, which would redress an expanding trade deficit with that country and boost the long-term prospects for Mexican economic growth. A domestic coalition composed of economic and business elites, the president and his allies, and some populist groups supported NAFTA. This multiclass, multigroup coalition hoped that NAFTA would strengthen economic restructuring, help large businesses in Mexico with exporting capacity to increase exports by taking advantage of a free trade environment, attract foreign investment from the United States, Asia, and Europe, and make Mexican products more competitive and better positioned vis-á-vis Asian and European common markets.

Despite Salinas's economic accomplishments, the massive privatization program was not a quick panacea for Mexico; it aggravated many problems instead of easing them. Closing or selling government enterprises led to major layoffs of workers. More than four hundred thousand jobs were lost in the last decade, which caused widespread social hardship in a country with an already high unemployment rate. Getting government out of business did not always result in greater efficiency, more competition, or a better life for the average Mexican. New owners sometimes proved to be just as unresponsive to workers and consumers as the old government bureaucrats.

The economy, which had expanded at a steady rate of 2.5 to 4.5 percent a year after Salinas took office in 1988, took a major dive in 1993. Unemployment rose, as many enterprises folded. There were failures among numerous companies producing goods such as textiles, furniture, and electrical products. The slowdown was partly the result of government policy, as officials became concerned with a massive $23 billion current-account deficit at the end of 1992. They increased interest rates and instituted strong austerity measures.

Salinas's economic reforms were accompanied with a modest political modernization program. His administration strove to level somewhat the lopsided electoral playing field and bolster its sagging credibility and prestige. It recognized an unprecedented number of opposition victories in state and municipal races. Yet, it was obvious that Salinas's

The signing of the North American Free Trade Agreement (NAFTA). Standing, from left to right, President Carlos Salinas de Gortari of Mexico, President George Bush of the United States, and Prime Minister Brian Mulroney of Canada. *Government of Mexico*

changes were implemented while attempting to preserve the hegemonic power of the PRI and to secure its continuous control of the presidency and Congress. During 1993, Congress passed reforms to regulate PRI's unchecked access to public funds and the mass media and introduce limits on campaign financing. In addition, for the first time in Mexican history, an offspring of foreign-born parents could become president in the election of 2000. Other reforms included opening the Senate to opposition representation by allowing a third, minority-party senator from each state; introducing some proportional representation in the way the lower chamber of Congress is elected; and setting up a federal body to oversee elections.

While the conservative National Action Party (PAN) supported the reforms, the most powerful opposition force, the leftist Party of the Democratic Revolution (PRD), failed to support them. The head of the PRD explained that "the changes are unacceptable. They show that the PRI is not prepared to think about losing elections." Other critics argued that the change in electing deputies would increase the PRI's current overrepresentation via a more proportional system of representation. Still others complained that electoral reforms would mean little until the electoral authorities were beyond government control and the overlap had closed between state and ruling party. They claimed that fraud had merely become more sophisticated.

As the 1994 elections approached, such criticism about the electoral process seemed mild compared with manifestations of political instability and violence, particularly in the south. Mexico was headed toward major upheavals.

CHAPTER 16

YEARS OF CRISIS: 1994–1995

The presidential election of 1994 focused Mexico's and the world's attention on the country's deepening problems. Suddenly, the Salinas administration and the PRI had to deal with increasing turmoil, a political elite in conflict, and a developing financial crisis.

The propensity toward violence in changing political, social, and economic conditions had been part of Mexico's history. Such violence now reappeared with a vengeance. In Mexico, 1994 began with a bang, but unfortunately it was not the cheering noise of drums welcoming NAFTA. Rather, it was the terrifying sound of bullets and bombs created by the Zapatista Army of National Liberation in the southern state of Chiapas.

On January 1, 1994, the date when the North American Free Trade Agreement took effect and the Cuban revolution commemorated its thirty-fifth anniversary, a well-organized military uprising of Mexican Indians and peasants overran several towns and cities in Chiapas—an impoverished, primarily Indian state. The Mexican past had again become the present. After a few days of fierce fighting, numerous buildings had been destroyed, which was partly the result of massive air force bombings by the Mexican military, and hundreds of rebels had been either killed or arrested. In Mexico City and other towns, sporadic bombings and terrorist threats followed the uprising. The immediate and overwhelming response of the Mexican military forced the Zapatistas (the rebels) to retreat to the mountains, while the government

The Zapatista Army of National Liberation is a well-armed, well-trained guerrilla group that was thrust into national prominence in 1994 when its members captured several towns in the southern state of Chiapas. They remain an active military force and a challenge to the Mexican government. *Alyx Kellington*

regained control of rebel towns. Peace negotiations between the rebels and the government helped diffuse a tense situation.

Although the initial uprising seemed to have been crushed, the Zapatista National Liberation Army maintained a large force in the south that demanded major concessions from the government. Questions remain, however, about the reasons and impact of this bloody event in the year of the Salinas administration's departure from power. Underlying reasons for the unhappiness among the native masses in southern Mexico seem to be the impoverished economic conditions of Chiapas, which is one of the poorest states in Mexico; years of governmental and private sector corruption, abuse, and exploitation of the indigenous population; and lack of arable land needed to satisfy the demands of a landless peasantry.

Chiapas, which primarily produces coffee and vegetables, ranks last among Mexican states both in literacy and in the availability of drinking water and electricity. The violence vividly reminded Mexico that the advances during the last half century had failed to reach significant sectors of the population. Subcommander Marcos, a rebel leader, suggested opposition to NAFTA and support for Indian rights as objectives of the movement.

Economic and ethnic reasons alone, however, cannot explain the violence. First and foremost these events highlight a profound crisis of confidence in the PRI. During the past two decades, the government and the PRI have been increasingly criticized—because of authoritarianism and corruption—for neglecting the poorer sectors of society and for abandoning the statism and populism that had characterized early administrations in favor of private enterprise, foreign investment, and laissez-faire capitalism. While the pendulum of social and economic reforms directed by the state has swung back and forth between right and left for much of the PRI's tenure in power, a marked movement away from statism, populism, and social change characterized the Miguel de la Madrid administration. This tendency accelerated under President Salinas, who privatized the economy, sold off hundreds of inefficient state enterprises, encouraged foreign and domestic investment, and catered to the business community.

These activities have been strongly challenged by a newly created group—the Democratic Revolutionary Party (PRD)—led by Cuauhtémoc Cárdenas. Cárdenas articulated the frustration and anger of a generation that has lived under the shadow of the PRI. Although he lost the presidential election of 1988 to Salinas, Cárdenas has continued to criticize the government and has called Mexico "a nation divided by inequality and injustice and governed by an autocratic, patrimonial system." He also lashed out against NAFTA and warned that the agreement would lead Mexico "beyond integration into absorption under conditions of at least partial subordination and submission."

Cárdenas's criticism has been echoed by other sectors of society. It is significant that the leader of the Zapatista group, Subcommander Marcos, emphasized that the "uprising was needed because Mexico's government was illegitimate and could not be changed by elections because of vote fraud." He added that the free trade agreement "would harm the indigenous population."

That the crisis erupted into violence in southern Mexico is also significant. Aside from its endemic poverty, this area has been overwhelmed by Central America's instability and civil wars during the past decade. Thousands of refugees from Guatemala and El Salvador have found a safe haven in southern Mexico. Guerrilla leaders and exiles from these countries have used this area as staging grounds for their antigovernment activities. The region has suffered from violence, and reports of guerrilla activity have appeared sporadically in the Mexican press. A porous border seemed to have allowed significant contacts between Central American and Mexican guerrilla groups. Although Mexican politics traditionally have been plagued by urban and rural violence, and there were certainly enough indigenous reasons for unhappiness in Chiapas, the Zapatista uprising can be interpreted, in part, as an extension of Central American struggles into Mexico.

It is important to note that the end of a presidential term in Mexico is usually a period in which the PRI reexamines its policies and sets the agenda for the next *sexenio*. This period has traditionally been used by various groups to advance their own agendas and to demand redress of specific grievances, occasionally through the use of violence and demonstrations. This cyclical unrest seemed to be dramatically evident now in the south and probably will continue to appear, hopefully in a milder form, in other parts of the country.

Although the violent uprising seemed brief, its effect upon Mexico will surely be longer lasting. The violence embarrassed both the Salinas administration and the PRI. Their public attempts to portray Mexico as a peaceful, stable society that welcomes foreign investment have been shattered by the reality of Mexico's ethnic, social, economic, and regional inequities; by the traditional inclination toward violence; and by the debate about the country's policies and the proper role of the state in directing the economy and in promoting social change.

The Zapatista uprising is forcing the PRI to reexamine its policies. Although the Salinas government made significant strides toward democratizing the political process, election fraud, corruption, and coercion still flourish in the system. Under the next president, more reforms may be instituted in this area.

The pendulum of social change may swing left, albeit gently. New social and economic programs that benefit the poorer sectors of society will intensify, the southern areas will receive special attention, and the bureaucracy and leadership in Chiapas and other southern states may be revamped and modernized. The PRI had already acknowledged the growing discontent and anticipated the need for social reforms by nominating Luis Donaldo Colosio as its candidate for the August 1994 presidential elections. A more populist leader, the former secretary of social development seemed well suited to institute a vigorous program of social reform and to cater to the poorer, indigenous sectors of the population.

Unfortunately, on March 23, 1994, in the midst of the presidential campaign, Colosio was assassinated, while campaigning in the north-

Luis Donaldo Colosio, leading PRI candidate in the 1994 presidential elections. He was mysteriously assassinated while campaigning in Tijuana in March 1994. *Alyx Kellington*

ern border town of Tijuana. Suspicion of a conspiracy centered on drug traffickers or old-guard conservative PRI henchmen who feared Colosio's reformist rhetoric. Several initial investigations failed to produce conclusions about either the motives for the assassination or whether a conspiracy existed.

The death of the popular PRI presidential candidate Colosio required a quick decision about a replacement. Violence and demonstrations, although at a much lower level, continued in the south and in the capital; the growing popularity of the Partido Acción Nacional's (PAN) able candidate, Diego Fernández de Cevallos, indicated an increased challenge from the right. The candidate from the left, Cuauhtémoc Cárdenas, maintained a confrontational stance, accusing the PRI of planning dishonest elections and portraying himself as the victim of electoral fraud durng the earlier 1988 elections. The PRI had to convince the Mexican electorate as well as the international community that the elections would be free and fair, which was not an easy task given Mexico's history of election fraud and the continuous accusations of the opposition that the PRI would repeat its traditional corrupt practices again in 1994.

The PRI presidential nomination was quickly transferred to Ernesto Zedillo Ponce de León. A forty-two-year-old, U.S.-educated economist, Zedillo was the most experienced public servant to seek the Mexican presidency. Born to a working-class family, Zedillo went to public school and worked his way through college. He earned a doctorate in economics from Yale in 1978. He enrolled in the PRI in 1971 and began working in the Office of Economic Policy in the Ministry of the Presidency. In 1978, he joined Mexico's Central Bank, and by 1982, he was assistant director of economic research at the bank. He became known in the world of international finance for skillfully renegotiating the

Elected in 1995, Ernesto Zedillo brings to the presidency a long and successful administrative career and a reputation for integrity and efficiency. *Government of Mexico*

private-sector debt. In 1983, Zedillo launched FICORCA (Fideicomisio para la Cobertura de Riesgos Cambiarios), a trust fund for hedging against exchange risks, which had been established to help Mexican companies restructure their foreign debt. Zedillo also publicly advocated adopting macroeconomic modernization policies and the further privatization of the economy. In 1987, he was appointed undersecretary of planning and budgetary control. In that position, Zedillo helped to develop Mexico's plan for fighting inflation with a wage and price control pact among government, unions, and businesses that reduced the inflation rate from 150 percent yearly to single digits by 1994.

Upon taking office in 1988, President Salinas appointed Zedillo as the secretary of planning and budget and, later, secretary of education. In the former position, Zedillo was one of the architects in the program to modernize Mexico's economy. He crafted Mexico's first balanced budget and pioneered the Solidarity Program, a massive antipoverty and development effort. As secretary of education, he overhauled and decentralized the country's education system, but he also became the focus of national controversy when he allowed the publication of new official history books that blamed the army for the 1968 killing of students at Tlatelolco in Mexico City.

Although an able administrator and negotiator, Zedillo lacks the charismatic appeal of his slain predecessor. Cold, analytical, and pragmatic, he admires Benito Juárez, the ninteenth-century liberal leader, and intends to continue the policies initiated by the Salinas administration, particularly expanding the economy, supporting NAFTA, reforming the judicial system, improving the educational system, and accelerating Mexico's move toward full democracy. He also, however, shocked some of the old guard in his party by proposing, if elected, to hold primary elections to select the party's future candidates—a practice unknown in PRI history—and to become a "passive member" of the PRI, which is a nontraditional role for Mexican presidents, who dominated both the party and the government. "I firmly believe," he proclaimed in a campaign speech, "that democracy calls for a healthy distance between my party and the government."

The preelectoral climate was permeated by political instability, fears of increased violence, and suspicions of widespread electoral corruption. Opposition candidates accused the PRI of manipulating the electoral process to ensure Zedillo's victory. In particular, Cárdenas, the Party of the Democratic Revolution (PRD) candidate, warned that fraudulent elections would not be tolerated and that his followers would stage massive demonstrations, if the balloting were questionable.

In addition to these internal demands, the recently signed NAFTA agreement exerted pressure on the PRI to provide fair and open elections. There was increasing criticism in the United States about the Mexican electoral process and the weakness of Mexican democracy in general. The violence in Chiapas revived past images of an unstable and violent country. Some U.S. opponents of NAFTA seized the occasion to warn about the dangers of a closer relationship with Mexico. Others worried about the security implications of possible turmoil in a neighboring country with an extensive frontier. Still others insisted that U.S. policy promoting democracy in other countries in the hemisphere should apply equally to Mexico.

The Mexican leadership had difficulty in demonstrating that a new Mexico was emerging and that the image of a third world country in political turmoil was not the reality. Both Salinas and Zedillo pledged to abide by the results and promised "a transparent, honest and democratic election."

The Salinas administration undertook significant measures and spent millions to legitimize the election. New photo IDs were issued; domestic observers were given legal status; foreign observers were permitted for the first time; opposition parties obtained greater access to the media. The role of PRI sympathizers at the head of the electoral machinery was reduced.

Yet, despite those improvements, the PRI retained significant advantages such as huge campaign coffers, widespread media support, and PRI sympathizers in lower levels of the electoral machinery. The vast state machinery was also geared to support Zedillo.

As the campaign progressed, Cárdenas seemed to be the more popular candidate and a real threat to PRI power. He advocated a greater state role, large public-sector investments, and the breakup and regulation of privatized monopolies. He also voiced reservations about NAFTA, criticized the United States, and bitterly attacked the Salinas government. Yet, his support began to evaporate following a May 12, 1994, publicly televised debate—the first in the history of Mexico—among the three candidates. Declared the uncontested victor by nearly all sectors of the population, the PAN candidate Fernández de Cevallos's popularity increased dramatically. Cárdenas's campaign floundered, and his popularity plummeted.

Yet, the left's apparent weakness had other more profound causes. The elections were taking place amid perceived prosperity and optimism about Mexico's future, although the economy had shown a meager growth rate of 0.4 percent in 1993. Many admired the accomplishments of the Salinas administration. Most of the issues that the left focused on in 1988 had been dealt with by the PRI during the past six years. The Salinas period had ushered in five years of economic growth, falling inflation, and sweeping economic reforms. Salinas had astutely instituted Solidarity, a multibillion-dollar antipoverty public works program targeted most directly at the poorest states, where Cárdenas's support was strongest.

The PRD leadership was also divided, and the party did little to build a national grassroots organization. The worldwide collapse of leftist policies and regimes hurt the left in Mexico. Relations between Cárdenas and the other PRD leadership remained tense and occasionally unfriendly. Cárdenas's confrontational and intransigent stance and his refusal to acknowledge the depth of the Salinas administration's electoral reforms divided the party and weakened its appeal. Voters were frightened by Cárdenas's constant warnings about violence in the event of election fraud, and his ill-timed trip to Chiapas to meet with Zapatista rebel leader Marcos. With little charisma and weak national appeal, Cárdenas tried to rally opposition to the PRI. As the elections approached on August 21, few expected him to win.

The Chiapas uprising may have hurt Cárdenas's bid for the presidency. Although he quickly distanced himself from events in Chiapas, the perception remained that his criticism of the system and his appeal to the Indian poor may have encouraged the violence. Some considered him too radical or too unpredictable, and thought that the PRI would be the best guarantee of continuous political stability and economic growth.

As the results of the elections were made public, what was unexpected was the clear victory of the PRI candidate, the strong showing of the PAN candidate, and the poor showing of Cárdenas and his PRD. Zedillo won with 49 percent of the vote; Fernández de Cevallos obtained 26 percent; and Cárdenas received a mere 16 percent, well down from the 30 percent he received in 1988. Six smaller parties and spoiled ballots accounted for the remainder of the presidential vote. What was more unexpected was that Zedillo and Fernández de Cevallos won more votes in working-class districts than Cárdenas. Poorer Mexicans voted 51 percent for Zedillo, 27 percent for Fernández de Cevallos, and 16 percent for Cárdenas.

Although some electoral irregularities occurred, international observers confirmed that the elections were generally honest. A very large number (78 percent) of the country's registered voters participated in the elections, and observers reported that many voters seemed determined to show the world that Mexico could hold open elections and that the country has a true democracy. It was also likely that an overwhelming majority of the Mexicans preferred ballots to bullets, rejected the violence of the Zapatistas, and were willing to trust Zedillo to continue the process of democratization and economic development.

Zedillo seems committed to solidifying and extending the free-market reforms begun under President Salinas. The major economic challenge for the new administration may be the shift from macro to micro economic policies. Zedillo must move from formulating broad macroeconomic programs to instituting industry-specific microeconomic policies designed to expand the benefits of Salinas's reform efforts to the middle and lower classes. Salinas's economic successes failed to filter down to the working masses and those most in need.

In September 1994, a pact among labor, industry, and government to hold down prices and wages was renewed until the end of 1995. The pact called for a 4 percent inflation rate for 1995, a 4 percent salary increase for workers, allowance for productivity increase in wages, up to a 3 percent tax credit for business, a commitment to maintain the current exchange rate policy, achieving an economic growth rate double that of population growth, and investment promotion. In an address following the signing of the pact, Zedillo stated that his administration's challenge will be to raise the Mexican family's standard of living by creating permanent jobs, promoting production, and keeping public finances healthy. "The pact will be successful," he emphasized, "to the degree that all parties comply with the agreement."

The signing of the pact indicates that the Zedillo administration will seek to continue the strong anti-inflation policies of the Salinas period. As in the past, labor's complaints about wage levels and inflation were largely ignored. The country's trade and current account deficits increased under President Salinas and emphasized the overvaluation of the Mexican peso. Yet, President Zedillo ruled out a sharp devaluation of the peso "because exports were growing and foreign investment was strong."

Zedillo's promises, however, were overtaken by events. Only three weeks later, on December 20, the drain on foreign currency reserves caused him to devalue the peso dramatically, which quickly dropped in value by more than 50 percent from its high. A U.S. product that once cost one dollar or three pesos suddenly cost over six pesos. Mexican interest rates shot up to 50 percent. Weaker companies were closed, and banks were taken over by the government. Jobs were lost. Mexican stocks that had attracted international investors, particularly from the

United States, dropped dramatically in value. The collapse of their prices caused significant losses throughout the world.

Mexico, the United States, and the world were shocked. Optimism about Mexico's future was replaced by skepticism. Foreign investment slowed down. Mexican stocks were sold at great speed. Investors' faith in "emerging markets," not only in Mexico but throughout the world, was badly shaken.

The United States, led by the Clinton administration, proposed $40 billion in U.S. loans guaranteed by the government. The new Republican leadership of the House and Senate agreed, but they could not guarantee passage of legislation to support a "foreign bailout." Acting under his executive authority, President Clinton organized international support of more than $50 billion in credits, loans, guarantees, and support of the peso's value. The U.S. share was estimated at $20 billion.

The scope and effect of this latest crisis clearly demonstrated both the growing importance of Mexico to the world and the rapidly growing linkage between Mexico and the United States. Although this dramatic financial crisis seriously affected the United States, one should not underestimate the severity of this calamity to all Mexicans. Their standard of living and the very ability of the poorest to maintain bare necessities have been depleted for the foreseeable future. The austerity measures required by both the U.S. and the international community will prevent any major social programs and will lead Mexico into a deeper economic recession. This, in turn, will provoke greater social and political unrest.

Although President Zedillo obviously inherited much of the financial and foreign exchange crisis from former President Salinas's administration, eventually it will become his crisis and will preoccupy his administration for years to come. Unfortunately, the new president must also deal with additional strong pressures in the economic, social, and political realms.

Zedillo has explained that he would definitely not open any more opportunities to private investment in such state-owned companies as Petróleos Mexicanos (PEMEX). Meanwhile, domestic business groups, which are participating in politics more openly than ever before, are lobbying the administration on everything from lower taxes to agricultural subsidies.

One of the concerns of the Mexican business community is that NAFTA and the rush of U.S. foreign investments to the country will hurt Mexican industries. Foreign U.S. direct investment reached $3.3

billion in 1993 and may have reached $7 billion in 1994. Unable to compete with American technology, capital, expertise, and access to foreign markets, middle and small Mexican industrialists will increasingly pressure the Zedillo administration to slow the pace of foreign investments. As in the past, the forces of nationalism, motivated in part now by the economic need to survive, will reassert themselves. While no one anticipates the repudiation of NAFTA or a rise in anti-Americanism similar to the 1940s, the long-term road to U.S.–Mexican cooperation will be bumpy and full of obstacles. The Porfiriato and foreign investment excesses still live in the Mexican historical memory.

The assassination on September 28, 1994, of José Francisco Ruiz Massieu was another dramatic indication of the difficulties of reforming the PRI. The shooting of the secretary general of the party, an apparent ally of outgoing President Salinas, may have been intended to warn those who want rapid reforms as well as government officials who are combating the narcotics trade in Mexico. When Mario Ruiz Massieu (who was the deputy attorney general) was asked about those who he believes masterminded his brother's assassination, he explained that "the investigation goes more along the political road than the road of drug trafficking. Perhaps the most solid hypothesis is that of a political affair with aid or financing from drug traffickers."

In early 1995, President Zedillo was reeling under criticism about his weakness and vacillation. Burdened by the anger over the collapse of the financial system and by the unsolved assassinations of a presidential candidate and the head of the PRI, Zedillo was then faced with an upsurge in the Chiapas armed revolt. He ordered the military to crush the rebellion, but then quickly changed his mind and called a halt to the mission. There were rumors of discontent in the Mexican military. Suddenly, in an unprecedented move in March, Zedillo dramatically violated the unwritten rule that a new president protects the reputation and honor of past presidents by never criticizing them. President Zedillo astounded the nation by directly blaming the crash of the peso and the economy on his predecessor, President Salinas; by arresting Salinas's older brother, Raul Salinas de Gortari, as the mastermind of the assassination of PRI Secretary General Ruiz Massieu; and by accusing President Salinas's administration of a cover-up in the investigation of the murder of presidential candidate Colosio. Zedillo temporarily catapulted himself into public favor, but now that he has shattered the mold of PRI behavior, it could be years, or only months, until Mexico passes final judgments on these actions.

This is one of those important moments in Mexican history when the past shaped the present, but where a sudden bold act or unique crisis ensures that a new phase of history will be written. How past trends may affect Mexico's future into the next century will be assessed in the last chapter. Before that speculation, however, it is essential to complete the story of Mexico and its people by noting that, although the United States has had a long-standing and profound effect upon Mexico, the influence of Mexican-Americans on and in the United States of America is also important, and will continue to expand in the future. No history of Mexico would be complete without an understanding of the impact of both Mexican-Americans and Mexican culture.

CHAPTER 17

MEXICANS AND MEXICAN-AMERICANS

Mexican-Americans constitute the second largest minority group in the United States after African-Americans. There are more people of Mexican heritage in Los Angeles than in any city in Mexico, except Mexico City. Mexican-Americans represent 64 percent of all Latinos in the United States. They colonized and settled the American Southwest long before the Anglo-Americans did. Yet, Mexican-Americans are a somewhat neglected group. They are the least known, least sponsored, and least vocal minority in the United States. Their important cultural impact has been generally unrecognized by the majority of the non-Hispanic populace, and traditional stereotypes dominate the thinking of Anglo-Americans toward Mexican-Americans. Although the vast majority of Mexican-Americans are citizens, the media and non-Hispanic Americans often perceive them as illegal aliens who have come to the United States to take jobs away from hard-working Americans. Mexican-Americans are not a homogeneous group, and the majority perceive themselves as loyal citizens of the United States—not as citizens of Mexico. Furthermore, geographical continuity has provided the Mexican immigrant with a relocation experience vastly different from that of the European immigrant.

The Mexican-origin population in the United States traces its antecedents to those who colonized the Southwest before 1848. Between 1528 and 1602, before the English colonization of North America, the first Spaniards entered what is now the American Southwest, lured by the promise of Indian wealth.

The city of Santa Fe was founded in 1609. Extensive colonization of the area did not occur for another hundred years. The early settlements in the Southwest stretched more than two thousand miles along the northern edge of Mexico, but they seldom extended more than one hundred fifty miles north of the present-day border. In Texas, most settlers lived along the lower Rio Grande River. Indian attacks limited the number of people in the Southwest, and in places such as Arizona nearly all the Spanish colonists had to seek shelter within the city of Tucson.

Throughout this period, Mexico exerted weak and distant political control over the area. After the war between Mexico and the United States, the Treaty of Guadalupe-Hidalgo in 1848 stipulated that Mexico relinquish California, New Mexico, Utah, Texas, and Colorado to the United States. Subsequently, Mexico sold part of Arizona to the United States.

These acquisitions, however, affected only a small number of Mexican nationals. The American government gave the Mexicans residing in the area the option of either returning to Mexico or becoming U.S. citizens. The government also promised those who stayed, and whose land deeds had been issued before annexation, that those deeds would be honored, and that their culture and language would be legally respected. Approximately eighty thousand Mexicans chose to remain in the Southwest and became U.S. citizens.

Although Anglo-American immigration to the Southwest increased before annexations, the trend accelerated after 1848, which exacerbated the conflict between the two cultures. The gold rush in California attracted more than one hundred thousand U.S. citizens to the area in only a few years. Many Mexicans lost their land, despite U.S government promises. In many places, the new settlers imposed land taxes, questioned Spanish land deeds, and conducted legal proceedings in English, which was detrimental to the interests of the Spanish-speaking Mexicans. These maneuvers by the new settlers enabled them to displace many Mexicans and seize their lands.

The gold rush brought clashes between English-speaking and Mexican-American miners. Although Mexicans had discovered gold first, and Mexican miners from Sonora had already staked out claims, the newcomers plotted to chase the Mexican miners out, lynched Mexicans, and burned and destroyed Mexican mining encampments. Such events occurred so frequently that newspapers in Los Angeles stopped reporting the details. In response to the harassment, social banditry increased among the Mexicans. Men like Gregorio Cortéz, Joaquin Murieta, Jacinto Trevino, and Tiburcio Vásquez became the Robin Hoods of the Southwest. Their defiance made them legendary in the Mexican-American communities.

In Texas, the conflict between American and Mexican cattlemen and sheepherders exacerbated racial tensions. Americans were constantly afraid that the Mexicans might explode in rebellion. As a result, lynching Mexicans was commonplace. These acts of violence against Mexican-Americans received a boost from the legal system because few juries in Texas would convict a white man for the death of a Mexican. Moreover, the Texas Rangers often shot Mexicans, eliciting a warning from the U.S. secretary of state to the Texas governor that measures would be taken unless atrocities against Mexicans ceased.

Mexican-Americans disparagingly called the Americans "gringos." The term *gringo* referred to anyone who spoke with a foreign accent. On the other hand, Americans referred to Mexicans as "greasers." Although the origin of the word is disputed, many believe that it began when Americans observed Mexicans in New Mexico greasing the wheels of their wagons; hence, a Mexican was literally a "greaser." In California, the term has been traced to the days of the hide-and-tallow trade and is said to have been applied by American sailors to the Indians and Mexicans who loaded the greasy, tick-ridden hides on the clipper ships.

The conflict between Americans and Mexicans in the New Mexico territory never reached the level that it did in Texas and California. New Mexico was more isolated, and its American population grew very slowly. By 1870, there were only 91,784 residents, and 90 percent of them were of Spanish origin.

Until 1910, the total population of the Southwest remained small. It increased substantially soon afterward, partly because of the influx of refugees from the Mexican revolution. Following the turbulence in Mexico, great numbers of wealthy, middle-class, and even poorer Mexicans came to the United States. Naturally, many of them settled in the Southwest. This migration, coupled with the outbreak of World War I, led to renewed tension and violence between Mexican-Americans and Americans, during which several hundred from both sides lost their lives. Further exacerbating the situation, the media and law enforcement officials questioned the loyalty of Mexican-Americans and claimed to have uncovered plots that called for a Mexican uprising in the Southwest, which caused mass hysteria and violent outbursts by the American population. To alleviate American fears, various Mexican-American organizations emerged to promote their loyalty to the United States. One organization, the Order of the Sons of America, restricted its membership to U.S. citizens of Mexican origin and promoted assimilation and mastery of English. This group splintered around 1929, which resulted in the League of United Latin American Citizens (LULAC).

Although Mexican-Americans were repeatedly harassed and persecuted, their labor was needed to help build the American Southwest. At the turn of the century, Mexican labor was extensively used in constructing the Southern Pacific and Santa Fe railroad lines. Thousands of Mexicans were recruited from Mexico, and such recruitment of Mexican labor by the United States would repeatedly occur throughout this century. Subsequently, Mexican workers became critical to the agricultural production of the Southwest. In addition, Mexicans were being employed in California and Chicago in industrial areas. The U.S. government recognized the importance of Mexican labor to the economy, and Congress exempted Mexican migrants from the quota immigration system that it instituted during the 1920s. Although a border patrol was created in 1924 to prevent illegal immigration, Mexican migrants found that crossing the border was an easy task.

The Great Depression rekindled American frustrations and fears about Mexican-Americans. Many believed that they were taking away jobs. During the early 1930s, approximately three hundred thousand Mexicans were returned to Mexico, although some of them were U.S. citizens. According to official records, about one third of the Mexicans counted in the 1930 census were repatriated. Furthermore, the United States Bureau of Immigration involved itself in numerous labor conflicts by deporting any Mexicans who went on strike. Mexican-Americans suffered from poor working conditions, low wages, the inability to protest, and fear of deportation.

As World War II raged, the U.S. press shifted its coverage of Mexican-Americans from "fiesta" and "old California culture" stories to negative accounts of the Mexican-American youth subculture dramatized by the zoot suit. Years later, the zoot suit incidents that occurred during the early 1940s became symbols among civil rights activists of the persecution endured by the Mexican-American population in the United States. Zoot suits were the clothes worn by Mexican-American youths in the Los Angeles area. Such clothing featured long, broad-shouldered

Zoot-suiters under arrest in Los Angeles. In California in the 1940s and 1950s, the American press portrayed Mexican Americans, who favored this distinctive clothing, as gang members bent on violence. *Library of Congress*

coats, extra-baggy pants that were pegged at the ankles, and a broad-brimmed hat, occasionally sporting a feather. Unfortunately, along with this fashion, the first Mexican-American gangs appeared to be composed of youths who were caught between two worlds in search of their cultural identity. These gangs would become an intrinsic part of the Mexican-American subculture.

Los Angeles newspapers trumpeted the juvenile crime wave occurring throughout the city, and a grand jury was convened to investigate the gangs. Some newspapers started reporting that fascist organizations were manipulating the zoot-suiters to sow turmoil on the West coast. On August 2, 1942, tensions turned violent. A man named José Díaz was found dead near the Sleepy Lagoon area, a prominent hangout for zoot-suiters. The newspapers cried out for justice. On August 10 and 11, the police blocked all streets going into East Los Angeles. They searched and arrested over six hundred Mexican-Americans on various charges. Many were beaten by the police.

Following this incident, eleven sailors of the U.S. Navy claimed they had been attacked by a Mexican gang. The sailors retaliated by gathering two hundred comrades to cruise through East Los Angeles and attack anyone wearing a zoot suit. This action precipitated a week of rioting. Thousands of white locals and servicemen fought zoot-suiters and blacks throughout the city. They stripped the Mexican-Americans of their clothes. Many people were hurt; miraculously, no one was killed.

While tensions in the western United States continued, several thousand Mexican-Americans fought gallantly against the Axis powers. Many were killed, and they became highly decorated for their bravery in combat.

On the home front, the U.S. government concluded an agreement with Mexico on August 4, 1942, to supplement the U.S. labor force with workers from Mexico. This agreement became known as the bracero program. Various labor recruiters went to Mexico to convince Mexicans to relocate to the United States in exchange for a job. The agreement stipulated that imported workers were to be assured of free transportation to and from their homes, that they were to be provided sustenance en route, that they were not to be used to displace other workers or to reduce wage rates, and that certain minimum guarantees governing wages and working conditions would have to be observed.

Originally, the bracero program was designed as a short-term measure. At the behest of agricultural growers, however, the U.S. government extended its lifetime until 1964. Under this program, hundreds of thousands of Mexicans came to the United States. Ironically, during the early 1950s, the U.S. government simultaneously instituted Operation Wetback to control the flow of unauthorized Mexicans across the border. Once again, immigration officers rounded up thousands of Mexicans and repatriated them to Mexico.

The 1960s brought many changes to the Mexican-American community. Along with other minority groups, Mexican-Americans demanded guarantees for their civil rights, called for basic labor rights, and advocated pride in their cultural heritage. In 1962, César Chávez organized California grape pickers and farmworkers into a group that later became famous as the United Farm Workers' Union. Mexican agricultural labor had been abused and laborers were working for less than minimum wage, with neither overtime pay nor disability benefits, and were living in horrible conditions. Congress had exempted the growers from national labor laws because it believed that farmers could not compete if they had to pay higher wages. During the early 1960s, most farm workers earned less than three thousand dollars a year. In 1965, Chávez's organization decided to strike against grape growers, after they refused to negotiate fairly. Chávez waged a high-profile media campaign. He marched his followers to Sacramento and organized a national boycott of California grapes. Finally, he went on a hunger strike to protest the violent measures being used by the grape growers to break the strike. His actions made him internationally famous. After five years, the grape growers gave in to Chávez's demands, and for the first time in United States history, farmworkers would be legally protected by national labor laws.

The Civil Rights Act of 1964 and the Voting Rights Act of 1965 improved the legal status of Mexican-Americans throughout the Southwest. Although Mexican-Americans never suffered the degree of racism and violence experienced by blacks, these federal acts eliminated some of the more egregious practices of segregation that were being committed against Mexican-Americans. The Voting Rights Act, and the Twenty-Fourth Amendment eliminated barriers that discouraged Mexican-Americans from voting. These measures outlawed the poll tax, literacy requirements, and English-only ballots.

During the 1960s, many Mexican-Americans began to call themselves Chicanos and their actions became known as El Movimiento. Led by young people and college students, Chicano groups promoted ethnic pride and claimed that assimilation into American culture was unnecessary. The term *Chicano* tended to denote ethnic pride and an assertive, defiant political stance. These Chicanos saw the American Southwest as the ancient homeland of their ancestors. They viewed themselves as culturally repressed because their heritage had existed in the Southwest long before any other. Many middle-class Mexican-Americans reacted negatively to these Chicanos. Mexican-American and Chicano activists waged high-profile debates over the degree to which their ethnicity should be emphasized in their political and social future. In many ways, the Chicano movement emulated the black civil rights struggle and the anti–Vietnam War protest in tactics and style. The critical event in the Chicano movement occurred in 1968, when high school students walked out of classes, demanding to be instructed in the history and literature of their people. During this period, various radical parties emerged, such as La Raza Unida and the August Twenty-Ninth Movement, and the Chicano movement managed to gain some political power. By the late 1970s, however, the movement splintered over ideology and tactics, allowing more moderate groups, such as LULAC, to reassert themselves.

César Chávez organized California Mexican-American farm workers and led a high-profile strike. His actions improved the legal status and wages of grape pickers and other farm laborers. *Library of Congress*

The last two decades have witnessed the reemergence of the "Mexican problem" in American political rhetoric. Once again, illegal immigration, the loss of U.S. jobs, and English-only issues resurfaced. In response to these pressures, Congress passed the Immigration Reform and Control Act of 1986. It granted amnesty to anyone who had lived in the United States longer than five years, but it penalized any employer who had knowingly hired undocumented workers. In late 1990, Congress passed the Immigration Act of 1990. The act's primary focus was to increase total allowable immigration under an overall flexible cap, but it also expanded the antidiscriminatory provisions of the 1986 act and increased the penalties for unlawful discrimination. The media also heightened fears by describing the border area as chaotic, and some people advocated the use of the military to police the border. The negotiations for NAFTA in 1993 between Mexico and the United States caused the shifting of political coalitions in the United States, which united two hitherto opposing groups—labor and the environmentalists—in opposition to NAFTA. Obviously, some problems remain, and traditional perceptions of Mexico and Mexican-Americans persist.

American frustration over undocumented Mexican immigrants reached to a fever pitch in the November 1994 election in the critical state of California. Voters then passed a referendum by a margin of almost two to one—the now famous Proposition 187—which would deny illegal immigrant families state-funded programs such as medical care and schooling. As the California economy and the tax base shrank in a serious local recession, citizens led by Governor Pete Wilson organized against costs estimated at between two and three billion dollars a year. The state's voters rejected paying their taxes for aliens crossing the border in violation of American laws. The vote reflected real, but lesser, anger against unfunded federal mandates on the states and the high costs of crime committed by illegals.

It is interesting that a significant minority of the Californian Mexican-American population supported Proposition 187, despite the fact that the reductions may eventually primarily affect illegal Mexican-American immigrants. It is unlikely that provisions of this popular referendum will be implemented soon, as lawsuits against it have already halted enforcement. Based upon national reporting (and the Republican sweep of the national legislature), one can expect illegal immigration to be a national issue in future U.S. elections.

Migration to the United States is a sensitive issue in Mexico because it highlights the Mexican inability to create sufficient jobs at decent wages. Mexico regularly expresses concern about U.S. abuses suffered by Mexican workers whom it considers "undocumented workers," not illegal immigrants. Mexico is joined by liberal U.S. politicians and intellectuals in making this distinction.

Mexico benefits in several ways from continuous migrations, which provide an "escape valve" that dissipates political discontent at home. Tensions produced by unemployment and recent austerity measures could lead to increased opposition and even violence. In addition, many migrants send back a portion of their wages, as well as goods, to relatives in Mexico. Estimates of total yearly remittances are in the several billions of dollars, which constitute an important source of foreign exchange for Mexico. Many Mexican-Americans visit their former country and spend an important share of the tourist dollars Mexico receives every year.

In any normal year, more than a million Mexicans cross the border illegally into the United States. According to some estimates, the total may be even higher because of the underreporting of undocumented migrants. Most survey data report that 80 percent of these immigrants are male, which is a pattern that has been established since the turn of the century. Tales abound of molestation by unscrupulous smugglers, and most men will not subject their female relatives to the risks involved in surreptitious entry. Most of the migrants are between the ages of twenty and thirty-four. Very few children migrate, but many of the migrants are married heads of household.

Usually, the Mexican immigrant is better educated than his countrymen in Mexico. Only 3 percent of the migrants are illiterate compared with 10 to 15 percent for the general Mexican population. These figures tend to support the notion that there is a bit of a brain drain from Mexico to the United States. Only a small number of the immigrants entering the United States in the 1980s indicated that they had previously been involved in agricultural work. The majority claimed that they were skilled or unskilled industrial workers, craftsmen, foremen, operatives, and laborers. Most of them did not want farm jobs in the United States. The numerous undocumented workers make such data suspect, however, as it is difficult to gather accurate socioeconomic information from this population.

The majority of the migrants come from eight states in Mexico: Michoacán, Guanajuato, Jalisco, Zacatecas, Durango, San Luis Potosí, Baja California, and Chihuahua. They originate in traditional mining and agricultural areas of Mexico that have been in constant economic decline. Zacatecas and Michoacán represent two of the poorest non-Indian areas of the country. The heavily Indian and more southern areas of Mexico, however, such as Chiapas and Yucatán, send relatively few immigrants to the United States.

According to the U.S. 1990 census, there are an estimated 13,393,208 people who claim Mexican ancestry. The median age of this population is twenty-three and more than 51 percent of the population is male. In addition, 95 percent professed their adherence to the Roman Catholic faith. Mexican-Americans are primarily concentrated in five southwestern states: California, Arizona, Colorado, New Mexico, and Texas. California was home to slightly more than half the Mexican-American population, and three-fourths of Mexican-Americans in California live in major cities.

Although Mexican-Americans constitute the second largest minority group in the United States, their political participation and power have been negligible until recently. Aside from the institutional barriers that prevented Mexican-Americans from voting, census figures overestimate the population that holds citizenship and is eligible to vote. The differences between the citizen and noncitizen segments of the Mexican-origin population preclude it from becoming a unified political community. The noncitizen segment of the population is politically inactive and likely to remain so. Population totals that combine citizens and noncitizens distort the real political clout of Mexican-Americans. Furthermore, the geographic concentration of Mexican-Americans in a few congressional districts may have reduced their power. For example, 50 percent of all Mexican-Americans in California reside in only thirteen of the fifty-two congressional districts. In addition, many Mexican-Americans are only now reaching voting age, and Mexican-American voting participation has increased from 31 percent in 1974 to over 44 percent by 1990. This swelling political activism has allowed the number of Hispanic representatives selected to state legislatures to outpace the growth of the population. For example, between 1973 and 1990, thirteen additional Hispanic representatives joined the state legislature in Texas.

Historically, Mexican labor provided the manpower necessary to build the American Southwest. Through various programs sponsored by the U.S. government, thousands of Mexican laborers were brought to this country. During the nineteenth century, they worked on railroads, in mines, and on large ranches, for poorer wages than their white counterparts. In addition, by the 1930s and 1940s Mexican laborers

Among the numerous Mexican-Americans in leading government and private-industry positions, Rep. Henry B. Gonzalez (D-Texas) is ranking member of the House Banking and Financial Services Committee. *U.S. Congress*

were heavily involved in industrial work. Currently, Mexican-Americans are employed in all types of jobs, so they no longer conform to the U.S. stereotype of them as farm laborers or maids.

Mexican-Americans, however, still have a high unemployment rate and low incomes. The median family income for Mexican-Americans is about 60 percent of that of all U.S. families, and the unemployment rate is generally 50 percent higher than for white Americans. According to the 1990 census, the unemployment rate for Mexican-Americans born in the United States was 10.1 percent, for those born in Mexico it was 11.3 percent, and for whites it was below 6 percent.

As is true of educational levels, there is also a difference in the earnings of Mexican-Americans born in the United States and those born in Mexico. Median household income for Mexican-Americans born in United States was $25,396. Under 2 percent of the households have earnings over $100,000 and over 8 percent of the households earn less than $5,000. The median household income for Mexican-Americans born in Mexico is $21,913; about 1 percent have earnings over $100,000, and under 8 percent earn less than $5,000. Over 20 percent of the Mexican-American households born in the United States live below the poverty line, and 27 percent of those born in Mexico live below it, while the number of households below the poverty line for the non-Hispanic population is 9 percent.

Although these figures might seem to reflect a bleak picture of the economic status of Mexican-Americans, a recent survey showed that 45 percent of Mexican-Americans believed that they are better off now than they were before; 39 percent believed that their financial situation was the same; and 15 percent believed that they are worse off. Compared with their potential situation if they lived in Mexico, the situation in the United States may seem good.

Since the Treaty of Guadalupe-Hidalgo, Americans have viewed Mexican-Americans as only partially loyal to the United States. The geographic proximity of Mexico convinced many that Mexican-Americans' real loyalty might be to Mexico. The loyalty question has prompted violence between the two cultures, especially in times of U.S. national crisis. Yet, data suggest that overwhelming numbers of Mexican-Americans view themselves as U.S. citizens, and that they are as loyal to the United States as any other ethnic group. Mexican-Americans look neither to Mexico nor to the closed, protective communities of the past for identity, but to an ongoing struggle on behalf of their rights as American citizens, including the right to continue to enjoy their Mexican heritage. Mexican-Americans have their own U.S. problems, and will not jeopardize their position by identifying too closely with the problems of their homeland. Generational influences, however, do play a role in the identification process. Not surprisingly, it is only among first-generation Mexican-Americans that ties to Mexico are the strongest. Recent census data even indicated that 19 percent of

Mexican-Americans identified themselves in a way that hid their Mexican heritage.

Intermarriage between Mexican-Americans and non-Mexicans is another indicator of identification, and Mexican-Americans have a high rate of marriage to people of non-Mexican origin. By marrying people outside their culture, Mexican-Americans are weakening their ties to Mexico. The rate of intermarriage for Mexican-Americans outside the Southwest has reached almost 40 percent for both sexes. In contrast, African-Americans marry nonblacks less than 1 percent of the time.

Language use is another indicator of identification patterns. In California, 79 percent of Mexican-Americans whose mother tongue was Spanish identify English as their usual language. The percentage is over 84 percent for the Rocky Mountain region. Both the high rates of English use and intermarriage indicate a willingness among most Mexican-Americans to break ties with Mexico.

It is important to realize that the Mexican-American population is heterogeneous and reflects the fact that the Mexican nation itself is not homogeneous. There are divisions between Mexican-Americans who want to become Americanized and those who want to preserve their heritage. Although most Mexican-Americans want to maintain some cultural aspects of their heritage, they feel almost no political loyalty to Mexico.

The Mexican-American population in the United States has experienced different forms of racism and discrimination. Besides physical abuse and lynching, Mexican-Americans had to carry passes to attest to their citizenship during the California gold rush. Arizona outlawed Mexican fiestas. In 1896, Corpus Christi, Texas, established the first Mexican-only schools in the United States. Other states in the Southwest soon followed Texas's example. As a consequence, Mexican-American schoolchildren were given shorter school terms, ramshackle school buildings, and inadequate supplies and teachers. In Gonzales, Texas, Mexican laborers were chained to posts guarded by men with shotguns. Moreover, many places posted English-only signs. The property restrictions imposed by the state of California on Mexican-Americans created and perpetuated the barrio of East Los Angeles. In the past, fashionable movie theaters in Los Angeles or Hollywood did not admit Mexican-Americans, and many restaurants refused to serve them. Public parks and swimming pools had signs that read, "Wednesdays reserved for Negroes and Mexicans only."

Many white Americans viewed Mexican-Americans in stereotype and as a homogeneous group that spoke Spanish, ate tortillas and beans, and worked in the fields. Early writers suggested that the Mexican was just plain lazy and deserved to lose out, as he surely would, to the energetic and productive northerner. A small Texas town during World War II refused to have a wake at a funeral home for a slain Mexican-American serviceman, which prompted Mexican-Americans to form the American GI Forum to protect veterans' rights.

Although many of the institutional barriers have been eliminated by federal legislation, some prejudice against Mexican-Americans continues. In a 1990 poll, Americans perceived Latinos second only to blacks in terms of being lazy rather than hardworking and as living off welfare rather than being self-supporting. The survey also reported that Hispanics are seen as the nation's least patriotic group.

Yet, American society traditionally has given migrant groups an opportunity to escape persecution at home and to thrive in a new and freer environment. Few countries or cultures in the world have accepted great numbers of immigrants with different languages, values, and cultures into their midst without great hostility or rejection. The wonder is that, given the continuous migrations of Mexicans and other nationalities into the United States, there has not been more hostility and less integration.

Divisions within the Mexican-American population must also be recognized. There is a great emphasis on the shade of the skin, and a rejection among some of an Indian past. Some longer-term Mexican-American residents have exhibited considerable disdain toward more recent arrivals. At one time, LULAC, the American GI Forum, and other Mexican-American political associations argued against mass immigration from Mexico because it undermined the position of those already in the United States. A 1983 Gallup poll reported that nearly 75 percent of Mexican-Americans believed that hiring undocumented workers should be considered a criminal act.

Mexican-Americans have also experienced stress in their family structure. For the Mexican-American, the family traditionally represents a source of great strength, and there is great value in preserving family unity, respect, and loyalty. Mexican-American family structure is based upon respect for parental authority, not an egalitarianism between parents and offspring that is often found in American society. Strong ties exist among relatives for whom closeness and interdependency are encouraged, which contrasts with the sense of independence or autonomy most members of American society seek to achieve. American culture clashes with traditional Mexican family values, as it has with the values of earlier waves of immigrants.

On the other hand, the stresses and pressures of American urban society have eroded the role of the Mexican-American family. Therefore, greater problems exist with drugs, alcohol abuse, child abuse, divorce, juvenile delinquency, school dropouts, and malnutrition than would be found in a more supportive cultural environment.

Then again, Mexican-Americans have also had a tremendous impact on the dominant culture of the United States, and Mexican-American influences can be found in every aspect of American culture. Many places and streets have Spanish-origin names, and Spanish words such as piñata, taco, and fiesta have become part of the regular English vocabulary. Mexican restaurants are favorites across the United States, and there is now more salsa than ketchup sold in the United States! The famous cowboy of the American Southwest is a direct cultural descendent of the Mexican vaquero whose clothes, spurs, and roping techniques he copied. The language of the cowboy is heavily influenced by Spanish, so the words *rodeo* and *corral* are spelled and mean the same in Spanish and English.

During the past century, Mexican and Latin American music in general have had by far the greatest external influences on the popular music styles of the United States. Mexican rhythms and styles have affected virtually all of the major forms—Tin Pan Alley, stage and film music, jazz, rhythm-and-blues, country western, and rock. Roy Rogers appropriated Mexican ballads, and marching bands across the United States regularly play tunes of Spanish origin. The Mexican-American band Los Lobos reintroduced the Mexican folk song "La Bamba" to appreciative American audiences, and famous Mexican-Americans— Linda Ronstadt, Sheena Easton, Vikki Carr, and Carlos Santana—have left their mark on the music scene. The Grammy award has recently added a Mexican-American category.

In the Southwest during the nineteenth century, the Mexican *corrido* and the Anglo-American ballad met and mutually reinforced each other. Some cross-fertilization occurred as Anglo and Mexican-American cowboys gathered on the range to have musical contests. At the turn of the century, Mexican music became popular in New Orleans. In addition, the country music of the Southwest appropriated some of its guitar techniques and songs from Mexican sources. The periodic popularity of mariachi and marimba groups in the United States has helped introduce to American audiences the songs "Besame mucho," "Cuando

Calienta el Sol," "Granada," and "La Cucaracha." At this point, the meshing is sufficiently complete to warrant a name—"Tex-Mex" music.

The dominant Latin musical area in the Southwest is Texas, whose flourishing culture not only preserved Mexican forms, but also developed an indigenous Mexican-American style called Norteño music. It is played by an ensemble, consisting of an accordion lead, a guitar, and sometimes a double bass. The music played by these groups leans heavily on *corridos* and on dances such as the polka, waltz, and schottische.

Throughout the United States, but particularly in the South and West, one can see the influence of Mexican-American architecture. Adobe homes with ceramic tiled roofs, cool in the summer and warm in the winter, predominate in fashionable neighborhoods from Florida to California. The rear of these homes often faces an enclosed patio or garden, imitating the Spanish colonial style. The use of earth colors, pastels, red tile hipped roofs, and Mexican tiles and patterns enlivens the aesthetic appeal of homes and buildings. Many older churches or missions in the Southwest were vernacular interpretations of Mexican church buildings in the Baroque style. Hybrid buildings combine Mexican colonial styles with Victorian architecture.

Mural painting is another aspect of Mexican-American culture that has made its mark on America. Mexican-American (and then American) muralists have expressed themselves by drawing and painting on public buildings and businesses. One famous work in Los Angeles is the "Great Wall" by Judy Baca, whose mural stretches eight hundred yards and incorporates other mural art that tells the history of California and its people through the decades.

Mexican-American literature has added to the traditional United States canon the simple fact of an earlier Spanish presence in the American Southwest. Before the emergence of the Chicano literature of the 1960s, a rich folk tradition rooted in traditional Spanish and (later) Mexican tales existed among Mexican-Americans. These folk tales were passed orally from generation to generation, from the arrival of the Spanish in the sixteenth century until today. The great variety of Mexican-American newspapers during the first half of this century provided proof that the Mexican-American culture of that time was experiencing tremendous growth and vitality. These newspapers were a rich avenue for Mexican-American literary expression.

The Chicano movement of the 1960s awakened publishers to the rich vitality of Mexican-American literature. The great theme of this literary period was the search for identity against the powerful and overbearing U.S. culture. In 1967, Rudolph Gonzáles published his famous poem "Yo Soy Joaquín" that became a milestone for writers after him. Many Chicano writers clutched at the idea of Aztlan, which promoted the American Southwest as the mythic homeland of the Aztecs.

With few exceptions, Hollywood has not presented Mexican-Americans in a very positive light. Clint Eastwood, John Wayne, and Yul Brynner westerns show a few mighty Anglo-Americans protecting poor Mexican villagers from bandits or an evil government, while seducing exotic and passionate Mexican women. Although Hollywood does not use the term *greasers* anymore, the majority of Mexican-Americans are still presented as gangsters, bandits, gang members, undocumented workers, and people who have bad accents. The positive images in *The Mark of Zorro* do little to help offset such stereotypes.

Mexican-Americans, Puerto Ricans, Cubans, and Central Americans interact very little with one another. Most do not recognize that they have much in common culturally, and they do not express strong mutual affinity. Each Hispanic group predominates in a specific part of the United States. When other Hispanics appear in these home areas, they are forced to adapt to local circumstances and, therefore, to the dominant Hispanic group. Indicative of the animosity Mexican-Americans feel toward other Latino groups was their protest at a California television station over the appearance of too many Cubans on their Spanish nightly news. Anglo-Americans tend to identify Spanish descendants as Hispanic, but many Mexican-Americans do not consider themselves the same as Central Americans, Puerto Ricans, or Cubans. Most Mexican-Americans prefer to identify themselves with a Mexican-origin label rather than with a Hispanic identification.

Survey data report that only 10 percent of Mexican-Americans indicate that they have a great deal or some contact with Puerto Ricans, and only 6 percent claim that they have a great deal or some contact with Cubans. Furthermore, an overwhelming majority of Mexican-Americans could only identify, from a list of Hispanic organizations, groups that have been traditionally affiliated with Mexican-Americans, such as LULAC, United Farm Workers, and the Council of La Raza. Very few could name organizations that dealt with Cuban or Puerto Rican causes. Almost 50 percent of Mexican-Americans believe that they do not have political concerns in common with Puerto Ricans or Cubans. It is extremely difficult for any politician to circumvent the nationality issue and unite these groups under one Latino banner.

Obviously, most Mexican-Americans have not yet fully realized the dream that lured them to America, although they seem to continue to believe in that dream. Perhaps as they look south to the homeland of their ancestors, they understand that Mexico, too, has promise, but that there are enormous problems to overcome in Mexico's future.

CHAPTER 18

MEXICO'S FUTURE, MEXICO'S PAST

Mexico, at the end of the twentieth century, faces a difficult path to the next millennium. Problems abound, yet these are part of Mexican history—violence, economic crisis, maldistribution of wealth, rebellious peasants, corruption and graft, accusations of illegal elections, an autocratic elite hoarding political and economic power, ambivalent feelings about the United States, rural-urban conflict, left-right conflict, and north-south tensions. All of these issues are more understandable and somewhat less threatening when viewed in the Mexican historical context. Yet, a discussion of the major problems, even in their context, illustrates clearly that life in Mexico will be strained, at least in the foreseeable future.

The Mexican revolution that began in 1910 was unique in many ways. It was the first revolution of the twentieth century and preceded the Russian Revolution of 1917. It started as a political upheaval against an oppressive dictatorship that could not acknowledge the reality of a changing Mexico and developed into a full-blown social, economic, and political revolution. The objectives of this revolution were to destroy the caste system based on the hacienda and large land holdings, to weaken the power of the foreign capitalists, the church, and the military, and to redeem the indigenous Indian population. These objectives were not fully realized. In the first decade, it was primarily an agrarian revolution, which grew piecemeal—initially as a local, and later as a regional, upheaval, which then developed into a national movement.

The revolution that resulted was experimental and pragmatic; it lacked a defined ideology or foreign models to deal with the problems of Mexico. In its foreign policy aspects, its main tenets were nationalistic and anticolonialist. It advocated self-determination and nonintervention and challenged U.S. policies and involvement in Mexico.

In a very real sense, the Mexican revolution and, perhaps, the Chiapas rebellion are a continuation of the movement that began with independence when some of the leaders of the war against Spain advocated the destruction of the caste system, the elimination of church power, the distribution of large land holdings and laissez-faire capitalism. This revolutionary tradition was reinforced by Juárez and the liberals in the mid-nineteenth century and reemerged forcefully during the first decades of the twentieth century.

The revolutionary leaders of this century modified the earlier liberalism, placing the interest of the state above individuals and groups and abandoning the laissez-faire economic policies so prevalent in the nineteenth century. Those policies were replaced by others emphasizing strong statism and government intervention in all aspects of society. The central government was strengthened, and major social programs were implemented, including massive redistribution of land and nationalization of foreign investments; in addition, a new unified and authoritarian political party—the PRI—emerged to rule the country. Rival institutions were weakened, and the control of the party became institutionalized.

By the 1940s, the pendulum of revolution swung right. The process of rapid social and economic change slowed down considerably. Many argued that the revolution had ended. The earlier revolutionary hopes and programs were abandoned or transformed in the quest for modernization and economic development. Foreign capital was again welcomed, and subsequent administrations introduced measures to encourage private investment and the growth of domestic industries, usually through protectionist measures. The state, however, remained a major employer, and the government bureaucracy swelled with every new administration. With increasing resources, patronage expanded, as did graft and corruption.

Mexican–U.S. relations moved beyond confrontation and hostility toward cooperation and integration during the recent past. The earlier Mexican bitterness over the loss of half of its territory to the United States and over the continuous U.S. meddling in Mexican affairs seemed to have subsided as time passed. This is not to say that latent hostility and xenophobia have disappeared completely from the Mexi-

A 1942 engraving by Alfredo Zalce contrasts Mexico's modernization with its poverty, graft, and corruption—all still in existence today. *Library of Congress*

can attitude. Mexican children still learn about the northern colossus and its previous expansionist policies. The constructive policies of the United States during the past several decades and the awareness of the Mexican leadership of the necessity for closer commercial relations with its northern neighbor have created a climate of guarded trust and respect.

The recent signing of the North American Free Trade Agreement is the culmination of an era of closer collaboration between the two countries as well as an example of mutual realization of their economic interdependence. "I realized," said President Salinas, "that if Mexico stayed outside the commercial blocs, it was not possible to grow with the dynamism required by a country of 82 million inhabitants, to whom almost two million are added every year."

In the past decades, Mexico has become the U.S.'s third most important trading partner after Canada and Japan, and its fourth most important foreign source of petroleum. Mexico is also one of the leading countries in Latin America in terms of U.S. investments. The United States is Mexico's most important customer, accounting for 70 percent of Mexico's exports—including petroleum, automobiles, auto

The Bolsa Building in Mexico City, which houses the International Stock Market. Numerous international companies have established offices and plants in Mexico City, now a major center for investment and commerce. Since the signing of NAFTA, U.S. investments in Mexico have grown significantly. *Alyx Kellington*

parts, and vegetables. The United States is not only Mexico's largest source of foreign investment but also its primary source of important tourist dollars.

"Change" has been achieved in other areas as well. Even the Catholic Church, which formerly was the victim of anticlerical legislation and persecution, now enjoys rather cordial relations with the Mexican state. Government criticism of the church focuses primarily on the radicalism of some clerics who speak out against such matters as poverty and social injustice and the church's support of and ties to the National Action Party (PAN).

There is a striking philosophical continuity in the attitudes of the Church hierarchy earlier in this century and those prevalent today. During the past three decades, the Mexican Church has been characterized by greater direct involvement in social issues in response to the challenges presented by the growth of Protestantism in Mexico and Fidel Castro's rise to power in Cuba. This latter challenge reinforced the Church's serious concern about preventing communism in Mexico.

Currently, the Catholic Church in Mexico is demonstrating sharply conflicting opinions concerning political and social issues. It is experiencing discord over its appropriate role in Mexican society, increasing challenges to Church leadership by Church-affiliated groups regarding liberation theology, and the growing episcopal demands for an abolition of constitutional limitations on political participation. This last issue, which involves the hierarchy's wish to be more politically active and visible, potentially places the Church in direct conflict with the government in the future.

Church and state in Mexico have recently sought to promote harmony through a dialogue intended to build bridges and diminish tensions. Nevertheless, the Church hierarchy has criticized what it perceives as election fraud and institutionalized corruption by the PRI. In sum, Church and state have slowly and sometimes secretly come to terms, but it is an uneasy truce, based on behind-the-scenes cooperation and compromise between two powerful institutions.

Recently, there have been other significant changes in Mexico. Modernization and industrialization have advanced significantly, particularly in the northern states. The government has taken critical steps to bolster public finance through privatization and deregulation of state-owned enterprises, elimination or reduction of subsidies to inefficient industries, dramatic reduction of tariff rates, and shrinkage of the overall financial deficit. The process of transforming the agricultural sector has also begun. Its restructuring will change one of the oldest and most venerated of institutions—the *ejido* system of communal land-holding—and will increase tensions with indigenous populations still fond of their ancestral traditions.

Monetary and fiscal discipline and a wage-price stabilization program reduced inflation from 150 percent in the 1980s to less than 10 percent in the 1990s. With the introduction of market-oriented reforms, Mexico's gross domestic product growth rate went from 2 percent annually in the 1980s to over 3.5 percent in the 1990s. The Mexican economy has also decreased its dependence on petroleum exports, while diversifying its export base. Mexico was making progress until the crisis of 1994 and 1995.

Since 1988, the economy has experienced a moderate recovery from the six-year economic crisis that began in 1982. The long-term objectives of the Salinas administration were to renew sustained economic growth with inflation similar to levels in the industrialized countries, to make the economy more competitive internationally, to achieve greater integration with the United States and Canada, and to reduce poverty levels. The medium-term strategy was to stimulate the economy progressively by promoting increased availability of goods and services, while tempering growth of domestic demand to avoid inflationary pressures.

Despite these economic changes, poor and working-class Mexicans have benefited only partially. Because half of the government's budget is spent to meet the country's debt obligation, little remains for spending on domestic programs that directly help the poor. In the 1980s, for instance, real spending on education and health care programs was cut by more than 50 percent. The government recognized that there is a housing shortage of six million units and that 25 percent of the houses do not have electricity. Moreover, 29 percent of the population does not have access to safe water, 22 percent does not have access to health services, and 55 percent does not have access to sanitation. Even more troubling for Mexico's poor and working classes has been the decline in the real value of their wages.

According to foreign organizations such as the United Nations Food and Agriculture Organization (FAO), approximately 41 million Mexicans do not obtain adequate food. Of these, 17 million live in extreme poverty and suffer from malnutrition. Although poverty is found throughout the country, it is heavily concentrated in the areas of Chiapas, Oaxaca, Veracruz, Puebla, and Guerrero, where as many as 80 percent of the peasants are poor.

Despite significant modernization and economic development, Mexico still suffers from widespread poverty. This is one of the country's major challenges: how to satisfy the demands of the poorer elements in society at a time of significant government austerity and economic recession. Many Mexican Indians still live in poverty. *Alyx Kellington*

The Salinas administration's answer to the population's growing discontent was a new antipoverty campaign called the National Solidarity Program (PRONASOL). This program, which combined community involvement and volunteer work with government funding for public works, included improvement in health care facilities, schools, electricity, and telephone service, as well as the granting of land titles, mostly to the urban poor. It should be noted, however, that while PRONASOL was seen by many as a model for regional development and achieved moderate success during the Salinas years, critics maintain that it did not represent a fiscal commitment to help the needy, as it was merely the astute renaming and regrouping of the limited funds previously directed to the poor. The program, the critics suggest, targeted former opposition areas in an attempt to co-opt them.

Poverty has been accentuated in part by the uneven economic development of various regions. Although the southern states have traditionally been the poorest, the Mexican government has consistently devoted its resources, including the bulk of federal financial support, to the capital city and the prosperous northern areas, while providing limited help to the southern region.

As a result, many Mexicans have migrated from rural areas that lack job opportunities—such as the underdeveloped southern states and the crowded central plateau—to the industrialized urban centers and the developing areas along the U.S.–Mexico border or have illegally entered the United States. According to 1991 census estimates, the population of greater Mexico City is roughly twenty million, making it the largest urban concentration in the world. The border region and Guadalajara, Monterrey, and other major metropolitan areas have also undergone a sharp rise in population. This phenomenon is generating widespread perceptions that demographic and geographic centralization is excessive, and that significant decentralization must somehow be achieved. Some recent statistics illustrate this problem.

Mexico has not managed to decentralize industry and has chosen growth over redistribution. Of the seventeen cities that have industrial parks, fourteen are in the north of Mexico. Moreover, the northern and central sections of the country contain over 90 percent of small and medium-sized businesses. Eighty-four percent of the *maquila* industries are located in the north.

In addition, 56 percent of the gross national product (GNP) is accounted for by only five of the thirty-two Mexican administrative units: the federal district accounts for roughly 27 percent, Mexico State for 11 percent, Jalisco for 7 percent, Nuevo León for 6 percent, and Veracruz for 5 percent. The imbalance is even greater in investments, with the federal district accounting for 63 percent of the total. This concentration suggests that the economic policies of the government have concentrated, rather than dispersed, national wealth.

Excessive degrees of centralism have resulted in continued provincial hostility toward people from Mexico City, who are perceived in the rest of the country to be arrogant and pompous. Such disdain for people from the capital can be considered as a protest against the federal district's dominance of almost every aspect of Mexican life. When regional leaders, however, adopt confrontational approaches that can potentially divide a nation that needs to be united, they become a dangerous force.

Along with these economic changes, there has been a simultaneous attempt at opening Mexico's political system. After emerging from the controversial 1988 and 1994 presidential elections with just over 50 and 49 percent of the vote, respectively—the lowest acknowledged percentage ever for PRI candidates—the government began to democratize

The indigenous past is very much alive in contemporary Mexico, where the glory of Indian civilization is still revered. *Author's Collection*

the electoral process. With congressional support, electoral laws have been revised, and new electoral organizations have been created. In 1990, legislators approved the Federal Code of Electoral Institutions and Procedures (COFIPE), which significantly reformed the manner in which elections are conducted and adjudicated.

Expanded freedoms have accompanied electoral reforms. There are stronger opposition voices, and the press is freer and more militant. Business, middle-class, and even grassroots popular groups have now organized autonomously and are far more critical of the regime. Pressures have increased for honest elections and debates in the legislature about the need to eradicate fraud and corruption.

Yet, the prospect for complete democratization in Mexico remains clouded. Although the country is emerging from a semiauthoritarian state toward a more pluralistic one, it is important to emphasize that authoritarianism has been firmly entrenched for so long that it has become institutionalized. Even if the country were to change quickly and the opposition were permitted to gain power through elections, it would not necessarily mean the acceptance of democratic norms, especially tolerance of opposition, respect for human rights, and observance of legal and constitutional guarantees. It would take more than a mere transfer of power to instill these values in Mexican society and to modify accepted beliefs and attitudes.

Both the centralization of power in the executive and the *personalista* nature of Mexican politics also weaken the development of democratic government. Although congressional and judicial powers have recently been strengthened, the figure of the president is still supreme and his power is extensive. This tradition is unlikely to be changed very dramatically in the near future.

The political opposition, while increasingly advocating democratization, is neither unified nor united in its views of what constitutes democracy or the way in which it should be implemented in Mexico. Voices on the right, mostly connected with PAN, argue that a highly centralized state with massive power concentrated in an unchecked presidency, which exercises extensive control over politics and the economy, is incompatible with democracy. By contrast, voices of the left, represented primarily by the Partido de la Revolución Democrática (PRD), argue that democratization requires a strong, revitalized, and large state that assumes a central role in economic policy and social change. In a sense, their longing for a powerful, centralized, welfare state is a throwback to the pre–World War II Mexican state of Cuauhtémoc Cárdenas's father, with all its problems and weaknesses.

Obviously, the Mexican road to full democratization will be full of obstacles.

The Zapatista uprising will surely strengthen the role of the military. Although it is subject to civilian control, the Mexican military has been an institutional pillar of the government and the PRI, and a force for authoritarian domination. In addition, the inclusion of the military leadership in high-level decision making appears to have been a factor in preventing that pattern of political instability and militarism common to other countries of the region.

The Salinas administration repeatedly used the military to implement policies and to enforce its objectives. The Mexican military has had as its primary mission the defense of national sovereignty. In past decades, it has become increasingly involved in civic action programs. More recently, the military has engaged in counternarcotics operations, which has led to charges of corruption, and military leaders seem unhappy about the military's involvement in antidrug campaigns.

One area in which the military seemed ill-equipped was that of counterinsurgency operations. While the decision not to launch a major military offensive against the guerrillas in Chiapas seemed to have been politically motivated, the uprising highlighted the need for changes in the military's command and intelligence structures as well as for modern equipment to fight this type of insurgency. It is still troubling that by midyear 1995, the situation in Chiapas remained unresolved. The army had surrounded the Zapatistas and confined them to a limited geographical area. The Zapatistas have acted cautiously, although they have used modern telecommunications to marshal international support for their cause. They clearly understand that they are in a weak position militarily. Given the results of the elections, and the popular repudiation of Zapatista violence, the rebels may be forced to seek accommodations with the government. The government may offer major concessions to diffuse a potentially explosive situation. One major signal by the government and PRI was the resignation in February 1995 of the recently elected PRI governor of Chiapas, which satisfied a major demand of the rebels. On the one hand, the prolonged peace negotiations between the Zapatistas and government representatives, led by Manuel Camacho Solis—the charismatic and able former secretary of foreign affairs—failed to negotiate an end to the conflict. On the other hand, they seemed to indicate some willingness by the Zapatistas and the government to seek mutual accommodation.

The assassinations and propensity toward violence that have recently plagued Mexico will also increase the role of the military. The government will be forced to rely more heavily on the armed forces for security and to maintain a climate of public safety, and the military may exact a greater price from the PRI and the government for this new role. Although the military probably will maintain its support of PRI and continue its previous close working relationships with the political leadership, in the future there will likely be a more independent military that is concerned with the integrity and role of the institution and less subservient to the government and party leadership.

Another casualty of the uprising may be full implementation of NAFTA. The new administration elected in 1994 will be cautious in the process of integration with the United States, and U.S. investments in Mexico may slow down, especially if violence continues and spreads to Mexico City and the northern states, and Mexico's economic crisis deepens. This is not to say that NAFTA will be rejected, but under a climate of tension and questioning about the benefits of closer relations with the United States, the Mexican president may proceed cautiously. Integration will continue more slowly, as increased attention is paid to the potential impact on internal developments of U.S. relations with Mexico.

A final consequence of the Chiapas events will probably be a tougher policy on immigration, particularly on the southern flank. There has been growing concern in Mexico about the refugee camps in the southern region resulting from increased immigration from Central America. This will now translate into a more vigilant and tightly controlled atmosphere that will perhaps involve dismantling camps and repatriating refugees.

Whatever the outcome, the recent uprising in the south, similar to the massacre of Tlatelolco in Mexico City in 1968 (when a student demonstration was violently suppressed by the army), will have a chilling effect on the country's political process. As has happened frequently in the past, the winds of radical change are blowing in Mexico. Hopefully, such winds will not weaken, or even destroy, the admittedly painful and partial attempt at democratization underway.

On another level, the potential for instability has increased owing to the strains caused by years of economic stabilization and structural reforms. Groups that were hurt by past policies are taking advantage of the political opening and are uniting against the PRI. In the major cities, grassroots movements have acquired greater importance, and in the rural areas, dissident movements are challenging PRI policies and leadership. The opposition PAN actually elected a governor and local officials in Jalisco in early 1995.

Discontent in rural areas has increased as a result of both deteriorating economic conditions and government policies. Mexico is experiencing an agrarian crisis. Farmers, unable to eke out an existence, are abandoning the rural areas in increasing numbers. Low prices for their products, high interest rates, reduction of agricultural subsidies, and small, unproductive plots of land are creating desperate rural conditions. At least nine million Mexicans live in extreme poverty in rural areas.

To ease hardships among farmers, the Mexican government introduced PROCAMPO, a rural support program. Over the next fifteen years, PROCAMPO will provide the approximately 3.5 million farmers, who produce basic commodities, with a fixed payment for each hectare of cropland. Whether this program will be sufficiently effective to reverse the migration from rural areas and restore some level of economic stability to the agrarian sector remains to be seen. Meanwhile, the rural areas, particularly in the southern region, remain in need of immediate and continuous government attention.

Another obstacle that President Zedillo must face is the unstable political climate in the wake of the Chiapas uprising and the Colosio and Ruiz Massieu assassinations. Most Mexicans see Zedillo's victory as a cry for stability and continuity, but not as a personal mandate for Zedillo. Accordingly, the president still needs the "old guard" of PRI, "the dinosaurs," as they are known in Mexico, to maintain political calm within the party. Despite campaign promises, Mexico probably will not soon see any major overhaul of the party structure.

Major reforms within PRI and the separation of PRI from the government, as Zedillo promised, would affect the pockets of hundreds of local party officials who have profited from government privileges and handouts. The PRI bosses have benefited from numerous activities entrusted to them by the state, such as selling licenses to street vendors. In many states, the government also paid huge sums to help local party leaders get elected. Dislodging these party officials will be a difficult and long-term proposition.

Zedillo's handling of the confrontation between democracy and patronage within PRI will be a critical indicator of his power and his ability to set Mexico's direction. As Salinas's second choice for president, Zedillo did not enter office with unchallenged power. He will have to try to build support and expand his power base.

Indeed, President Zedillo may be the first Mexican president in decades to face a covert or even an open threat of a coup. In addition to all of the systemic problems discussed, he must cope simultaneously with four recent crises—the Chiapas uprising, investigation of the two assassinations, the economic chaos accompanying peso devaluation, and the fragmenting of the once solid PRI. It will not be an easy six years.

Yet, Mexican stability is critical to continue economic development as well as to attract foreign, particularly U.S., investments. A continuing tendency toward violence could frighten away foreign visitors and investors and would weaken the close relationship that is developing between the United States and Mexico. Any major turmoil and social unrest in Mexico will have an impact on the United States, as large numbers of Mexicans might flee north across the border. If violence and guerrilla activities expand, the United States could decide to defend and militarize its border. Any threat to Mexico's oil production will threaten U.S. national interest and security, especially if Middle Eastern oil supplies were interrupted or reduced.

Drug traffic has also become a major recent problem. Mexico's position is that the United States focuses on control of the supply side of this traffic because it is unable to control the demand side, and Mexico has, therefore, become a scapegoat for what is essentially a U.S. domestic problem. The United States, however, accuses Mexico of producing not only illicit drugs, but also of allowing them to move freely through its territory. Furthermore, it has accused government officials of corruption and complicity in the drug business. The drug traffic generates major tensions in U.S.–Mexican relations and could potentially derail cooperation between the two countries in other critical areas.

Immigration remains another major troubling issue in U.S.–Mexican relations. Illegal immigration has become a focus of major concern in the United States, which has the sovereign right to set immigration policy and to protect its borders. Anti-immigration laws, especially initiatives such as Proposition 187 in California, increase unhappiness in Mexico, strain U.S.–Mexican relations, and could produce social unrest in Mexico by closing an escape valve for poor and unemployed Mexicans. There appears to be no easy solution to this issue.

The era of close economic cooperation ushered in by NAFTA has somewhat reduced the importance of these problems. Yet, they remain key irritants in an evolving relationship between the two countries. The U.S. public campaign to nudge Mexico into a more democratic, less corrupt system also causes unhappiness among Mexico's political elites and is considered to be continuing interference in Mexico's internal affairs.

From the U.S. point of view, Mexico is an important, large, populous, bordering country. It is the third largest U.S. trading partner, a source of much needed energy, and a major investment destination for U.S. capital. It is in the U.S. interest for Mexico to remain stable, prosperous, and friendly. Policies that exacerbate tensions between the two countries should be avoided. A policy based on prudence and patience may be best in dealing with Mexico. Such a policy would accept the evolution of Mexico's social, political, and economic system; it would encourage gradual change to a more open democratic society; and it would continue to build on the recent good will generated by NAFTA.

Mexico's exciting and colorful history will undoubtedly continue to influence its future through the same trends and patterns that are blended in its past.

SUGGESTED READING

Although numerous books, periodical articles, and newspapers in various languages were consulted in the preparation of this volume, only a select list of books in English have been included in the following list, which is intended mainly as a guide to further reading.

Aiton, Arthur S. *Antonio de Mendoza, First Viceroy of New Spain.* Durham, N.C.: Duke University Press, 1927.

Alba, Victor. *The Mexicans.* New York: Frederick A. Praeger, 1967.

Anna, Timothy V. *The Mexican Empire of Iturbide.* Lincoln: University of Nebraska Press, 1990.

Anton, Ferdinand. *Women in Precolumbian America.* New York: Abner Schuram, 1973.

Archer, Christon I. *The Army in Bourbon Mexico, 1760–1810,* Albuquerque: University of New Mexico Press, 1977.

Ashby, Joe C. *Organized Labor and the Mexican Revolution under Lázaro Cárdenas.* Chapel Hill: University of North Carolina Press, 1967.

Azuela, Mariano. *The Underdogs.* Translated by V. Munguia. New York: New American Library, 1963.

Bagley, Bruce M., and Sergio Aguayo Quesada, eds. *Mexico: In Search for Security.* New Brunswick, N.J.: Transaction Publishers, 1993.

Bailey, David C. *¡Viva Cristo Rey!: The Cristero Rebellion and the Church-State Conflict in Mexico.* Austin: University of Texas Press, 1974.

Bakewell, Peter J. *Silver Mining and Society in Colonial Mexico: Zacatecas, 1546–1700.* Cambridge: Cambridge University Press, 1971.

Bancroft, Hubert H. *History of Mexico.* 6 vols. San Francisco: A. L. Bancroft & Co., 1883.

Bannon, John F. *The Spanish Borderland Frontier, 1513–1821.* New York: Holt, Rinehart and Winston 1970.

Barker, Nancy N. *The French Experience in Mexico, 1821 to 1861: A History of Constant Misunderstanding.* Chapel Hill: University of North Carolina Press, 1979.

Bazant, Jan. *Alienation of Church Wealth in Mexico: Social & Economic Aspects of the Liberal Revolution, 1856–1875.* Cambridge: Cambridge University Press, 1971.

———. *Concise History of Mexico from Hidalgo to Cárdenas, 1805–1940.* Cambridge: Cambridge University Press, 1977.

Beals, Carleton. *Porfirio Díaz: Dictator of Mexico.* Philadelphia: J. B. Lippincott, 1932.

Benitez, Fernando. *The Century After Cortés.* Translated by Joan Maclean. Chicago: University of Chicago Press, 1965.

Benson, Nettie Lee, ed. *Mexico and the Spanish Cortés 1810–1822.* Austin: University of Texas Press, 1966.

Bernal, Ignacio. *Mexico Before Cortés.* Translated by Willis Barnstoni. Garden City, N.Y.: Doubleday & Co., 1975.

———. *The Olmec World.* Translated by Doris Hayden and Fernando Horcasitas. Berkeley: University of California Press, 1969.

Blasio, José L. *Maximilian, Emperor of Mexico: Memories of His Private Secretary.* Translated by Robert H. Murray. New Haven: Yale University Press, 1934.

Borah, Woodrow. *Early Trade and Navigation Between Mexico and Peru.* Berkeley: University of California Press, 1954.

———. *New Spain's Century of Depression.* Berkeley: University of California Press, 1951.

Brading, David A. *Miners and Merchants in Bourbon Mexico, 1763–1810.* Cambridge: Cambridge University Press, 1971.

Brady, Haldeen. *Pershing's Mission in Mexico.* El Paso: Texas Western College Press, 1966.

Brandenburg, Frank. *The Making of Modern Mexico.* Englewood Cliffs, N.J.: Prentice-Hall, 1964.

Brenner, Anita, and George Leighton. *The Wind That Swept Mexico: The History of the Mexican Revolution, 1910–1942.* Austin: University of Texas Press, 1971.

Brown, Lyle C. *The Mexican Liberals and Their Struggle Against the Díaz Dictatorship 1900–1906.* Mexico City: Mexico City College Press, 1956.

Brushwood, John S. *Mexico in Its Novel: A Nation's Search for Identity.* Austin: University of Texas Press, 1966.

Callcott, Wilfrid H. *Church and State in Mexico, 1822–1857.* Durham, N.C.: Duke University Press, 1926.

Calvert, Peter. *The Mexican Revolution, 1910–1940: The Diplomacy of the Anglo-American Conflict.* Cambridge: Cambridge University Press, 1968.

Camp, Roderick A. *Generals in the Palacio: The Military in Modern Mexico.* New York: Oxford University Press, 1992.

———. *Mexico's Political Stability: The Next Five Years.* Boulder: Westview, 1986.

———. *Politics in Mexico.* New York: Oxford University Press, 1993.

Charlot, Jean. *The Mexican Mural Renaissance, 1920–1925.* New Haven: Yale University Press, 1963.

Chevalier, François. *Land and Society in Colonial Mexico: The Great Hacienda.* Trans. by Alvin Eustis. Berkeley: University of California Press, 1963.

Clark, Marjorie. *Organized Labor in Mexico.* Chapel Hill: University of North Carolina Press, 1934.

Clendenen, Clarence C. *The United States and Pancho Villa: A Study in Unconventional Diplomacy.* Ithaca, N.Y.: Cornell University Press, 1961.

Cline, Howard. *Mexico: Revolution to Evolution, 1940–1960.* New York: Oxford University Press, 1963.

———. *The United States and Mexico.* New York: Atheneum, 1963.

Cockcroft, James D. *Intellectual Precursors of the Mexican Revolution 1900–1913.* Austin: University of Texas Press, 1968.

Coe, Michael. *America's First Civilization: Discovering the Olmecs.* New York: Van Nostrand, 1968.

———. *The Maya.* New York: Frederick A. Praeger, 1967.

———. *Mexico.* New York: Frederick A. Praeger, 1967.

Cook, Sherburne F., and Woodrow Borah. *The Aboriginal Population of Central Mexico on the Eve of the Spanish Conquest.* Berkeley: University of California Press, 1963.

Cornelius, Wayne A. *Politics and the Migrant Poor in Mexico City.* Stanford, Calif.: Stanford University Press, 1975.

———. *Politics in Mexico: An Introduction and Overview.* San Diego: University of California Center for U.S.–Mexican Studies, 1991.

Corti, Egon. *Maximilian and Charlotte of Mexico.* 2 vols. Trans. by Catherine Alison Phillips. New York: Alfred A. Knopf, 1928.

Cosio Villegas, Daniel. *Change in Latin America: The Mexican and Cuban Revolution.* Lincoln: University of Nebraska Press, 1961.

———. *The U.S. Versus Porfirio Díaz.* Lincoln: University of Nebraska Press, 1963.

Cumberland, Charles C. *Mexican Revolution: Genesis Under Madero.* Austin: University of Texas Press, 1968.

———. *Mexican Revolution: The Constitutionalist Years.* Austin: University of Texas Press, 1972.

————. *Mexico: The Struggle for Modernity.* New York: Oxford University Press, 1968.

Dabbs, Jack A. *The French Army in Mexico, 1861–1867.* The Hague: Mouton & Co., 1962.

Davies, Nigel. *The Aztecs: A History.* London: Macmillan & Co., 1973.

Davies, R. Trevor. *The Golden Century of Spain, 1501–1621.* New York: Harper & Row, 1961.

Díaz del Castillo, Bernal. *The True History of the Conquest of New Spain, 1517–1521.* Trans. by A. P. Maudslay. New York: Ferrar, Straus, 1966.

Dulles, John W. F. *Yesterday in Mexico: A Chronicle of the Revolution, 1914–1956.* Austin: University of Texas Press, 1961.

Elliott, John H. *Imperial Spain, 1469–1716.* New York: St. Martin's Press, 1963.

Farriss, Nancy. *Crown and Clergy in Colonial Mexico, 1759–1821.* London: University of London Press, 1968.

Fisher, Lillian V. *The Background of the Revolution for Mexico's Independence.* Gainesville: University of Florida Press, 1966.

————. *The Intendant System in Spanish America.* Berkeley: University of California Press, 1929.

Flores Caballero, Romeo. *Counterrevolution: The Role of the Spaniards in the Independence of Mexico.* Trans. by Jaime E. Rodriguez. Lincoln: University of Nebraska Press, 1974.

Flynn, Gerard. *Sor Juana Inés de la Cruz.* New York: Twayne Publishers, 1971.

Galarza, Ernesto. *Merchants of Labor: The Mexican Bracero Story.* San Jose, Calif.: Rosicrucian Press, 1964.

Gibson, Charles. *The Aztecs Under Spanish Rule.* Stanford, Calif.: Stanford University Press, 1964.

————. *Spain in America.* New York: Harper & Row, 1967.

Gilderhus, Mark J. *Diplomacy and Revolution: U.S.–Mexican Relations Under Wilson and Carranza.* Tucson: University of Arizona Press, 1977.

Gillmor, Frances. *The King Danced in the Market Place.* Tucson: University of Arizona Press, 1964.

González Casanova, Pablo. *Democracy in Mexico.* Trans. by Danielle Salti. New York: Oxford University Press, 1970.

Grayson, George. *The Church in Contemporary Mexico.* Washington, D.C.: Center for Strategic and International Studies, 1992.

————. *The United States and Mexico: Patterns of Influence.* New York: Praeger Publishers, 1954.

————, ed. *Prospects for Democracy in Mexico.* New Brunswick, N.J.: Transaction Publishers, 1990.

Grebler, Leo, Joan W. Moore, and Ralph C. Guzmán. *The Mexican-American People: The Nation's Second Largest Minority.* New York: Free Press, 1970.

Greenleaf, Richard E. *The Mexican Inquisition of the Sixteenth Century.* Albu-
    querque: University of New Mexico Press, 1971.

————. *Zumarraga and the Mexican Inquisition, 1536–1543.* Washington, D.C.:
    Academy of American Franciscan History, 1969.

Greib, Kenneth J. *The U.S. and Huerta.* Lincoln: University of Nebraska Press,
    1969.

Guzmán, Martin Luis. *The Eagle and the Serpent.* Trans. by Harriet de Onis. New
    York: Doubleday & Co., 1965.

Haddox, John H. *Vasconcelos of Mexico.* Austin: University of Texas Press, 1967.

Hale, Charles A. *Mexican Liberalism in the Age of Mora, 1821–1853.* New Haven:
    Yale University Press, 1965.

————. *The Transformation of Liberalism in Late Nineteenth-Century Mexico.*
    Princeton, N.J.: Princeton University Press, 1989

Hamill, Hugh. *The Hidalgo Revolt: Prelude to Mexican Independence.* Gaines-
    ville: University of Florida Press, 1966.

Hanke, Lewis V. *The Spanish Struggle for Justice in the Conquest of America.*
    Philadelphia: University of Pennsylvania Press, 1949.

Hanna, Alfred Jackson, and Kathryn A. Hanna. *Napoleon III and Mexico.* Chapel
    Hill: University of North Carolina Press, 1971.

Hannay, David. *Díaz.* New York: Holt, 1917.

Haring, Clarence H. *The Spanish Empire in America.* New York: Oxford Univer-
    sity Press, 1947.

Humboldt, Alexander von. *Political Essay on the Kingdom of New Spain.* Ed. with
    an introduction by Mary Maples Dunn. New York: Alfred A. Knopf, 1972.

Hundley, Norris, Jr. *Dividing the Waters: A Century of Controversy Between the
    U.S. and Mexico.* Berkeley, University of California Press, 1966.

————, comp. *The Chicano.* Santa Barbara, Calif.: Clio Books, 1973.

Israel, J. I. *Race, Class and Politics in Colonial Mexico, 1610–1670.* London: Oxford
    University Press, 1975.

Johnson, Harold R. *From Reconquest to Empire: The Iberian Background to Latin
    American History.* New York: Alfred A. Knopf, 1970.

Johnson, Kenneth F. *Mexican Democracy: A Critical View.* Boston: Allyn & Bacon,
    1971.

Johnson, William Weber. *Heroic Mexico: The Violent Emergence of a Modern
    Nation.* Garden City, N.Y.: Doubleday & Co., 1968.

Jones, Oakah L., Jr. *Santa Anna.* New York: Twayne Publishers, 1968.

Katz, Friedrich, ed. *Riot, Rebellion and Revolution: Rural Social Conflict in Mex-
    ico.* Princeton, N.J.: Princeton University Press, 1988.

Kaufman Purcell, Susan, ed. *Mexico in Transition: Implications for U.S. Policy.*
    New York: Council on Foreign Relations, 1988.

Keen, Benjamin. *The Aztec Image in Western Thought.* New Brunswick, N.J.: Rut-
    gers University Press, 1971.

Kirkpatrick, F. A. *The Spanish Conquistadores*. New York: World Publishing Co., 1962.

Knight, Alan. *The Mexican Revolution*. Lincoln: University of Nebraska Press, 1990.

Lafaye, Jacques. *Quetzalcoatl and Guadalupe: The Formation of Mexican National Consciousness 1531–1815*. Trans. by Benjamin Keen. Chicago: University of Chicago Press, 1976.

Langley, Lester. *Mexico and the United States: The Fragile Relationship*. Boston: Twayne Publishers, 1991.

Lanning, John Tate. *Academic Culture in the Spanish Colonies*. London: Oxford University Press, 1940.

Leonard, Irving. *Baroque Times in Old Mexico*. Ann Arbor: University of Michigan Press, 1971.

———. *Books of the Brave*. Cambridge, Mass: Harvard University Press, 1949.

———. *Don Carlos de Sigüenza y Góngora: A Mexican Savant of the Seventeenth Century*. University of California Publications in History, vol. 18. Berkeley: University of California Press, 1929.

Leon-Portilla, Miguel, ed. *The Broken Spears: The Aztec Account of the Conquest of Mexico*. Trans. by Lysander Kemp. Boston: Beacon Press, 1972.

Levy, Daniel, and Gabriel Szekely. *Mexico, Paradoxes of Stability and Change*. Boulder, Colo.: Westview Press, 1953.

Lewis, Oscar. *The Children of Sánchez: Autobiography of a Mexican Family*. New York: Vintage Books, 1961.

———. *Five Families: Mexican Case Studies in the Culture of Poverty*. New York: Science Editions, 1962.

Lieberman, Mark. *Hidalgo: Mexican Revolutionary*. New York: Praeger Publishers, 1970.

Lieuwen, Edwin. *Mexican Militarism: The Political Rise and Fall of the Revolutionary Army, 1910–1940*. Albuquerque: University of New Mexico Press, 1968.

Liss, Peggy K. *Mexico Under Spain, 1521–1556*. Chicago: University of Chicago Press, 1975.

Liss, Sheldon. *A Century of Disagreement: The Chamizal Conflict, 1864–1964*. Washington, D.C.; University Press of Washington, D.C., 1965.

López y Fuentes, Gregorio. *El Indio*. New York: Frederick Ungar Publishing Co., 1961.

Lynch, John. *Spain Under the Hapsburgs*. New York: Oxford University Press, 1964.

MacNutt, F. A. *Hernando Cortés and the Conquest of Mexico*. New York: G. P. Putnam's Sons, 1909.

Madariaga, Salvador de. *Hernan Cortés, Conqueror of Mexico*. Chicago: H. Regnery Co., 1955.

McAlister, Lyle N. *The "Fuero Militar" in New Spain, 1764–1800*. Gainesville: University of Florida Press, 1957.

McBride, Robert. *Mexico and the U.S.* Englewood Cliffs, N.J.: Prentice Hall Inc., 1981.

McWiliams, Carey. *North from Mexico: The Spanish-Speaking People of the United States.* New York: Greenwood Press, 1968.

Merriman, Roger P. *Mexico: A Country Study.* Washington, D.C.: Foreign Area Studies, The American University, 1983.

———. *The Rise of the Spanish Empire in the Old World and the New.* 4 vols. New York: Cooper Square Publishers, 1962.

Meyer, Lorenzo. *Mexico and the U.S. in the Oil Controversy, 1917–1942.* Trans. by Muriel Vasconcelos. Austin: University of Texas Press, 1977.

Meyer, Michael C. *Huerta: A Political Portrait.* Lincoln: University of Nebraska Press, 1972.

Meyer, Michael C., and William L. Sherman. *The Course of Mexican History.* New York: Oxford University Press, 1979.

Middlebrook, Kevin, ed. *Unions, Workers and the State in Mexico.* San Diego: Center for U.S.–Mexican Studies, University of California, 1991.

Miller, Robert R. *Mexico: A History.* Norman: University of Oklahoma Press, 1985.

Millon, Robert P. *Mexican Marxist: Vincente Lombardo Toledano.* Chapel Hill: University of North Carolina Press, 1966.

Morner, Magnus. *The Expulsion of the Jesuits from Latin America.* New York: Alfred A. Knopf, 1965.

———. *Race Mixture in the History of Latin America.* Boston: Little Brown & Co., 1967.

Mosk, Sanford. *Industrial Revolution in Mexico.* Berkeley: University of California Press, 1950.

Murray, Paul V. *The Catholic Church in Mexico: Historical Essays for the General Reader.* Mexico: Editorial EPM, 1965.

Needler, Martin C. *Mexican Politics: The Containment of Conflict.* New York: Praeger, 1990.

———. *Politics and Society in Mexico.* Albuquerque: University of New Mexico Press, 1971.

Newell, G. Roberts, and Luis V. Rubio. *Mexico's Dilemma: The Political Origin of Economic Crisis.* Boulder, Colo.: Westview Press, 1954.

Niemayer, E. V., Jr. *Revolution at Queretaro: The Mexican Constitutional Convention of 1916–1917.* Austin: University of Texas Press, 1974.

Padgett, L. Vincent. *The Mexican Political System.* Boston: Houghton Mifflin Co., 1966.

Parkes, Henry Bamford. *A History of Mexico.* Boston: Houghton Mifflin Co., 1966.

Parry, John H. *The Age of Reconnaissance.* Cleveland: World Publishing Co., 1963.

———. *The Audiencia of New Galicia in the Sixteenth Century.* Cambridge: Cambridge University Press, 1948.

Pastor, Robert A., and Jorge G. Castañeda, eds. *Limits to Friendship: The United States and Mexico.* New York: Random House, 1989.

Paz, Octavio. *The Labyrinth of Solitude: Life and Thought in Mexico.* Trans. by Lysander Kemp. New York: Grove Press, 1961.

———. *The Other Mexico: Critique of the Pyramid.* Trans. by Lysander Kemp. New York: Grove Press, 1972.

Pérez López, Enrique, et al. *Mexico's Recent Economic Growth: The Mexican View.* Austin: University of Texas Press, 1967.

Peterson, Frederick A. *Ancient Mexico.* London: George Allen & Unwin, 1959.

Powell, J. R. *The Mexican Petroleum Industry, 1938–1950.* Berkeley: University of California Press, 1956.

Prescott, William H. *History of the Conquest of Mexico.* New York: Bantam Books, 1967.

Priestley, Herbert. *José de Gálvez: Visitor General of New Spain, 1765–1771.* Berkeley: University of California Press, 1916.

Quirk, Robert E. *An Affair of Honor: Woodrow Wilson and the Occupation of Veracruz.* New York: W. W. Norton & Co., 1962.

———. *The Mexican Revolution, 1914–1915; The Convention of Aguascalientes.* New York: Citadel Press, 1963.

———. *The Mexican Revolution and the Catholic Church, 1910–1929.* Bloomington: Indiana University Press, 1973.

Raat, W. Dirk, ed. *Mexico: From Independence to Revolution, 1810–1910.* Lincoln: University of Nebraska Press, 1982.

———. *Mexico and the United States: Ambivalent Vistas.* Athens: University of Georgia Press, 1992.

Ricard, Robert. *The Spiritual Conquest of Mexico.* Berkeley: University of California Press, 1966.

Riding, Alan. *Distant Neighbor: Portrait of the Mexicans.* New York: Alfred A. Knopf, 1984.

Rives, George L. *The United States and Mexico, 1821–1848.* 2 vols. New York: Charles Scribner's Sons, 1913.

Robertson, William S. *Iturbide of Mexico.* Durham, N.C.: Duke University Press 1952.

Rodriguez, Jaime E., ed. *The Evolution of the Mexican Political System.* Wilmington, Del.: Scholarly Resources Books, 1993.

———. *Patterns of Contention in Mexican History.* Wilmington, Del.: Scholarly Resources, 1992.

———. *The Revolutionary Process in Mexico: Essays on Political and Social Change, 1880–1940.* Los Angeles: UCLA Latin American Center, 1990.

Roeder, Ralph. *Juárez and His Mexico: A Biographical History.* 2 vols. New York: Viking Press, 1947.

Roett, Riordan, ed. *Mexico's External Relations in the 1990s.* Boulder, Colo.: Lynne Reinner Publishers, 1991.

Romanell, Patrick. *Making of the Mexican Mind: A Study in Recent Mexican Thought.* Lincoln: University of Nebraska Press, 1952.

Ross, Stanley R. *Francisco I. Madero: Apostle of Mexican Democracy.* New York: Columbia University Press, 1955.

————. *Is the Mexican Revolution Dead?* New York: Alfred A. Knopf, 1966.

Ruíz, Ramón Eduardo. *The Great Rebellion: Mexico, 1905–1924.* New York: W. W. Norton, 1980.

————. *The Mexican War: Was It Manifest Destiny?* New York: Holt, Rinehart & Winston, 1963.

————. *Mexico: The Challenge of Poverty and Illiteracy.* San Marino, Calif.: Huntington Library, 1963.

————. *Triumphs and Tragedy: A History of the Mexican People.* New York: W. W. Norton, 1992.

Rydjord, John. *Foreign Interest in the Independence of New Spain.* Durham, N.C.: Duke University Press, 1935.

Sauer, Carl O. *The Early Spanish Main.* Berkeley: University of California Press, 1966.

Schmitt, Karl M. *Communism in Mexico: A Study in Political Frustration.* Austin: University of Texas Press, 1965.

————. *Mexico and the United States: Conflict and Coexistence, 1821–1973.* New York: John Wiley & Sons, 1974.

Scholes, Walter V. *Mexican Politics During the Juárez Regime, 1855–1872.* Columbia: University of Missouri Press, 1957.

Schurz, William L. *The Manila Galleon.* New York: E. P. Dutton, 1939.

————. *This New World: The Civilization of Latin America.* New York: E. P. Dutton & Co., 1965.

Scott, Robert E. *Mexican Government in Transition.* Urbana: University of Illinois Press, 1959.

Sierra, Justo. *The Political Evolution of the Mexican People.* Trans. by Charles Ramsdell. Austin: University of Texas Press, 1969.

Simpson, Eyler N. *The Ejido: Mexico's Way Out.* Chapel Hill: University of North Carolina Press, 1937.

Simpson, Lesley B. *The Encomienda in New Spain.* Berkeley: University of California Press, 1965.

————. *Many Mexicos.* Berkeley: University of California Press, 1960.

Singletary, Otis. *The Mexican War.* Chicago: University of Chicago Press, 1960.

Sinkin, Richard N. *The Mexican Reform, 1855–1876: A Study in Liberal Nation Building.* Austin: University of Texas Press, 1979.

Smart, Charles Allen. *Viva Juárez: A Biography.* London: Eyre & Spothswoode, 1964.

Smith, Justin H. *The War with Mexico.* 2 vols. Gloucester, Mass: Peter Smith, 1963.

Smith, Peter H. *Labyrinths of Power: Political Recruitment in Twentieth-Century Mexico.* Princeton, N.J.: Princeton University Press, 1979.

Soustille, Jacques. *Mexico.* Trans. by James Hagarth. Cleveland: World Publishing Co., 1967.

Stein, Stanley J., and Barbara H. Stein. *The Colonial Heritage of Latin America: Essays on Economic Dependence in Perspective.* New York: Oxford University Press, 1970.

Stevens, Donald F. *Origins of Instability in Early Republican Mexico.* Durham, N.C.: Duke University Press, 1991.

Stevenson, Robert. *Music in Mexico: A Historical Survey.* New York: Thomas Y. Crowell, 1971.

Story, Dale. *The Mexican Ruling Party: Stability and Authority.* New York: Praeger, 1986.

Tannenbaum, Frank. *Peace by Revolution: Mexico After 1910.* New York: Columbia University Press, 1966.

Taylor, William P. *Landlord and Peasant in Colonial Oaxaca.* Stanford, Calif.: Stanford University Press, 1972.

Thomas, Hugh. *The Real Discovery of America: Mexico, November 8, 1519.* Mount Kisco, N.Y.: Moyer Bell, 1992.

Thompson, J. Eric S. *The Rise and Fall of Maya Civilization.* Norman: University of Oklahoma Press, 1966.

Timmons, Wilbert H. *Morelos: Priest, Soldier, Statesman of Mexico.* El Paso: Texas Western College Press, 1963.

Townsend, William Cameron. *Lázaro Cárdenas: Mexican Democrat.* Ann Arbor, Mich.: George Washington Publishing Co., 1952.

Tulchin, Joseph, ed. *Problems in Latin America History: The Modern Period.* New York: Harper & Row, 1973.

Turner, Frederick C. *The Dynamic of Mexican Nationalism.* Chapel Hill: University of North Carolina Press, 1968.

Turner, John Kenneth. *Barbarous Mexico.* Austin: University of Texas Press, 1969.

Vaillant, George. *The Aztecs of Mexico.* Garden City, N.Y.: Doubleday & Co., 1962.

Vanderwood, Paul J. *Disorder and Progress: Bandits, Police and Mexican Development.* Lincoln: University of Nebraska Press, 1981.

Vasconcelos, José. *A Mexican Ulysses: An Autobiography.* Trans. by William Rex Crawford. Bloomington: Indiana University Press, 1963.

Vernon, Raymond. *The Dilemma of Mexico's Development: The Roles of the Private and Public Sectors.* Cambridge: Harvard University Press, 1963.

Villareal, Roberto E., and Norma G. Hernandez, eds. *Latinos and Political Coalitions: Political Empowerment for the 1990s.* New York: Greenwood Press, 1991.

Von Hagen, Victor. *Man & Tribe.* New York: New American Library, 1961.

————. *World of the Maya*. New York: New American Library, 1960.

Von Sauer, Frank A. *The Alienated "Loyal" Opposition: Mexico's Partido Acción Nacional*. Albuquerque: University of New Mexico Press, 1974.

Wauchope, Robert. *The Indian Background of Latin American History: The Maya, Aztec, Inca and Their Predecessors*. New York: Alfred A. Knopf, 1970.

Weintraub, Sidney, Luis F. Rubio, and Alan D. Jones, eds. *U.S.–Mexican Industrial Integration: The Road to Free Trade*. Boulder, Colo.: Westview Press, 1991.

White, Jon M. *Cortés and the Downfall of the Aztec Empire: A Study in a Conflict of Cultures*. New York: St. Martin's Press, 1971.

Wilkie, James W. *The Mexican Revolution: Federal Expenditures and Social Change Since 1910*. Berkeley: University of California Press, 1967.

————, ed. *Society and Economy in Mexico*. Los Angeles: UCLA Latin American Center, 1990.

Wolf, Eric. *Sons of the Shaking Earth: The People of Mexico and Guatemala*. Chicago: University of Chicago Press, 1974.

Wolfe, Bertram D. *The Fabulous Life of Diego Rivera*. New York: Stein and Day, 1969.

Womack, John, Jr. *Zapata and the Mexican Revolution*. New York: Alfred A. Knopf, 1968.

Zea, Leopoldo. *Positivism in Mexico*. Trans. by Josephine H. Schulte. Austin: University of Texas Press, 1974.

INDEX

THE AUTHOR

JAIME SUCHLICKI, one of the world's foremost scholars on Latin America, has taught Mexican history for thirty years. Formerly executive director of the North-South Center at the University of Miami, he is now professor of history at the Graduate School of International Studies. He edits the *Journal of Inter-American and World Affairs,* consults for the U.S. government, and is the author of *University Students and Revolution in Cuba* and *Cuba: From Columbus to Castro.* Dr. Suchlicki lives in Coral Gables, Florida.